IRREVERENT

guide to

London

5th Edition

By
Donald Olson

original text by Ben Illis

WILEY

Wiley Publishing, Inc.

other titles in the

IRREVERENT GUIDE

series

About the Author

Donald Olson is a novelist, playwright, and travel writer. His novel *The Confessions of Aubrey Beardsley* was published in the United Kingdom by Bantam Press, and his play, *Beardsley*, was produced in London. His travel stories have appeared in the *New York Times, Travel & Leisure, Sunset, National Geographic* guides, and many other national publications. He is also the author of *England For Dummies* and *London For Dummies*, and has written guidebooks to Italy, Berlin, and Oregon.

Published by:
Wiley Publishing, Inc.

111 River St.
Hoboken, NJ 07030-5774

ISBN 0-7645-4298-2

Interior design contributed to by Marie Kristine Parial-Leonardo

Editor: Amy Lyons
Production Editor: Bethany André
Cartographer: John Decamillis
Photo Editor: Richard Fox
Production by Wiley Indianapolis Composition Services

For information on our other products and services or to obtain technical support, please contact our Customer Care Department within the U.S. at 800/762-2974, outside the U.S. at 317/572-3993 or fax 317/572-4002.

Wiley also publishes its books in a variety of electronic formats. Some content that appears in print may not be available in electronic formats.

Manufactured in the United States of America

5 4 3 2 1

A Disclaimer

Prices fluctuate in the course of time, and travel information changes under the impact of the varied and volatile factors that influence the travel industry. We therefore suggest that you write or call ahead for confirmation when making your travel plans. Every effort has been made to ensure the accuracy of information throughout this book and the contents of this publication are believed correct at the time of printing. Nevertheless, the publishers cannot accept responsibility for errors or omissions or for changes in details given in this guide or for the consequences of any reliance on the information provided by the same. Assessments of attractions and so forth are based upon the author's own experience and therefore, descriptions given in this guide necessarily contain an element of opinion, which may not reflect the publisher's opinion or dictate a reader's own experience on another occasion. Readers are invited to write to the publisher with ideas, comments, and suggestions for future editions.

Your safety is important to us, however, so we encourage you to stay alert and be aware of your surroundings. Keep a close eye on cameras, purses, and wallets, all favorite targets of thieves and pickpockets.

CONTENTS

Best park view (30) • May I get that for you, sir? (31) • Bargain beds (31) • The millionaire look, at Scrooge rates (31) • Family values (32) • For history buffs and Anglophiles (33) • For enemies of chintz and Regency (33) • Best health club (34) • Taking care of business (34) • The twilight zone (35) • Try these when there's no room (35)

Maps

2 DINING   **54**

Basic Stuff   **58**

Only in London   58
How to Dress   59
When to Eat   59
Getting the Right Table   59

The Lowdown   **60**

Book before you fly (60) • Celebrate here (60) • Suddenly starving in Covent Garden (61) • Caught in Portobello with low blood sugar (61) • Most comforting (62) • For grown-ups (62) • For kids (63) • Party hearties (63) • Pre- and post-theater (64) • Beautiful people (64) • Most romantique (65) • Britburgers (65) • Really old but still alive (66) • Overrated (66) • Auld London towne (67) • Cockneys and East Enders (67) • Vegging out (68) • Something fishy (68) • For oenophiles (69) • Neighborhood places where Londoners go (70) • Is this a pub or a restaurant? (70) • Cheap 'n' cheerful (72) • Indian institutions (72) • Best Asian (73) • The rest of the world (73) • The French connection (74) • Old Italian (74) • Noov Italian (75) • Best prix-fixe (75) • The great British breakfast (76) • Tea for two (77)

Maps

3 DIVERSIONS 104

Basic Stuff 108

The Lowdown 113

Maps

The Index 141

4 GETTING OUTSIDE 160

The Lowdown 164

Maps

5 SHOPPING 174

Basic Stuff 178

HOTLINES & OTHER BASICS 254

GENERAL INDEX 266

INTRODUCTION

The new millennium has outgrown its diapers and is now toddling along on its own two feet...but have we entered a brave new world or a corporate takeover of the old one? Hmmm...you decide. The specter of that hugely expensive dud, the Millennium Dome, still stands in London's Borough of Greenwich, only now instead of promoting the U.K.'s image of itself as an important world power, it's used as a venue for large rave-style parties. Unlike the unlicensed, illegal warehouse bashes of a decade or so ago, these raves are sponsored and run by the Ministry of Sound, the *über*-club of the 1990s that now represents the new youth establishment that the underground has become. This, in many ways, best sums up London: a constant cycle of underground growing into establishment while a new underground's being spawned. Be it fashion, food, literature, architecture, clubbing, theater, culture, or shopping, London leads the pack.

So why are *you* here? Well, it may be the history and culture; or perhaps it's the cutting-edge trends, from High Street to the dinner table...or maybe you prefer partying to museum visits. Who knows? The most important thing is that London endures. Like New York, that other self-proclaimed world leader of everything, London has been burnt out, bombed out, and bummed out, and yes, folks, it's still there, still ticking, with an irrepressible energy, even if the tourist figures are down.

But to tell the truth, there is a bit of America-bashing going on in London (and throughout western Europe) right now. How to explain it, since America and England have been such long-time allies? Well, the English superiority complex is always looking for something to feel superior to (especially since it lost all its colonies). This binds the nation together. There are two things an Englishman hates: arrogance and stupidity. The first is secretly desired, and the second is ruthlessly satirized. So the hottest ticket in London as I write this is for *Jerry Springer—The Opera,* a musical that portrays the dimwitted, dumbed-downed culture of exhibitionist American television shows as a simulacrum of American life in general. Fine—as long as they don't assume we're *all* like that! The more serious reason for disenchantment with America is—what else?—politics. Tony Blair was George Bush's one and only ally in the war with Iraq, but polls indicated that a majority of Brits did not support that war, no matter how hard the government tried to goose up approval for it. So, not unsurprisingly, the other hot ticket in the West End just now is a show that portrays George Bush as a teddy bear–hugging nitwit egomaniac. Be prepared to discuss American culture and politics at length if you get invited to any London parties, or strike up a conversation. It's important to *hold views* in London. Apathy will get you nowhere.

And don't worry, no one will spit in your face once they hear your unmistakable American accent (an accent they can never get right when they try to mimic it). The worst that can happen is that they'll feel sorry for you. But be compassionate and remember that they are probably pissed off because nothing works right in London. Especially the transit system.

So what makes a Londoner's tongue tick? Well, the royals do it every time. Their greatness/uselessness is a topic close to every Brit's heart. Why are the Brits so obsessed with the royals? Because, frankly, they're fed up with them but are afraid to lose the traditions they represent. The Brits know perfectly well that the royals are basically a successful tourist attraction (albeit incredibly expensive to maintain) and a slice of old-world history, and not much else. There is always a royal scandal to keep tongues wagging and palace officials scurrying to put out the public-relations fires.

The spotlight was first turned on Diana and the breakup of her marriage to Prince Charles. It then moved on to lazy Prince Andrew and his failed marriage to Sarah Ferguson (desperately selling her name to the highest bidder). After that, it moved back to Prince Charles and his mistress, Camilla Parker-Bowles, and then a couple of years ago it moved to the Queen's new daughter-in-law, Sophie Rhys-Jones, who married the Queen's youngest, Edward—the one everyone thinks is gay—and became the countess of Wessex. After getting hitched, the countess boasted about how much her royal connections were helping attract potential clients to her PR firm. Trouble is, said clients were actually undercover reporters...oops. Then her husband—still trying to make a go of his dreadful and hugely unprofitable TV company—got a very public dressing-down from big bro and first-in-line-to-throne Charles for following his nephew Will around the university with camera crews. This despite a friendly agreement between the Royal Household and TV flacks to leave the poor kid alone till he's all grown up. In 2002, the spotlight of scandal moved dangerously close to the queen herself. Just before Diana's butler was due to go on trial for allegedly stealing some of her things, the queen conveniently remembered that said butler had, in fact, told her not long after Diana's death that he was holding some items for safekeeping. It was a move both deft and clumsy on the queen's part. She got the trial—with its no-doubt-awful royal revelations—called off, but everyone naturally wondered why she had to wait until the very last minute to "remember" something that she could have mentioned a year earlier.

The monarchy isn't up there in the popularity polls, but it still wields terrific emotional power. Like it or not, the Windsors provide a great real-life soap opera, one that is rivaled in popularity only by that other great national soap, *Eastenders*. Catch it on BBC1 most weeknights at 7:30 or 8.

However blasé the Londoner may be about the royals, their continued existence raises a dilemma for the visitor. Do you do the royal thing, or act cool and ignore it? Do you, as you secretly are dying to, visit Buckingham Palace and take day trips to Windsor Castle? Oh, to hell with it; you *do* do the royal thing, knowing that the pomp and circumstance of royal London today is as hollow as St. Paul's dome. Still, the history is fascinating, and the riches are impressive (if you don't think too hard about how they were amassed).

To avoid disappointment, you should immediately release the common misconception that London is a beautiful city. Of course, there are many parts that are pretty, but great chunks of England's capital are also pretty hideous. Tottenham Court Road—where Londoners buy electronic, hi-fi, and computer goods, and you'll almost certainly exit the tube there at some stage—is one of the ugliest streets in Europe. Oxford Street is

Map 1: London Neighborhoods

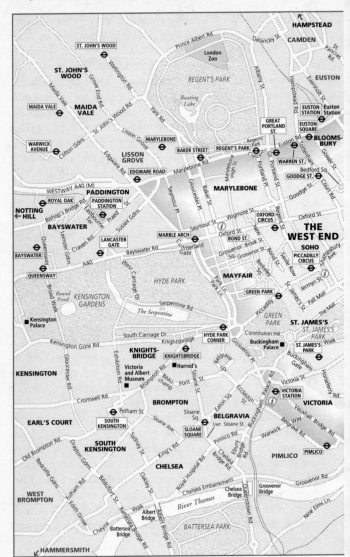

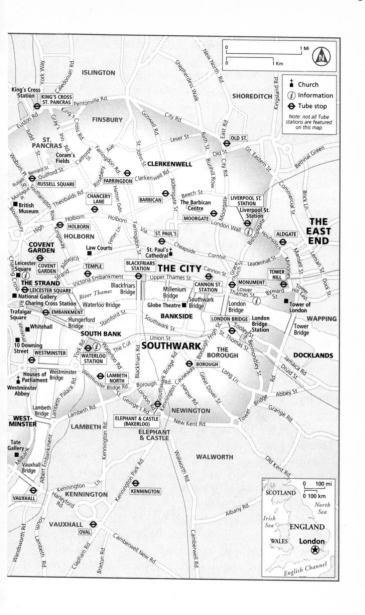

no great shakes either, and all over the place, including most of the City, there's plenty of uninspired architecture that got hurled up after the World War II blitz, plus acres of housing projects (called council housing), awful '60s office blocks, and grotesque monuments to '80s greed (the Thatcher years). There's a certain urban *jolie-laide* style about this real London, however, and if you want to know London, you shouldn't avoid it or avert your eyes.

Parts of the "new" London, though, are better than ever. Norman Foster's Millennium Bridge, though it had to be closed twice before it opened, is now a sleek and welcome addition to the London bridges, and so are the revamped pedestrian footbridges on either side of Hungerford Bridge between Embankment and the South Bank. The Fosterized glass roof over the Great Court in the British Museum is a fabulous improvement to the hallowed halls, and from any bridge in the city you can look east and see the glass gherkin shape of his newest skyscraper in the City. And right alongside the Thames, next to Tower Bridge, is yet another Foster creation: the new London City Hall, shaped like a wasp's behind but environmentally as green as they come. And someone finally had the brilliant foresight to close Trafalgar Square to traffic (at least one side of it) so that pedestrians can now walk right from the National Gallery onto the most famous square in England.

Some of the impressive improvements in London are not visible from the outside. For instance, there are great new galleries in the Victoria and Albert Museum, the Science Museum, and the Tate Britain. (And even more wonderful, all of London's great national museums are now completely free.) All the new spaces and courtyards and buildings and bridges—and the Starbucks that you now see on every corner—should put to rest the old images of London as a place where thick fogs swirl endlessly around Big Ben.

Another misconception that should be laid to rest before you walk out into the hermetically sealed corridors of Heathrow is that all the theater in London is great. If you believe that, you may as well tear up a dozen 10-pound notes right now for practice. Amidst bona fide theatrical greatness you'll find dreary dramas, uninspired musicals, unfunny comedies—just like New York!

Guidebooks—and many of the first-time visitors who buy them—would prefer it if London would stick to its old image, the one that worked through the 1950s, when the "Great" in Great Britain still seemed an appropriate qualifier, and ladies wore white gloves to tea. That city of polite rituals, colonial hauteur, and gracious monuments was demolished once and for all by the Swinging '60s, the punky '70s, and the money-mad '80s. All the change has rendered London a much more complicated place, harder to grasp and still harder to penetrate. The much-vaunted '90s re-swinging of London hasn't made the place more accessible either. Its latest title, the New Capital of Europe, is completely untrue (Berlin is the New Capital of Europe). All it's done is made the city more smug, while failing to increase the number of taxis.

Another preconception that should be scraped into the rubbish bin: that the local cuisine consists of dried-up meat, leathery Yorkshire pudding, and sad, colorless vegetables. Neophytes to London's food scene are astonished to find that a city with a glorious culinary confidence has set in, influenced by every cuisine of the world. There's just one problem: Eating out in many London restaurants is unbelievably expensive. A modest lunch for two with a couple of drinks at a current "in" spot recently set my (thankfully paying) host back about £100 ($165).

England is, of course, officially part of Europe now, and boundary-free work permits mean more cross-fertilization with neighbors. The underwater link with France via the Channel Tunnel has underlined that connection. London is also every bit as much a melting pot as New York, with West Indian, Bangladeshi, Indian, and Pakistani cultures firmly integrated. Look at Soho. Quite unlike its New York namesake, this roughly 2.5km (square mile or so) of the deepest West End, having hosted successive waves of immigrants and gone through a protracted sleaze period, never lost its cosmopolitan, bohemian spiciness, and has settled in as London's playground of clubs and restaurants and hot gay scene.

Of course, it's not wrong to seek *auld London towne,* but that is not the focus of this guide. The London that can't be packaged is harder to find but more rewarding because it's personal. How to get personal with people who stay inside by the fire, throw dinner parties for each other, and belong to exclusive clubs is a challenge, especially now that the chattering classes have fallen in love with The Restaurant. To begin a relationship with London, it's best to dilute, or eschew, the tourist trail. See all the big sights on one visit, and you'll come away with your stiff-upper-lipped British bulldog prejudices reinforced—but you won't meet a soul who isn't a fellow tourist.

If you'd rather befriend a Londoner, there's no foolproof method (except, perhaps, sex, and, of course, that doesn't always work either). For every American who visits twice a year with the adopted London family whom he or she met in the line at the National Theatre, there's a sad story of a lonely week being snubbed in pubs and dining at a table for one near the loos. Since knowing people is the best route to some version of the real London, though, you should reach out, regardless of the British reputation for non-garrulousness with strangers. It's only habit that keeps them from talking to people they don't know, and the worst you'll have to deal with is a withering glance or a muttered reply. Pubs—those communal sitting rooms with large drinks cabinets—sometimes offer the perfect environment to get chatting, though they do revolve around alcohol (and often billowing cigarette smoke), and still tend not to be the most comfortable environments for single women. But alcohol sure does loosen the British tongue. In fact, you might be tempted to wonder if they could survive a day without booze.

Go ahead, ask questions—the Brits love trying to explain their culture. Ask about the incomprehensible rules of cricket, the current state of the class system, the difference between a *Guardian* and a *Telegraph* reader, whether anyone has heard of John Grisham and who's Jeffrey Archer anyway (in fact, in light of his recent fall from grace, millionaire author/politician/liar Archer has become Britain's favorite love-to-hate figure: Drop his name and break the ice in all but the most frigid company). Ask what's with Brits and toilet humor; and, by all means, ask about the weather, which remains a popular and safe topic.

Where to go to meet the candidates for your friendly overtures depends on where you're coming from. Suburbanites and professionals may not bond with youth culture–oriented neighborhoods like Notting Hill, Camden Town, and Shoreditch. Perhaps only New Yorkers, San Franciscans, Angelenos, and other big-city babes, who speak the language of street style, will. On the other hand, Chelsea—the swinging King's Road of the '60s—is now full of the scenes made by models and trustfunders, Eurotrash and bankers, and is (along with neighboring Knightsbridge) quite the place to which Elvis Costello didn't want to go. For Chelsea's diametric opposite, try Brixton, a 'hood far more West Indian than white-guys-with-dreadlocks Notting Hill, and also home to dyke chic, bike messengers, and young families restoring Georgian houses. It also has a reputation for being unsafe, and all of that makes it a draw for the hip and intrepid city anthropologist. Professors and freelance creatives may find soul mates in Islington, where Camden kids go when they grow up. Islingtonians work in TV or the print media, or act, and never leave their borough of restaurants, pubs, bookshops, and the Almeida, London's best Off–West End theater.

But since you're not moving here, and time is limited, even the Almeida may be further off the West End than you have time to wander. Perhaps, like the priciest hotels on the British Monopoly board, you'll just keep landing on Mayfair and St. James's, following the royal path from Kensington to Belgravia, and merely grazing the green and pleasant surface of the city. That's okay. Whatever you do in London, you'll be left to get on with it.

YOU PROBABLY DIDN'T KNOW

How to get London smarts... You can't. Or at least it's not that easy. London's reputation for impenetrability is no myth. As a "bloody foreigner," you'll probably have to live here for at least 2 years just to qualify for a provisional Londoner license, and that's just for tourist rights. Still, many "Londoners" are imported from the British provinces and former colonies—so they may understand your desperation to fit in, though they will be loath to admit it. Tip for the top on this front is to think of London as a series of small towns. If you want to fit in, pick an area that appeals to you and stick to it—almost no one in London maintains rep in more than one area. Swallow your pride and be persistent.

Where to get a drink after hours... British licensing laws are bizarre. As things stand, alcohol cannot be sold after 11pm, when pubs are legally bound to give desperate imbibers 20 minutes drinking-up time before ejecting them into the night. Since everyone, including those responsible for them, considers these laws daft (they're a throwback to World War I, when the laws were geared to make munitions workers head home to beddy-bye at a reasonable hour), there has been an increasing laxity in their enforcement, and many bars are already open, and legal, until midnight or 1am. As you will read in the "Nightlife" chapter, rumors abound that licensing laws are going to be officially relaxed in the near future. The Brits want to be able to drink until breakfast, just like other European nations. Other rumors suggest, however, that the laws may be tightened even further in some residential areas. To locate late-drinking spots, avoid overly residential areas; instead, check out **Soho** and the largely commercial districts of **Clerkenwell/Farringdon** and **Shoreditch**). West London is also getting laxer—but, frankly, the best way to find out what's hot and what's not is to ask in the bar you're in for local recommendations. If all else fails, remember that most hotels are able to bypass the licensing laws regarding guests and can keep you tanked up into the wee small hours. Also, restaurants can serve booze until midnight if you're eating, and nightclubs often have late licensing, although rarely beyond 3am. Late bars are a lottery you may not want to play; many have rude doormen and an irritating entry policy (if you know/have slept with/will sleep with/might consider sleeping with me/my friend). Lastly, be prepared for cover charges, crowds, and lots of cigarette smoke in late-night bars.

Where are the insomniacs?... Bar Italia, on **Frith Street** in Soho. The tiny, echt-Italian, stand-up espresso bar with a Rocky Marciano altar and stale panettone contains London's only life—if you can call it that—after 4am.

Where the hot neighborhoods are... There are four. For an evening out, **Soho** is still the place, as it has been since the 1950s. It has a thriving and friendly gay and mixed scene and an atmosphere that is seriously relaxed. Soho is also restaurant land and home to London's small but worthwhile Chinatown. Many, however, have come to feel that Soho is too anonymous and too full of tourists and therefore not the place to experience London. In the 1980s, **Camden Town** took over the mantle, or at least helped to share the burden of it. Camden is still the center for live music, struggling bands, and scruffy, booted youth. It's also where you find street markets, vintage clothes, and even a smattering of goths and punks, those symbols of London's street-style roots (even though most of them these days are not even British, let alone Londoners). **Notting Hill** is an altogether more modern arbiter of what's hot in London town. Home to many of the artists who have put London on the style map, Notting Hill is another restaurant region, but it also offers bars, galleries, markets (such as Portobello, arguably London's finest), West Indian culture, the biggest street carnival in the northern hemisphere, and antiques galore. Native Notting Hillbillies look cool and deconstructed, so you can't tell if they're slackers or trustafarians with a bestseller under their belts. Lastly, **Shoreditch,** the newest kid on the block, is East London's capital of cool. The artists of Shoreditch are thought to be more "genuine, man" than their West London counterparts. A scarcity of residential space means later drinking, but some may be put off by the postapocalyptic landscape. Shoreditchers seem to believe that trees are passé, so bizarre sculptures serve the streets instead. To each his—or her—own.

> **Children's Hour**
> Some of our favorite characters in children's literature are Londoners. Mr. and Mrs. Dearly, who owned Pongo, Perdita, and the 99 other Dalmatians, lived on the Outer Circle of Regent's Park, while Wendy and Michael Darling left their Victorian house on the north side of Kensington Gardens for NeverNeverLand. As for bears, Paddington had a station named after him, from which British Rail trains still depart for the West Country, and a certain bear named Winnie had residence for a time in the Polar Bear pit at the London Zoo. Then, of course, there's Harry Potter. He isn't a Londoner but before he goes off to Hogwarts, his school, he visits Dagon Alley, a wizards' mall in London. Harry's author, by the way, is now the richest woman in England, even richer than the queen herself.

Where to park… Nowhere, because you didn't rent a car, did you? What's that? You did? Well, more fool you. Try to avoid broken meters, red lines, double yellow lines, single yellow lines before 6:30pm and after 8:30am, and residents' zones. You may be able to ignore a ticket but not one of the massive clamping units that roam the city, ruining lives.

The big yellow immobilizing wheel clamps will take a day to have removed and cost £120 ($198). Towing also happens and results in the same loss of time/cash, with the added bonus of trying to figure out exactly where they might have taken little Herbie. Unclaimed cars are crushed, so do not stall tracking down your errant roadster. If you're looking for safe and easy parking, find an NCP park; the rates are exorbitant but you can find these places all over London—and I can assure you that you will never, ever, find a legal space to park on the street in this city. The traffic problem is so bad that in 2003 a £5 ($8.25) daily "congestion charge" went into effect. Everyone who drives into Central London must pay it.

When to avoid London... Christmas. It's fun and buzzy right up to the day before Christmas Eve. Then everything shuts down for interminable turkey and the queen's oh-so-relevant speech about which members of the Commonwealth are going to attempt independence next.

Where the top chefs are... Oh please, where aren't they? Example: Once upon a time, 192, the Notting Hill restaurant, had a kitchen run by a fellow named Alastair Little. His protégés included Rowley Leigh, Dan Evans, Adam Robinson, and Angela Dwyer. Each of these people now has at least one establishment of his or her own, and many have nurtured other chefs who have gone on to run their own places. Other eateries can be traced to the Roux Brothers or Anton Mosimann or Prue Leith and Ruthie Rogers. To find the cuisine of your dreams, simply scan the million newspaper gastroporn sections. I can certainly tell you where the top chefs *aren't:* in the kitchens of the B&Bs where you'll probably be staying and eating that big greasy breakfast.

How to afford that grand dinner... Lunch, prix-fixe. The 3-hour lunch never did die here, so you'll be in good company. Also, each February, the *Financial Times* does a promotion where top tables go for a ridiculously cheap £5 or £10 ($8.25–$17); entrance ticket is a copy of *FT,* printed on its distinctive pink paper, and booking is essential.

What's that ringing sound?... A mobile, darling. Cellphones are to London what cockroaches are to New York, and just as annoying.

How to save buckets of cash on museums... Simple: Go to the free ones, which now includes all of London's top museums. Any museum with national collections now has free admission, that means biggies like the **Victoria and Albert** and its South Kensington neighbors the **Natural History Museum** and **Science Museum,** plus **Tate Britain** and **Tate Modern.** You still have to pay for runner-up places like the **Courtauld Institute Gallery** and the **Hayward** (see the "Diversions" chapter for full details).

How to stay with London friends when you haven't any... Upscale B&Bs are a new thing in a country where a B&B sign normally heralds a depressing room with mismatched furniture. Unlike American B&Bs, which are often small inns, these London digs are truly private homes with rooms to let to an exclusive few. The **Bulldog Club agency** (tel 020/7371-3202; fax 020/7371-2015; www.bulldogclub.com) is top-drawer—Maggie Jackson practically runs a credit check on you before you're allowed into her friends' tiny houses—and **Uptown Reservations** (tel 020/7351-3445; www.uptownres.co.uk) has some great places in Central London. And there's always home-swapping. This works like it sounds: trading places with your counterparts in London. Although nearly all participants describe their abode accurately in the home-swap catalogs, Americans often experience a degree of culture shock when staying in an English home, running into privations like snowed-up iceboxes, lack of central heat, doormanless walk-ups (a normal London flat), and stick-shift cars with the steering wheel on the wrong side. If you're persnickety, don't swap your home. Otherwise, register with **Intervac** (tel and fax 01225/892-011; www.intervac.co.uk); **Homelink International** (tel 01344/842-642; www.homelink.org.uk; Linfield House, Gorse Hill Rd., Virginia Water, Surrey GU25 4AS) or **Home Base Holidays** (tel 020/8886-8752; www.homebase-hols.com; 7 Park Ave., London N13 5PG).

Where the queen gets her groceries... Fortnum & Mason. But you'll never see Her Maj strolling down the aisles with a shopping cart: Her flunkies do all that.

How to order Indian food... With 1,500-odd Indian restaurants in London alone, curry is England's national cuisine. Everyone orders the following: onion *bhajia* (onion fritters), *murgh tikka masala* (yogurt-spice-marinated chicken breast, baked in the tandoor oven and served with thick sauce), *sag ghosh* (lamb with spinach), *mattar paneer* (peas with cubes of Indian curd cheese), *tarka dahl* (garlic lentil sauce), and *pulau* rice (cooked in ghee and stock). Another option is a meat and vegetable *thali*. Traditionally served in silver pots on a silver tray, a *thali* is like a curry sampler and a great way to taste several dishes when you just can't make up your mind. If you want heat, order vindaloo; for extra mild and creamy, have *korma*. Beware of young men in packs on Saturday nights ordering chicken *biriani* and buckets of lager.

How to get designer labels cheap... The best sources are "warehouse sales," where a single designer or a group offloads samples and surplus to the cognoscenti. Look in the *Evening Standard*'s Tuesday fashion section, and in *Time Out*'s "Buys and Bargains" section for notices. Or call the office of your favorite London designer (Katharine Hamnett, Jasper Conran, Nicole Farhi) and ask about the next sample sale. See the "Shopping" chapter for more.

How to hear Queen Victoria... The **National Sound Archive** at the **British Library** (tel 0207/412-7440; 96 Euston Rd. NW1) has a recording of Her Majesty made around 1880. Hear it (and about a million more historic sound bites) by appointment, which can usually be made for the same day.

How to get theater tickets when they're sold out... From the theater. Every theater holds at least one row of "house seats," which the management keeps for its own use. If no one fabulously important wants to see the show that night, or the theater didn't overbook, the tickets are sold at the last possible moment, along with the "returns"—unpicked-up bookings. Some theaters want you to queue up that morning, others an hour or two before curtain. Call ahead to each theater for the policy. The better hotel concierges—usually the ones at posh hotels—are good at getting hold of these in their special way.

What to do on Sunday... Sunday used to be a really dead day in London, before the Sunday trading laws, based on the Christian Sabbath notion, got eroded. Now Sunday is the busiest shopping day of the week, with accompanying lines and traffic jams. If that doesn't put you off, beware of the hours, since large stores are currently allowed only a 6-hour window, and *which* 6 hours they pick varies. But what most bona fide Londoners really do on Sunday is wade through a huge stack of Sunday papers—look on the newsagent's shelf that day and you'll see what I mean. What else could you do? Go to market (especially Camden and the East End ones: Brick Lane, Petticoat Lane, Columbia Road, Spitalfields); have an old-fashioned roast lunch; stroll in the park; see a movie. Some theaters are experimenting with performances on this traditionally "dark" day, too.

What not to do on Sunday... Don't go to the South Ken museums, or see the show at the Tate Modern or the Royal Academy, unless you adore crowds.

What the weather's like... This wouldn't be the number-one topic of conversation in London if anyone understood the British climate. Guidebooks tell you stories about 40°F (4°C) winters and 70°F (21°C) summers, but literally anything could happen. There was a hurricane in 1987, a 97°F (36°C) heat wave in 1989, the hottest August and the wettest June on record in 1997, and nearly always a fortnight in April when temperatures hit the upper 80s, after which frost may hit in May. Sometimes the rain sets in for a week, but not in dramatic downpours or picturesque thunderstorms—just relentless soaking drizzle. In fall 2000, it rained solidly for almost 2 months (Noah, eat your heart out). The local light is flat and diffuse, which is sheer misery on those endless wet days, but absolute perfection on a sunny day in a park.

Do we need a gun?... No. The police increasingly carry firearms, it's true, but London is still a relatively safe city, a result of the fact that personal firearms are not yet an issue in the U.K. Still, the usual commonsense city precautions for taking care of your property and your person apply. More distressing is the rise in the number of homeless people you'll see wherever you go...just like at home.

How to tell where you are... Look at a map of London. See how big it is? London, which grew out of a pack of once-separate villages, is still divided into 32 boroughs— plus the City of London—each separately governed by its own council. Every corner street sign (big white rectangles mounted on walls at about knee level) tells you which borough you're in, in smaller letters above the street name. But the borough system doesn't really tell you where you are; postcodes are marginally better, once you've deciphered them. The letters simply refer to compass points, with the *C* of EC1 and WC2 and so on denoting "central." The numbers seem helpful at first: West Central One is indeed sandwiched between West One, West Central Two, and East Central One, with North One and North West One to the (that's right) north. Travel a bit farther, however, and you find that W2 segues into W11, that W8 is next to SW7, and W9 is NW6's neighbor.

Why the Londoner crossed the river... To get back to the other side. South Londoners hate the snobbish attitude of the majority that lives on the north side and thinks it needs a passport to cross a bridge. Easily accessible South London highlights include the **British Airways London Eye** observation wheel; County Hall, the former headquarters of the London City Council (disbanded by Thatcher), which now is home to the screamingly sensational **Saatchi Gallery,** plus the **Dalí Museum** and the **London Aquarium; National Theatre** and **South Bank Centre, Tate Modern** (on every visitor's list); **Shakespeare's Globe** (which should be); the "Gastrodrome," the **Design Museum,** and the new (2003) **London City Hall** by Tower Bridge; the OXO Tower; Battersea Park and Clapham Common in which to escape other tourists; and neighborhoods to explore, such as Brixton.

How to enjoy Heathrow... Invest in a Virgin Atlantic business-class ticket—or Upper Class, as they cheekily call it. Virgin is the airline belonging to Richard Branson, that gently ridiculed, yet nationally beloved tycoon/visionary. The flight itself is groovy, with its masseuse/manicurist, wine tastings, seat-back gambling, and way-better-than-average grub, but you want to spend an actual vacation in the Upper

Class Lounge at Heathrow. Go early for a haircut, massage, and shoeshine; practice your putting; nap in the rooftop conservatory; listen to CDs in the soundproof lounge; play state-of-the-art computer games. The decor's funky and the Virgin staff friendly—it's an airport lounge fantasy.

ACCOMM

Do Not
Disturb

ODATIONS

Map 2: London Orientation—Accommodations

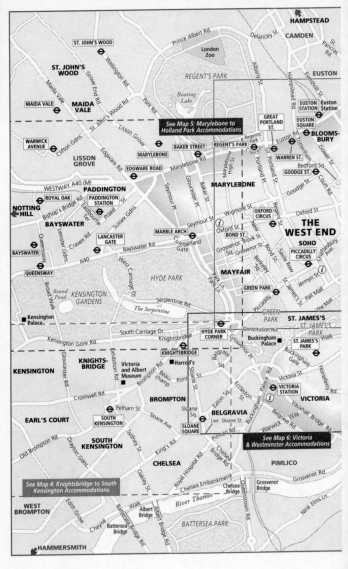

HAMPSTEAD
CAMDEN
St. Pancras Rd
Delancey St.
Prince Albert Rd
ST. JOHN'S WOOD
London Zoo
EUSTON
ST. JOHN'S WOOD
Wellington Rd
Grove End Rd
Park Rd
REGENT'S PARK
Euston Rd
EUSTON STATION Euston Station
EUSTON SQUARE
MAIDA VALE
MAIDA VALE
Maida Vale
St. John's Wood Rd
Hampstead Rd
Boating Lake
Albany St.
GREAT PORTLAND ST.
BLOOMSBURY
WARREN ST.
WARWICK AVENUE
Clifton Gdns.
Edgware Rd
Lisson Grove
See Map 5: Marylebone to Holland Park Accommodations
Regent's
Portland Pl.
Gr. Portland St.
Greenwell St.
Gower St.
Bedford Sq.
GOODGE ST.
LISSON GROVE
MARYLEBONE
BAKER STREET
REGENT'S PARK
Goodge St.
EDGWARE ROAD
Marylebone Rd
Marylebone High St.
Gt. Portland St.
Court Rd.
WESTWAY A40 (M)
PADDINGTON
ROYAL OAK
Seymour Pl.
Gloucester Pl.
Baker St.
Wigmore St.
Oxford St.
OXFORD CIRCUS
Oxford St.
THE WEST END
NOTTING HILL
Bishop's Bridge Rd
PADDINGTON STATION
Eastbourne
Praed St.
Sussex Gdns.
MARYLEBONE
BAYSWATER
Leinster Gdns.
Queensway
Craven Rd.
A40
MARBLE ARCH
Seymour St.
Cumberland Gate
Oxford St. i
BOND ST.
Grosvenor Sq.
New Bond St.
Regent St.
Same Row
SOHO
Shaftesbury Ave.
PICCADILLY CIRCUS
i
LANCASTER GATE
Bayswater Rd.
MAYFAIR
Berkeley Sq.
Jermyn St.
BAYSWATER
QUEENSWAY
West Carriage Dr.
HYDE PARK
GREEN PARK
Piccadilly
The Mall
Pall Mall
Broad Walk
Round Pond
KENSINGTON GARDENS
Serpentine Rd.
Park Ln.
GREEN PARK
ST. JAMES'S
ST. JAMES'S PARK Walk
The Serpentine
South Carriage Dr.
HYDE PARK CORNER
Constitution Hill
Buckingham Palace
ST. JAMES'S PARK
Kensington Palace
Kensington Gore Rd.
Knightsbridge
KNIGHTSBRIDGE
Grosvenor Pl.
Buckingham Gate
Horseferry
KENSINGTON
Exhibition Rd
Gloucester Rd
KNIGHTS-BRIDGE
Victoria and Albert Museum
Harrod's
Beau-champ
Belgrave Sq.
Sloane St.
Buckingham Palace Rd
Victoria St.
i
VICTORIA STATION
VICTORIA
Rd
Cromwell Rd.
Brompton Rd
Pont St.
Eccleston St.
Vauxhall Bridge Rd
EARL'S COURT
Pelham St.
BROMPTON
Sloane Ave.
Sloane Sq.
Eaton Sq.
BELGRAVIA
Belgrave Rd
Belgrave Way
SOUTH KENSINGTON
SOUTH KENSINGTON
Old Brompton Rd.
Drayton Gdns.
Sydney St.
SLOANE SQUARE
Lwr. Sloane St.
Pimlico Rd.
Warwick Way
See Map 6: Victoria & Westminster Accommodations
PIMLICO
King's Rd.
CHELSEA
Royal Hospital Rd
Chelsea Bridge Rd
Grosvenor Rd.
WEST BROMPTON
Edith Grove
Oakley St.
See Map 4: Knightsbridge to South Kensington Accommodations
Chelsea Embankment
Chelsea Bridge
Grosvenor Bridge
Cheyne Walk
Battersea Bridge
Albert Bridge
Battersea Bridge Rd.
Albert Bridge Rd.
River Thames
Queenstown Rd.
Nine Elms Ln.
HAMMERSMITH
BATTERSEA PARK

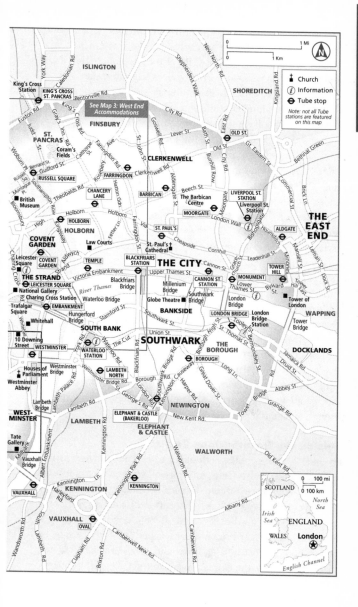

See Map 3: West End
Accommodations

Basic Stuff

Face it: This city makes you pay through the nose for a place to lay your head. You'll have to capitulate and consign half your vacation funds to the hotel bed. It's also true, though, that many London hotels have lowered their prices, and more and more of them are offering special "promotional" deals. They are doing what they can to lure back tourists, especially American tourists, who are particularly important to the London economy (though no one likes to admit this). But even with more empty rooms than usual, it pays to think ahead and spend those pounds wisely. London is blossoming with smaller "boutique" hotels. I list several, and they're very good bets, offering a much deeper London experience than those cookie-cutter chains or even some of the swankiest grand hotels. Then there are the legions of B&B hotels, the low- to mid-range hostelries that service low- to mid-range tourists. Some are great, but you have to be careful or you'll be stuck in a depressing room with a prefab bathroom no larger than what you'd find on an airplane. Some of these places are really pleasant, though, and you needn't feel ashamed to stay in them. Of course, the best (and cheapest) way of all to get under London's skin is to stay with friends. If you don't have any, you can buy the next best thing— the hospitality of strangers in upscale B&Bs, still a relatively new concept in town. These are rooms you rent in private homes through an agency. *And here's a tip:* One of the cheapest ways of all to experience London is in your own flat, rented through an agency.

Winning the Reservations Game

Try not to arrive roofless. Booking ahead not only gives you peace of mind, it also yields any special, weekend, or corporate rates that might be offered. Typically, though, it's the more expensive and bigger places that offer discounts, while the smaller hotels, guesthouses, and B&Bs don't reduce their already lower rates. If you book a packaged holiday, you may be given a hotel's most boring, boxy, and smallest room, but the rates are probably the lowest you could get for that property. Check into the air/hotel packages offered by most airlines that fly into London—you'll usually save a bundle and get a more-than-decent hotel room. Also check into the half-price programs—they're worth it if they include a hotel you like. Usually, you register, join, or buy a directory, which then accesses savings of up to 50% on the hotels in that program.

One to try is **Privilege Card International** (237 E. Front St., Youngstown, OH 44503; tel 800/236-9732; www.privilegecard. com). You can also book hotels online—usually with considerable savings—at the London Tourist Board's website, **www.visit london.com**, and also at www.londontown.com. If you arrive without a room (or want to book a room in advance by phone), try calling the **British Hotel Reservation Centre** (tel 020/ 7340-1616; www.bhrc.co.uk).

Is There a Right Address?

To a certain sort of Londoner (they're usually called Sloane Rangers, after their Sloane Square stomping grounds), **Knightsbridge** is the center not only of London, but of the world. For tourists, too, it's hard to beat, well served with tube, restaurants, and shopping—and Hyde Park on the doorstep. Just south of Knightsbridge, **Belgravia** is embassy territory, and home to some of the priciest real estate in town. As a tourist base it sure is peaceful, but there's not much more, except for pleasant strolls and Hyde Park.

Famously swinging in the '60s and boutique-heavy today, **Chelsea,** a onetime artists' ghetto west of Belgravia, is expensive to live in and lovely to walk in. Its main drawback for visitors is inaccessibility, since there's a weird dearth of tube stops. There are buses galore, though, and lots of fab-o shopping and dining in the borough. Also west of the West End, green, peaceful, and expensive residential **Holland Park** is 10 minutes by tube from practically anywhere, yet has a distinct out-of-the-maelstrom ambience and one of London's loveliest small parks. **Kensington** is busier and more urban than neighboring Holland Park, as well as being home to some good shopping, while sharing some of its green and pleasant peaceful feel. **South Kensington,** with its high-ceilinged houses, contains those giant Victorian cultural palaces—the museums. Streets are quieter and prices higher than farther north, except on the main roads (Brompton, Gloucester, Cromwell), where the opposite is the case. If you're a snob, you probably don't want to go much further west than **Earl's Court,** and maybe not even, though this formerly down-at-the-heels neighborhood is gradually gentrifying all over the place and has a few really nice hotels that would cost twice as much in another borough. Earl's Court isn't as gay as it used to be (Soho has taken over as Gay Central), and you probably wouldn't want to stick around for dining or evening fun. But it's only 15 minutes by tube to

Piccadilly. North of Holland Park, **Notting Hill** is the hippest district, centering on Portobello Road with its market. Antiques shops, a Caribbean-style carnival in August, and exciting young restaurants and galleries give Notting Hill a multicultural buzz. (With the arrival of the film *Notting Hill,* however, some say the area has lost it hip credibility, and have fled east to **Shoreditch** and **Clerkenwell.** While thin on accommodations, these districts see plenty of other action; see the Dining, Shopping, and Nightlife chapters.) East of Notting Hill is **Bayswater,** between Oxford Street and Queensway, between residential and midtown, and between swanky and seedy. It's full of cheapo hostelries in huge white wedding-cake Victorians. Those I list are on the upper end of this spectrum, though still bargains, easy to get around from, and bang on Hyde Park.

Mayfair is London's true center, and you'll feel most urbane and sophisticated staying here. Bond Street shopping, Cork Street art galleries, tree-filled squares, restaurants—it's all here. Less expensive and less tony are Oxford Street and the streets to its north. Just across Piccadilly from Mayfair, **St. James's** has been known as "Gentleman's London" on account of its anachronistic clubs and its legions of shops selling hats, canes, shaving sets, ties, shirts, and handmade shoes. It retains an old-fashioned and courtly air, has two beautiful parks, its own palace, good restaurants, and top hotel rates. East of Regent Street, **Soho** on weekend nights is the nightclubbers' theme park, with hordes of youths and a thriving gay scene. Other times, the confusing grid of streets is restaurant paradise. Great fun, but very few hotels.

On the east side of Charing Cross Road, **Covent Garden** is another center of London, not packed with hotel beds but rife with shopping, strolling, and eating places. It's as near as you can get to theaterland. North of Covent Garden lies **Bloomsbury,** made famous by Virginia Woolf and her circle. Convenient to the British Museum and lined with moderate small hotels, it's somewhat dusty and noisy but nevertheless a central place to stay. **Marylebone,** to the north of Bloomsbury and cupping giant Regent's Park, is a grab bag of the commercial and the cultural, though nobody can ever claim to feel uplifted by viewing the wax dummies in Madame Tussaud's, Marylebone's most famous—and overrated—tourist attraction. (If you have any class, you'll prefer the Wallace Collection instead.) If you know where to look, though, Marylebone has some very fine hotels. There are some, but I don't list any hotels in the **Docklands,** way downstream on the Thames about halfway to Greenwich. This is London's new business district that never quite took off—part de Chirico ghost town, part riverside theme park.

The Lowdown

Old faithfuls... The "Old Lady of Park Lane" is first in line. She is **Grosvenor House** (now, officially, **Le Meridien Grosvenor House**), built on the grounds of the earl of Grosvenor's late-18th-century estate. She's bulky, none too glamorous, and, like many an old friend, reassuringly homey and undemanding. The more glitzy **Savoy** never changes either, and we're glad of that, while the nearby **Fielding** is like the frumpy friend, dressed in sweats but seen in the right places. Some surprisingly wealthy people savor the continuity and fab location (in the heart of Covent Garden) of the little Fielding. Another old faithful that is refreshingly unglam and reassuringly welcoming is the **Hart House Hotel,** where the current owner carries on the traditions of his parents, who ran this small Marylebone B&B hotel for decades.

Grand duchesses... Masquerading as an old friend, but more of a snob than she cares to admit, is **The Connaught,** where you practically need a letter of introduction to get a room. It's considered very crass to ask for prices here. **The Dorchester** is the place to unpack your ball gown, or boogie in the nightclub if you lack an invitation to the ball. **Claridge's** is the epitome of understated elegance—royalty feels at home on the sweeping marble stairs here, as do ancient dowagers lunching on smoked fish in its restaurant, the Causerie.

Favorite uncles... Slightly racy, a little unpredictable, these are relatively new guys in town. In brazen Soho, **Hazlitt's 1718,** with its nooks and crannies, Victorian bathtubs, and many thousands of etchings, is popular with antiques dealers and literary lions; it's the oldest uncle of the lot, dating back to 1718. Its younger but bigger brother, **The Gore,** shares its style but expands on it, and features several over-the-top rooms. The **Stafford** has an interesting side: The carriage-house rooms, which have the names of racehorses on their stable doors, are fun. The **Landmark London** is full of surprises—it's a fully fledged grande dame with no dress code in an unstarchy part of town (Marylebone), with an outrageous atrium behind its unremarkable facade. More of a collection of pied-à-terre than a hotel, the slightly down-at-the-heel **Dolphin Square** is redolent of clandestine encounters, especially in the brasserie and in the bar overlooking the swimming pool with its 1950s-era murals, while the library at the **Covent Garden Hotel** is the very place for avuncular advice sessions over a glass of bubbly. **Twenty Nevern Square** is a younger and unsnobby uncle in Earl's Court (well, you have to be unsnobby in Earl's Court), full of stylistic verve and determined to go his own way.

Where to misbehave... The **Savoy** has always had a louche air about it, perhaps because it has its own theater, or maybe it's the handmade beds or the breezes rolling in off the Thames. Many Londoners who had a rock 'n' roll phase misspent part of their youth in the bar of the **Columbia,** which never closes to the bands in residence; the bedrooms, meanwhile, host photo shoots for sleazy fashion articles in famous glossy magazines. Completely the opposite form of chic has its home base at **The Hempel,** which is so pristine, hushed, and downright Zen-like, you can't help wanting to besmirch its immaculate surfaces. At **The Portobello,** the round-bed suite with a fully functioning Edwardian brass bathing machine is practically perverted. And let's not forget to mention the **St. Martin's Lane** near Leicester Square, where you can coordinate the color of the lighting in your room to match whatever naughty mood you might be in.

Britishest... Every other hotel in London has a faux-Brit chintzy decor, a couple of four-poster beds, and afternoon tea, but no hotel is more genuinely English than **The Connaught,** where oils hang in oak-paneled hallways and you get the feeling that your nanny may be lurking around the corner to scold you for making too much noise. The **Basil Street Hotel** is the cut-price version—it's like a dowager Knightsbridge aunt's house. The B&B agencies the **Bulldog Club** and **Uptown Reservations,** mind you, will book you into actual dowager aunts' houses in Knightsbridge, Kensington, and all the best addresses, while taking an apartment at **Dolphin Square** will make you the temporary neighbor of many members of Parliament, not to mention Princess Anne.

Worst simulated English... The clear winner of the Lionel Bart "London!" award is the **Lanesborough.** Great Britain was never as British as this—with drawing rooms, frills, and furbelows, and a genuine Jeeves on duty in every room (though the management is forever having to train new butlers, as American guests poach them). Honorable mention: **Browns,** especially for the venerable afternoon tea service, heavy on scones with lashings of clotted cream. Tea is better elsewhere (see the Dining chapter), but the tourists don't seem to know this.

Eurotrashiest... What with the Channel Tunnel and all, London now wants to pretend it is Europe's newest capital—without being a part of Europe. The question these days is really what neighborhood is *not* Eurotrashy. The style kids with cash would not be seen dead except in a very few hotels, and, frankly, darling, they'd rather stay with friends. But if they have to buy a bed, they get it at the **Sydney.** Those who don't sneer at hostelries flock to **The Metropolitan,** which was shamelessly designed expressly for them, though **Claridge's** is still okay, and while **Blakes** is a bit too music-biz, **The Hempel** continues to be a safe bet from the plebs—at least for the moment. **St. Martin's Lane** attracts some of the Continental martyrs to style, too.

Was that Gwyneth Paltrow in the elevator?... Before it closed, the Halcyon was the hands-down winner in this category. Now the truly hip slum it at the so-out-it's-in **Columbia.** Madonna and Michael Jackson have been known to choose fittingly ungroovy hotels: Ms. Ciccone queened it at the **Lanesborough** before she became a local, while the Weird One went to the **Montcalm** (which has London's only nonallergenic bedrooms. Surely no coincidence?). **The Metropolitan's** Met Bar has young Hollywood, half the music biz, and all the fashion crowd in a holding pattern (with Momo and the Soho House taking the overflow).

Suite deals... A person could move into the penthouse at **Dukes**—though not over-opulent, it's deeply carpeted, with plenty of space and a balcony, and you wake up looking at distant Westminster Abbey. **Hazlitt 1718**'s sole suite—a black oak Tudor fantasia with its own "Great Bed of Ware"—is fun for playing Lancelot and Guinevere, while Hazlitt's sister hotel, **The Gore,** has a suite with a bed Judy Garland once owned, and outrageous Grecian tiles in the bathroom. The **Stafford**'s carriage rooms have fireplaces and Jacuzzis (downstairs), and entrances off their own cobbled mews. Two bargains in accidental suites (they don't claim to be, but they are virtual suites): the none-too-handsome basement (number 77) at **Bryanston Court** and the **Commodore**'s wonderfully quiet, lemon-yellow duplex (number 11).

Silent nights... Yes, the **Commodore** is quiet, as is the above-mentioned **Stafford** and its neighbor, the even quieter—since it's set in its own gaslit alley—**Dukes.** Another group of neighbors with peaceful postcodes are the **Beaufort,** the **Franklin,** and the **Claverley,** tucked on a residential South Kensington side street just off the Brompton Road. Nearby, in Chelsea, the **Sloane Hotel** and the **Sydney Hotel** won't keep you up late—neither will ambient noise at **Blakes** or **The Portobello,** though your fellow guests' partying might. While at Blakes' sister, **The Hempel,** the peaceful garden square (which Anouska Hempel failed to have renamed Hempel Sq.) brings peace as deafeningly Zen as the decor. High rooms at the **London Hilton on Park Lane** don't even need their sound insulation. The most peacefully positioned hostelry of all is **Holland House Youth Hostel**—too bad its dorm-style sleeping arrangements take away your privacy.

Best park view... Holland House Youth Hostel, being inside Holland Park, has to lead this category. If you like to look upon green, though, this is a fine city. All the Park Lane grands (**Le Meridien Grosvenor House,** the **London Hilton on Park Lane, The Dorchester**), as well as the **Lanesborough** and **The Metropolitan,** overlook Hyde Park—if you get a room on the park side, of course—and at the latter, if you snag a corner suite, you are practically floating on top of the trees. From the **London Hilton**

on **Park Lane**'s highest floors, you can also see a corner of the queen's private gardens at Buckingham Palace. A different side of Hyde Park is available for half the rates at the **Columbia** and the **London Elizabeth**. Peep into private squares from **Dorset Square, Egerton House,** the **Franklin, The Hempel,** and **The Portobello.** Stay in room number 201 to 205 at the **Athenaeum** to get an eyeful of gorgeous Green Park.

May I get that for you, sir?... Service is a difficult commodity to pin down, since star individuals move on, but Donald and Alex, the pair of lovely concierges at the **Athenaeum,** have been there for a long time and show no sign of leaving. In general, this hotel apparently attracts kind people. The **Beaufort,** similarly, has an all-female staff that goes out of its way to make you happy, as does the neighboring crew at the **Claverley.** The ferociously modern **Halkin** looks like the kind of place where you'd get snubbed for no reason, but the Armani-uniformed Euro types who work there are especially nice, as are the informal staff at the very central **Covent Garden Hotel.** The small **London Elizabeth** has a loyal team of Irishly smiling staff, while the tiny **Sloane Hotel** retains gorgeous and conscientious young Spaniards and Swedes until their wanderlust moves them onward.

Bargain beds... Top-value prize goes to the high-end B&B agency the **Bulldog Club** for the ultimate in homey luxury. You get to live in the kind of house you'd want to own if you lived in London and will probably be given the insights of the family that actually does live there. **Uptown Reservations** does the same thing, offering relatively inexpensive but inspected and shipshape homes in all neighborhoods. **Hart House Hotel** in Marylebone is a bargain. It goes without saying that the **Holland House Youth Hostel** is cheap; those allergic to communal living should note that there are a couple of rooms (as opposed to dormitories) here.

The millionaire look, at Scrooge rates... All the hotels of David Naylor-Leyland and of Tim and Kit Kemp's Firmdale Hotels are beautiful to behold. **Egerton House** was Mr. N-L's first, and the one on which he lavished his best pieces and spared no expense. He takes the furniture home when it's too threadbare for his hotel. The penthouse suite at his **Dukes** hotel looks pricier than it is, and his **Franklin** hotel also gives a good deal of swank for the money. The Firmdale hotels I list are the **Covent Garden Hotel** and **the Pelham Hotel.** The **Dorset Square Hotel,** an ex-Firmdale beauty, has slightly lower rates. All three have probably been in the British decor-porn magazine, *World of Interiors* (I must have missed that issue). A relative newcomer to the millionaire look is **Twenty Nevern Square,** on the Earl's Court square of the same name, where lovely natural fabrics and finishes enhance every room and the prices are about half of what they'd be in another part of Central London. The two tiny independents that run away with the honors in this category, however, are the **Sloane Hotel** and the **Sydney.** Each is the love child of its doting owner, although Jean Luc of the Sydney has now moved on; each owner possesses such an eye! And at the Sloane, if you really love what Sue Rogers has done, you can take it home. Yes, every antique and gewgaw, along with the TV/VCRs, is for sale, and not at millionaire prices, either.

Family values... If your family wants to stay together in a family room, here are the best deals in town. Close to Madame Tussaud's and Regent's Park (the zoo!), **Hotel La Place**'s five family rooms are a great value, and **Hart House Hotel** has some reasonably priced family-size rooms as well. Both properties are child-friendly, as is **Basil Street Hotel.** Some of the many family rooms at the **Columbia** are big enough to play hide-and-seek in on a rainy after-noon; you can fit a family of five (one being a baby) in here for a hundred quid a night, English breakfast included. The **Commodore,** down the block, has better-looking multiple rooms, but they aren't the best rooms in the place—those are the two-level almost-duplexes, in which you could easily fit a family if you request a cot. For older kids who demand their own room, **Dolphin Square**'s larg-er apartments are the business. At the **Stafford** there are some triples, or you could fit an extra bed in a carriage-house room without feeling cramped.

For history buffs and Anglophiles... It was founded by Lord Byron's butler, honeymooned in by FDR, and was the place where Alexander Graham Bell made his first experimental telephone call. No wonder **Browns** is the number-one pick for amateur historians, especially when you consider the fame of its afternoon tea (you'd do better, actually, to take tea elsewhere). **Le Meridien Grosvenor House** has quite a history, or at least the land it stands on does. The oils in and around the fake library depict the former earl of Grosvenor's estate on this site. And above the fireplace in the main lobby (the other end from Park Lane), look for the painting of Victorian ice skaters on a rink that is now the Ballroom. **The Savoy** celebrated its centenary a few years ago and has certainly had its share of rollicking parties and happenings. For a re-creation of the lifestyle of the late cousin-to-the-queen Lord Mountbatten, check in at what used to be the plain old **Mountbatten,** now the branded **Radisson Edwardian Mountbatten Hotel. Dorset Square,** conversely, has only cricket-bat motifs and memorabilia to remind guests that the first lord's cricket ground was in the very square they're overlooking. The oldest house of all? The surviving Jacobean parts of the **Holland House Youth Hostel.**

For enemies of chintz and Regency... You're in trouble. Cabbage roses, brocade, and Regency stripes are de rigueur, with the English-country-house look beating all others hands down. Relief is possible in places where low budgets forbid decor, like the youth hostel **Holland House,** and also at the **Columbia,** and certain floors of **Dolphin Square. The Portobello** has a faded Victorian look filtered through the owners' 1960s heyday, all very reminiscent of sets from the Mick Jagger/James Fox cult movie *Performance.* Standouts for different decor include Anouska Hempel's also-slightly-'60s (and '70s) **Blakes,** and the stunning, Milano-modern **Halkin,** both of which have been overtaken by their own younger siblings, **the Hempel** and **The Metropolitan,** respectively. Even less dependent on chintz 'n' china is the **St. Martin's Lane,** designed by Philippe Starck with a minimalist flair that turns slightly surreal in the lobby. **Twenty Nevern Square**

in Earl's Court manages to look elegant in a comfortable but non-Englishy way, and so does the nearby **Kensington International Inn,** where the interior with its wheaty-colored fabrics and sleek pale-wood headboards looks more truly European than anything else for miles around.

Best health club... **Dolphin Square** has a big pool, squash courts, and weight machines, but the public's allowed in, so it's busy. The health club at **Le Meridien Grosvenor House** has a big pool, plus a good gym that also gets busy with nonresidents. The **Landmark London** has a pool that's on the small side but chlorine-free and pretty. Fitness on Five at the **London Hilton on Park Lane** is the flashiest and newest facility. It has personal trainers, plus sessions of acupuncture or hypnotherapy, but no pool. Best for sybaritic spas, with the only sweat generated by the sauna, are the **Athenaeum**'s little basement salon and the Elizabeth Arden–run pampering joint at **The Dorchester.** **The Metropolitan**'s reflexology, aromatherapy, and shiatsu rooms are the best for alternative care.

Taking care of business... **The Savoy** wins surprisingly many accolades from the corporate world; it's handily located, too, in a part of the West End that's as near to the City as the West End gets (10 minutes in a cab). The **Halkin** is a fantastic business base—rooms have two phone lines with conference-call capability, a fax (request it), and the Reuters news service—and the very look seems so efficient, with none of the flounces and curlicues that are endemic to London hotels. The **London Hilton on Park Lane,** like most Hiltons, is okay for business stays, and there'll probably be a convention group around to prove it; ditto at **Le Meridien Grosvenor House,** where there's a huge business center. The **Athenaeum**'s apartments are great for anyone who needs to entertain in a homey atmosphere, while the **Commodore,** which also has a business center, is a good pick for small businesses that don't splurge on expenses. Many hotels are upgrading their computer-friendly aspects, with ISDN lines and the like. Most hotels listed have websites (see index), and it is worth checking facilities in advance, as this is an area that is in constant flux.

The twilight zone... There's eccentric on purpose and then there's plain weird. In the first category, **The Portobello** wins the "individual piece of furniture" award for the Edwardian bathing machine in its suite—a perverted though functional contraption of brass rods and faucets. The **Sloane** easily takes the conceptual prize for its bright idea of selling not only time in a room, but the furnishings of the room itself, should you be interested. Since the non-conformist is highly prized in England, it's not necessarily an insult to succeed in the "plain weird" category. The **Basil Street Hotel** isn't weird, but it is deeply anachronistic, with its Parrot Club, counterpanes, and slightly threadbare Persian rugs. **Dolphin Square** is a time warp of a different stripe, with a mini-mall of shops that seems still stuck in the 1950s, and an atmosphere to match. The **Fielding** has the charm of a warmhearted person who dresses appallingly; meanwhile, **The Metropolitan** has the froideur of a cold-hearted person who dresses like a fashion plate—yes, London's wannabe swankiest hotel belongs in the twilight zone for the quantity of complaints we've heard about its haughty staff, both in the hotel and its ultra-trendy basement bar, The Met.

Try these when there's no room... You won't have a hope at the grands during sold-out times (admittedly rare nowadays), but the **Landmark London,** being a little off center, has been known to have a spare bed at the 11th hour. So has the very expensive **Lanesborough.** The **London Hilton on Park Lane** and **Le Meridien Grosvenor House,** being huge, might have rooms, too. Paradoxically, some of the less-known tiniest places are worth calling at the last minute—specifically the **Sloane Hotel,** the **Sydney, Hart House Hotel, Twenty Nevern Square, Kensington International Inn,** and **Hotel La Place.** Three Bayswater addresses that might yield a late-booking success are (in descending order of cost) **Thistle Hyde Park,** the **London Elizabeth,** and the **Columbia.** Among more central properties, try the **Radisson Edwardian Hotels: The Radisson Edwardian Mountbatten** and **The Marlborough.**

Map 3: West End Accommodations

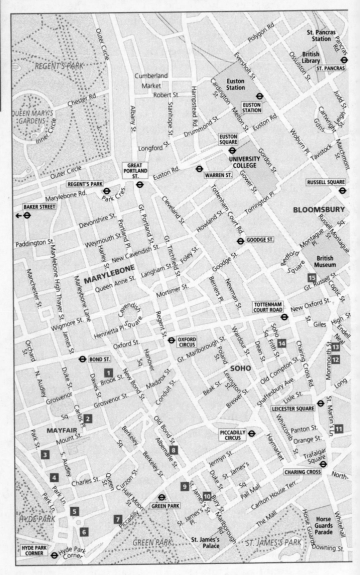

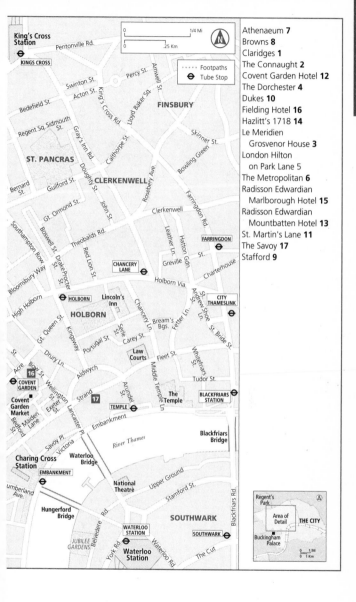

Athenaeum **7**
Browns **8**
Claridges **1**
The Connaught **2**
Covent Garden Hotel **12**
The Dorchester **4**
Dukes **10**
Fielding Hotel **16**
Hazlitt's 1718 **14**
Le Meridien
Grosvenor House **3**
London Hilton
on Park Lane 5
The Metropolitan **6**
Radisson Edwardian
Marlborough Hotel **15**
Radisson Edwardian
Mountbatten Hotel **13**
St. Martin's Lane **11**
The Savoy **17**
Stafford **9**

Map 4: Knightsbridge to South Kensington Accommodations

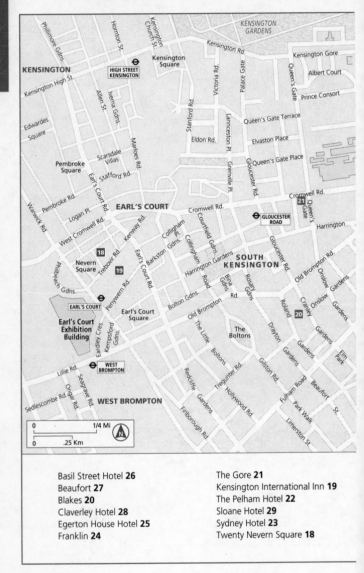

Basil Street Hotel **26**
Beaufort **27**
Blakes **20**
Claverley Hotel **28**
Egerton House Hotel **25**
Franklin **24**

The Gore **21**
Kensington International Inn **19**
The Pelham Hotel **22**
Sloane Hotel **29**
Sydney Hotel **23**
Twenty Nevern Square **18**

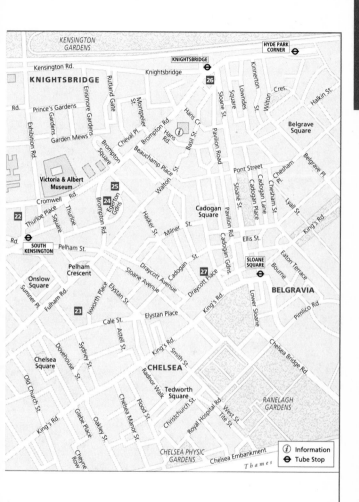

KENSINGTON GARDENS

HYDE PARK CORNER ⊖

KNIGHTSBRIDGE ⊖

Kensington Rd.

Knightsbridge

26

KNIGHTSBRIDGE

Rd.

Prince's Gardens

Ennismore Gardens

Exhibition Rd.

Gardens

Garden Mews

Rutland Gate

Montpelier St.

Cheval Pl.

Brompton Rd.

Beauchamp Place

Brompton Square

Hans Cr.

Hans St.

Basil St.

Sloane St.

Knightsbridge Square

Lowndes Square

Kinnerton St.

Wilton

Cres.

Halkin St.

Belgrave Square

Pavilion Road

Pont Street

Sloane St.

Chesham Pl.

Chesham St.

Lyall St.

Belgrave Pl.

King's Rd.

Victoria & Albert Museum

Cromwell

Thurloe Place

Thurloe Square

Brompton Rd.

Egerton Gdns

Walton

Hasker St.

Milner St.

Cadogan Square

Cadogan Square

Cadogan Lane

Cadogan Place

Pavilion Rd.

Sloane St.

Ellis St.

Eaton Terrace

25

24

22

Rd. ⊖

SOUTH KENSINGTON

Pelham St.

Pelham Crescent

Onslow Square

Summer Pl.

Fulham Rd.

Ixworth Place

Elystan St.

Draycott Ave.

Sloane Avenue

Cadogan St.

Draycott Place

27

Cadogan Gdns

King's Rd.

SLOANE SQUARE ⊖

Bourne

Lower Sloane

BELGRAVIA

Pimlico Rd.

23

Ixworth Place

Cale St.

Elystan Place

Astell St.

Sydney St.

Dovehouse St.

Chelsea Square

Old Church St.

King's Rd.

Smith St.

King's Rd.

Radnor Walk

CHELSEA

Tedworth Square

Chelsea Bridge Rd.

Chelsea Manor St.

Flood St.

Christchurch St.

Royal Hospital Rd.

West St.

Tite St.

RANELAGH GARDENS

Glebe Place

Oakley St.

Cheyne Row

CHELSEA PHYSIC GARDENS

Chelsea Embankment

T h a m e s

ⓘ Information

⊖ Tube Stop

Map 5: Marylebone to Holland Park Accommodations

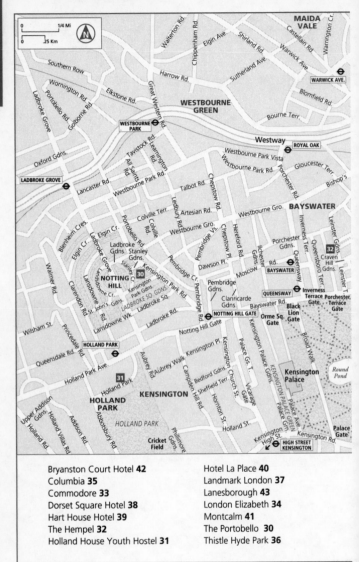

Bryanston Court Hotel **42**
Columbia **35**
Commodore **33**
Dorset Square Hotel **38**
Hart House Hotel **39**
The Hempel **32**
Holland House Youth Hostel **31**

Hotel La Place **40**
Landmark London **37**
Lanesborough **43**
London Elizabeth **34**
Montcalm **41**
The Portobello **30**
Thistle Hyde Park **36**

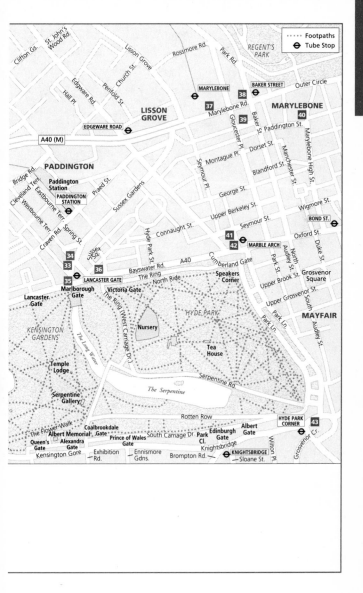

Map 6: Westminster & Victoria Accommodations

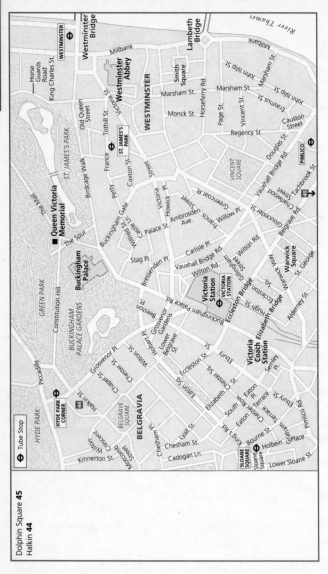

Dolphin Square **45**
Halkin **44**

⊖ Tube Stop

The Index

$$$$$	over $429	over £260
$$$$$	over $429	over £260
$$$$	$330–$429	£200–£260
$$$	$215–$330	£130–£200
$$	$132–$215	£80–£130
$	under $132	under £80

Athenaeum (p. 31, 34) WEST END This Regency-meets-Art-Deco-at-Laura-Ashley-style independent is the nonobvious Mayfair choice, scoring for low-attitude service, cute little health club, and attention to detail (just check out the minibar); the Athenaeum is also good to remember for its 34 apartments. Its restaurant, Bullochs, is Mediterranean-esque, semicasual, and relatively inexpensive (remember, I said *relatively*).... Tel 020/7499-3464 (800/335-3200 in the U.S.). Fax 020/7493-1860. www.athenaeumhotel.com. 116 Piccadilly W1J 7BJ. Tube: Green Park. 133 rooms. AE, DC, MC, V. $$$$–$$$$$

See Map 3 on p. 36, bullet 7.

Basil Street Hotel (p. 28, 32, 35) KNIGHTSBRIDGE Staying at this venerable hotel, you can breakfast at Harrods, yet it's peacefully set back from the Knightsbridge maelstrom. Antiques are strewn about, though it's not remotely designed. Guests—American academics and English country ladies (who get use of the private ladies' club)—come back and back and back, until they're "Basilites" and thus eligible for frequent-stayer miles.... Tel 020/7581-3311. Fax 020/7581-3693. www.thebasil.com. Basil St. SW3 1AH. Tube: Knightsbridge. 92 rooms. AE, DC, MC, V. $$$–$$$$

See Map 4 on p. 38, bullet 26.

Beaufort (p. 30, 31) SOUTH KENSINGTON One of the first of the swelling genre of boutique hotels, where you have a latchkey instead of a reception desk and a sitting room instead of a lounge, this one includes breakfast and afternoon tea. Run by a mainly female team of fiendish efficiency, the Beaufort's even nearer to Harrods than the Basil Street Hotel. It gets top marks for friendliness, squashy-couch designer decor, and not charging premium phone rates.... Tel 020/7584-5252. Fax 020/7589-2834. www.thebeaufort.co.uk. 33 Beaufort Gardens SW3 1PP.

Tube: Knightsbridge/South Kensington. 27 rooms. AE, DC, MC, V.
$$$–$$$$
See Map 4 on p. 38, bullet 27.

Blakes (p. 29, 30, 33) SOUTH KENSINGTON Anouska Hempel, once synonymous with swinging Beatles London, became Lady Weinberg and opened this glamorous stage-set hotel. Her eclectic visual vocabulary (Biedermeier and black lacquer, moiré walls and halogen spotlights, oatmeal raw silk) has since been imitated to cliché, but despite some very tiny rooms, the Blakes style still stuns. So do the ridiculous prices in Blakes the restaurant.... *Tel 020/7370-6701. Fax 020/7373-0442. www.blakeshotels. com. 33 Roland Gardens SW7 3PF. Tube: South Kensington. 49 rooms. AE, DC, MC, V. $$$$–$$$$$*
See Map 4 on p. 38, bullet 20.

Browns (p. 29, 33) WEST END Ever-popular with Connecticut Yankees, Browns does the ersatz Victorian country house thing fairly well, though its soulless afternoon tea is overrated. Labyrinthine corridors and dark-stained wooden staircases connect the various town houses that comprise this hotel begun in 1837 by Lord Byron's butler. There's now a health club, too.... *Tel 020/7493-6020. Fax 020/7493-9381. www.brownshotel. com. 30 Albermarle St. W1X 4BP. Tube: Green Park. 118 rooms. AE, DC, MC, V. $$$$–$$$$$*
See Map 3 on p. 36, bullet 8.

Bryanston Court Hotel (p. 30) WEST END Best Western affiliation brings Americans to this functional, better-since-its-1997-refurbishment, hotel. Most rooms are small, with postage-stamp–size bathrooms, but rates are great for this area behind Marble Arch. There's a rather elegant lounge with leather chesterfield sofa, oils, and a fireplace, plus a restaurant and a bar.... *Tel 020/7262-3141. Fax 020/7262-7248. www.bryanston hotel.com. 56–60 Great Cumberland Place W1H 8DD. Tube: Marble Arch. 54 rooms. AE, DC, MC, V. $$*
See Map 5 on p. 40, bullet 42.

Bulldog Club (p. 28, 31) For a $25 3-year membership, you can book a room in one of Maggie Jackson's many gorgeous houses in good neighborhoods. Accommodations will be similar to the best U.S. B&Bs, but most unusual in London. You'll get bargain-deluxe treatment—full British breakfast, tea/coffeemakers, mineral water, flowers, fruit, newspaper, and robe in your room, plus use of the family phone.... *Tel 020/7371-3202 (877/727- 3004 in the U.S.). Fax 020/7371-2015. www.bulldogclub.com. 14 Dewhurst Rd. W14 0E1. MC, V. $$*

Claridge's (p. 27, 29) WEST END Palatial, peaceful, and nearly perfect, this Savoy Group classic hosts the royal, political, and business worlds in spacious rooms, some of which feel like 1930s ocean-liner staterooms, others like the setting for a fox-hunting weekend. Take tea in the foyer, dine in the Gordon Ramsay– helmed restaurant, or—best—do the smorgasbord in the cozy Causerie.... *Tel 020/7629-8860 (800/637-2869 in the U.S.). Fax 020/7499-2210. www.savoy-group.co.uk. Brook St. W1A 2JQ. Tube: Bond St. 204 rooms. AE, DC, MC, V. $$$$–$$$$$*

See Map 3 on p. 36, bullet 1.

Claverley Hotel (p. 30, 31) KNIGHTSBRIDGE The Beaufort's neighbor, the quaint and friendly little Claverley has decor of rampant color and occasional four-poster beds. An enormous English breakfast is included, plus tea, coffee, and hot chocolate anytime in the wood-paneled reading room or lounge. The very few single rooms without bath are inexpensive.... *Tel 020/7589-8541. Fax 020/7584-3410. www.claverleyhotel.co.uk. 13–14 Beaufort Gardens SW3 1PS. Tube: Knightsbridge. 33 rooms. AE, DC, MC, V. $–$$$*

See Map 4 on p. 38, bullet 28.

Columbia (p. 28, 29, 31, 32, 33, 35) BAYSWATER An anomaly— half rock 'n' roll hangout, half family tourist bargain—this vast Victorian opposite Hyde Park (which many rooms overlook) is clean and bright, if no great shakes in the decor department. Acres of first-floor lounges, a 24-hour bar, a breakfast room that serves dinner, too, and an echoing lobby. The bedrooms are not very big.... *Tel 020/7402-0021. Fax 020/7706-4691. www. columbiahotel. co.uk. 95–99 Lancaster Gate W2 3NS. Tube: Lancaster Gate. 100 rooms. AE, MC, V. $–$$$*

See Map 5 on p. 40, bullet 35.

Commodore (p. 30, 32, 34) BAYSWATER Another bargain, down the block from the Columbia, this well-run, quiet hotel has some special duplex rooms in subdued colors. Rates include continental buffet breakfast in the separately owned Spanish restaurant in the basement.... *Tel 020/7402-5291. Fax 020/7262-1088. 50 Lancaster Gate W2 3NA. Tube: Lancaster Gate. 90 rooms. AE, DC, MC, V. $$*

See Map 5 on p. 40, bullet 33.

The Connaught (p. 27, 28) WEST END The honorary consul would feel at home here among the spacious corridors, the invisible staff of old retainers, and the sizable rooms. Beneath the air of picturesque aristocratic decay, all is shipshape, spotless, and silent as Sunday. The eponymous Anglo-French restaurant and its Grill are among the best in town.... *Tel 020/7499-7070 (800/ 223-6800 in the U.S.). Fax 020/7495-3262. www.savoy-group. co.uk. Carlos Place W1K 2AL. Tube: Bond St. 90 rooms. AE, DC, MC, V. $$$–$$$$$*

See Map 3 on p. 36, bullet 2.

Covent Garden Hotel (p. 28, 31, 32) COVENT GARDEN A designer/ architect couple, Tim and Kit Kemp have a clutch of haute couture baby grand hotels around town (see also Pelham), all distinctively English-countrified with loads of swagged drapes, lace antimacassars, antique cushions, and candlesticks, in the best possible taste. This one outdoes its sisters in theatrical ambience, achieved through layer upon layer of calorific drapes, antiques (including trademark dressmakers' dummies), and an adorable library, with an open fire, where the tea—or champagne—is always flowing.... *Tel 020/7806-1000. Fax 020/ 7806-1100. www.firmdale.com. 10 Monmouth St. WC2H 9HB. Tube: Covent Garden. 45 rooms. AE, DC, MC, V. $$$–$$$$$*

See Map 3 on p. 36, bullet 12.

Dolphin Square (p. 28, 29, 32, 33, 34, 35) WESTMINSTER This 1930s-era quadrangle, a 5-minute cab ride from the Houses of Parliament (many MPs keep a pied-à-terre here), is one of the few all-suite hotels in London. The overall look is functional rather than beautiful. What it lacks in hotel services it makes up for with its 1.4 hectares (3.5 acres) of gardens, health club (with its famous pool mural, squash courts, and gym), its brasserie (with jazz brunches), its shops, and even a Laundromat.... *Tel 02/07834- 3800. Fax 020/7798-8735. www.dolphinsquarehotel. co.uk. Dolphin Square, Chichester St., SW1V 3LX. Tube: Pimlico. 148 rooms. AE, DC, MC, V. $$–$$$*

See Map 6 on p. 42, bullet 45.

The Dorchester (p. 27, 30, 34) WEST END A legend among hotels, there is no faulting the opulent Dorchester, with its miles of gold leaf, marble, and antiques, plus climate control, marble bathrooms, cable TV, etc. There's not only a beauty spa and gym, but also a nightclub, lounges, shops, ballrooms, and three restaurants.... *Tel 020/7629-8888. Fax 020/7409-0114. www. dorchesterhotel. com. Park Lane W1A 2HJ. Tube: Hyde Park Corner. 244 rooms. AE, DC, MC, V. $$$$$*

See Map 3 on p. 36, bullet 4.

Dorset Square Hotel (p. 31, 32, 33) MARYLEBONE The Dorset Square is in a pair of Regency houses behind Oxford Street, overlooking the garden square where cricket was born. Its decorated to the teeth, in a swoony English-chintz style.... *Tel 020/ 7723-7874. Fax 020/7724-3328. www.dorsetsquare.co.uk. 39–40 Dorset Sq. NW1 6QN. Tube: Baker St. 38 rooms. AE, MC, V. $$$–$$$$*

See Map 5 on p. 40, bullet 38.

Dukes (p. 30, 32) ST. JAMES'S In the heart of St. James's, this flagship of small-hotel maven David Naylor-Leyland has its own gaslit driveway; oil portraits of assorted dukes in the foyer justify its name. Rooms have great detail (heated towel rack, real hair dryer, portable mirror, many outlets), and the staff is young, friendly, efficient. Green Park is steps away.... *Tel 020/7491-4840. Fax 020/7493-1264. www.dukeshotel.co.uk. 35 St. James's Place SW1A 1NY. Tube: Green Park. 64 rooms. AE, DC, MC, V. $$$–$$$$$*

See Map 3 on p. 36, bullet 10.

Egerton House Hotel (p. 31) KNIGHTSBRIDGE The first Naylor-Leyland property (also see "Dukes," above) is still strong, liked by bankers in particular for some reason. They are greeted by good antiques, a lovely garden view in back (but no access), and a charming staff. Trademarks of the N-L hotels are intimate size, no restaurant (but 24-hour room service), good-value rates, and a greater tendency toward vivid colors than your average English-country–style place.... *Tel 020/7589-2412 (800/473-9492 in the U.S.). Fax 0207/584-6540. www.egertonhousehotel.co.uk. Egerton Terrace SW3 2BX. Tube: Knightsbridge. 30 rooms. AE, MC, V. $$$–$$$$*
See Map 4 on p. 38, bullet 25.

Fielding Hotel (p. 27, 35) COVENT GARDEN This somewhat eccentric guesthouse occupies a choice spot in the dead center of Covent Garden, where shopping, theater, and opera collide. Expect narrow stairs instead of an elevator, showers instead of tubs in the tiny bathrooms, and no room service or restaurant, although there is a breakfast room and a tiny bar.... *Tel 020/7836-8305. Fax 020/7497-0064. www.the-fielding-hotel.co.uk. 4 Broad Court, Bow St. WC2B 5QZ. Tube: Covent Garden. 24 rooms. AE, DC, MC, V. $$*
See Map 3 on p. 36, bullet 16.

Franklin (p. 30, 31, 32) KNIGHTSBRIDGE Yet another Naylor-Leyland lodging, you can spit on this one from its sister Egerton House, with which it shares most of its characteristics. There's a handsome double parlor for a lounge, with stairs leading down to a long private garden.... *Tel 020/7584-5533. Fax 020/7584-5449. www.franklinhotel.co.uk. 28 Egerton Gardens SW3 2DB. Tube: Knightsbridge. 47 rooms. AE, DC, MC, V. $$$–$$$$$*
See Map 4 on p. 38, bullet 24.

The Gore (p. 27, 30) SOUTH KENSINGTON Very near the Albert Hall and Kensington Gardens is this big Victorian house hung with trillions of prints and strewn with antiques. Some rooms are funny follies—one with Judy Garland's former bed, another all leopard skins, another with a Tudor minstrels' gallery and oaken four-poster. Bistrot 190 serves as restaurant.... *Tel 020/7584-6601. Fax 020/7589-8127. www.gorehotel.com. 189 Queen's Gate SW7 5EX. Tube: Gloucester Rd. tube stop. 53 rooms. AE, DC, MC, V. $$$–$$$$*
See Map 4 on p. 38, bullet 21.

Halkin (p. 31, 33, 34) WEST END The Halkin stands out by a mile, with its exotic wood trim and paneling and many-hued marble, its nonfogging mirrors and keypad lighting controls. Once totally Milanese, the Halkin recently exchanged its Italian restaurant for an expensive Thai joint called Nahm; good, but at these prices, so it should be. The hotel is tucked away from the traffic, behind the Lanesborough (see below) in tiny Belgravia. In-room VCRs. Faxes and two-line phones please image-conscious Wall Street

types. See also its brash sister, the Metropolitan (below)....
*Tel 020/7333-1000. Fax 020/7333-1100. www.halkin.co.uk. 5
Halkin St. SW1X 7DJ. Tube: Hyde Park Corner. 41 rooms. AE, DC,
MC, V. $$$$–$$$$$*

See Map 6 on p. 42, bullet 44.

Hart House Hotel (p. 27, 31, 32, 35) WEST END This is one of the
best small B&B hotels in London, with only 16 rooms and no
attitude. Forget about elevators—they didn't exist back in the
Georgian era when this mansion was built—but expect an
extremely warm welcome and recently refurbed bedrooms with
small, immaculate bathrooms. Some of the rooms are large
enough for families. A full English breakfast is included in the
bargain rate.... *Tel 020/7935-2288. Fax 020/7935-8516. www.
harthouse.co.uk. 51 Gloucester Place W1U 8JF. Tube: Marble
Arch. 41 rooms. AE, MC, V. $$–$$$*

See Map 5 on p. 40, bullet 39.

Hazlitt's 1718 (p. 27, 30) SOHO The self-styled "only hotel in
Soho" has kept its fans, though its funky antiquey style has
been appropriated by others. Visual trademarks include
Victorian claw-foot tubs in the bathrooms and multitudes of
prints on all walls; it has no elevator, only a small lounge, and
no restaurant (but that's the last thing you need on this street
of restaurants).... *Tel 020/7434-1771. Fax 020/7439-1524.
www.hazlitts. co.uk. 6 Frith St. W1D 3JA. Tube: Leicester Sq. 23
rooms. AE, DC, MC, V. $$$$–$$$$$*

See Map 3 on p. 36, bullet 14.

The Hempel (p. 28, 29, 30, 31, 33) BAYSWATER Seen Blakes?
This, Anouska Hempel's other place, is its diametric opposite. In
its smooth white lobby, you lounge on a padded dip in the floor
by a single blue flame of a fireplace, having entered via a room
of single orchids upstanding in serried ranks. It's rather precious, but appealingly Zen-like.... *Tel 020/7298-9000. Fax 020/
7402-4666. 31–35 Craven Hill Gardens. W2 3EA. Tube:
Paddington. 48 rooms, 6 apts. AE, DC, MC, V. $$$$–$$$$$*

See Map 5 on p. 40, bullet 32.

Holland House Youth Hostel (p. 30, 31, 33) HOLLAND PARK
Possibly the world's best city youth hostel setting, though the
accommodations themselves are as basic as dormitories get.
It's housed partly in the remains of a Jacobean mansion and
partly in a modern block, set in the middle of gorgeous little
Holland Park.... *Tel 020/7937-0748. Fax 020/7376-0667. www.
yha.org. uk. Holland Walk, Holland Park W8 7QU. Tube: Kensington
High St. 201 beds. AE, MC, V. $*

See Map 5 on p. 40, bullet 31.

Hotel La Place (p. 32, 35) MARYLEBONE Just-off-center, not far
from Regent's Park, this small, sweet hotel has good facilities
for the price and an appealing English decor. Single women

feel comfortable staying here.... *Tel 020/7486-2323. Fax 020/7486- 4335. www.hotellaplace.com. 17 Nottingham Place W1M 3FF. Tube: Baker St. 21 rooms. AE, DC, MC, V. $$–$$$*

See Map 5 on p. 40, bullet 40.

Kensington International Inn (p. 34, 35) EARL'S COURT Like the elegant Twenty Nevern Square, this newly refurbed hotel might make you change your mind about Earl's Court. Okay, many of the rooms are minuscule. But they all have a sleek, minimalist, international-style decor that's quite welcome after the overblown English-chintz look found in most places. There's no restaurant here, but there is a small bar and a break-fast room.... *Tel 020/7370-4333. Fax 020/7244-7873. www.kensingtoninternationalinn.com. 4 Templeton Sq. SW5 9LZ. Tube: Earl's Court. 60 rooms. AE, MC, V. $$–$$$*

See Map 4 on p. 38, bullet 19.

Landmark London (p. 28, 34, 35) MARYLEBONE The extraordinary feature of this Marylebone giant—once the Great Central Hotel, then British Rail offices—is the soaring, palm-filled, eight-story Winter Garden atrium, which about half the bedrooms overlook. Rooms are very spacious and quite glamorous, with marble bathrooms and fax machines, and there's a pretty pool in the basement health club. There's an excellent French restaurant, but many prefer the small menu served right in the Winter Garden itself.... *Tel 020/7631-8000 (800/323-7500 in the U.S.). Fax 020/7631-8080. www.landmarklondon.co.uk. 222 Marylebone Rd. NW1 6JQ. Tube: Marylebone. 309 rooms. AE, DC, MC, V. $$$$$*

See Map 5 on p. 40, bullet 37.

Lanesborough (p. 29, 30, 35) WEST END A Disneyesque version of Regency London, converted from the former St. George's Hospital. The bar is lined with random leather-bound books; check-in is achieved by signing the visitors' book; bedrooms con-tain fax machines, personalized stationery, an umbrella, big jars of bath unguents, a disturbing infrared security system that knows where you are—and (no joke) a butler of your own. The hotel's Conservatory restaurant is somewhat twee.... *Tel 020/7259-5599. Fax 020/7259-5606. www.lanesborough.com. Hyde Park Corner SW1X 7TA. Tube: Hyde Park Corner. 95 rooms. AE, DC, MC, V. $$$$$*

See Map 5 on p. 40, bullet 43.

Le Meridien Grosvenor House (p. 27, 30, 33, 34, 35) WEST END Now a Le Meridien flagship, the "old lady of Park Lane" is into heavy color, marble floors and fireplaces, velvet couches, and flowers. Best of all: one of the city's most impressive hotel health clubs, complete with pool. There's also a lounge for tea, and two more restaurants. In spring 2002, the Grosvenor unveiled its new rooms—light wood, glass, and the last word in functional luxury. Expect to be pampered and impressed.... *Tel 020/7499-6363. Fax 020/7629-9337. www.lemeridienhotels.com. Park Lane W1K 7TN. Tube: Marble Arch. 444 rooms. AE, DC, MC, V. $$$$–$$$$$*

See Map 3 on p. 36, bullet 3.

London Elizabeth (p. 31, 35) BAYSWATER Set near the depressing guesthouses of Sussex Gardens, this likable and friendly family-run hotel was redesigned by the owner's American wife. Rooms are fresh and English-chintzy in pale blues and yellows; some have tiny balconies, deluxe rooms have Hyde Park views. There's an old-fashioned Continental restaurant, the Rose Garden, and 24-hour room service.... *Tel 020/7402-6641. Fax 020/7224-8900. www.londonelizabethhotel.co.uk. Lancaster Terrace W2 3PF. Tube: Lancaster Gate. 49 rooms. AE, DC, MC, V. $$–$$$$*

See Map 5 on p. 40, bullet 34.

London Hilton on Park Lane (p. 30, 34, 35) WEST END It's not the only grand hotel on the block, but it is the tallest, with great high-floor views for which you pay a premium. The boring room decor has Regency stripe brocade and repro Chippendale. The fabulous feature here is the Fitness on Five health club, with personal trainers, three studios, a gym, and a spa. There's a brasserie/cafe and a bar; on floor 28 is the restaurant Windows; in the basement, Trader Vic's hokey Polynesian.... *Tel 020/7493-8000 (800/445-8667 in the U.S.). Fax 020/7208-4142. www.hilton. com. 22 Park Lane W1K 1BE. Tube: Hyde Park Corner. 446 rooms. AE, DC, MC, V. $$$$–$$$$$*

See Map 3 on p. 36, bullet 5.

The Metropolitan (p. 29, 30, 33, 34, 35) WEST END London's latest louche pocket grand, from the owner of the Halkin, is to its neighbors—The Dorchester, Four Seasons, Le Meridien Grosvenor House—what Kate Moss is to Liz Taylor. The Met Bar is the hangout du jour—or was for about a year—and Nobu (compare and contrast Nobu New York, and Matsuhisa L.A.) does service as the dining room. The best rooms have many windows overlooking Hyde Park; all are beige and cream, with pear-wood fittings, minibars stocked with Budvar beer and Red Bull natural stimulation beverage, and Kiehl's products in cool bathrooms. Cool all 'round. ***Beware:*** Reports of snottiness from Armani-clad doormen are rife.... *Tel 020/7447-1000. Fax 020/7447-1100. www.metropolitan.co.uk. Old Park Lane W1K 1LB. Tube: Hyde Park Corner. 155 rooms. AE, DC, MC, V. $$$$–$$$$$*

See Map 3 on p. 36, bullet 6.

Montcalm (p. 29) WEST END Once the hippest deluxe lodging, with a Studio 54–style club in the basement, this Japanese-run (Nikko) establishment is now a haven of peace, complete with Japanese breakfast and London's first hypoallergenic rooms.... *Tel 020/7402-4288. Fax 020/7724-9180. www.montcalm.co.uk.*

Great Cumberland Place W1H 7TW. Tube: Marble Arch. 106 rooms. AE, DC, MC, V. $$$$–$$$$$
See Map 5 on p. 40, bullet 41.

The Pelham Hotel (p. 32) SOUTH KENSINGTON Another, earlier number from Tim and Kit Kemp (see "Covent Garden Hotel," above), this one is slightly grander, being in a high-ceilinged South Kensington town house, though the abundant antiques and drapery are familiar. Kemps restaurant is up to the neighborhood competition, and it offers 24-hour room service.... *Tel 020/7589-8288 (800/553-6674 in the U.S.). Fax 020/7584-8444. www.firmdale.com. 15 Cromwell Place SW7 2LA. Tube: South Kensington. 51 rooms. AE, MC, V. $$$–$$$$*
See Map 4 on p. 38, bullet 22.

The Portobello (p. 28, 30, 31, 33, 35) NOTTING HILL Once the haunt of major rock stars and other celebs, the peaceful and still hip Portobello has seen better days. A beautiful lounge leads to huge private gardens (no access for hotel guests, but many rooms enjoy a view over them). Decor features such follies as freestanding canopied Victorian tubs, a four-poster bed with its own stairs, and wood-paneled cabin rooms that make a virtue out of being small. The place has style, all right—plus breakfast is included in the rate and a 24-hour basement bar serves food.... *Tel 020/ 7727-2777. Fax 020/7792-9641. www.portobello-hotel. co.uk. 22 Stanley Gardens W11 2NG. Tube: Notting Hill Gate. 24 rooms. AE, DC, MC, V. $$–$$$*
See Map 5 on p. 40, bullet 30.

Radisson Edwardian Marlborough Hotel (p. 35) BLOOMSBURY From here you can spit on the British Museum, shop Covent Garden, and take in a few plays. It's a Radisson Edwardian, a reliable if unexciting chain, with decor that nods to that era. It has an unnecessary brasserie; rooms are fairly large and well insulated from traffic-heavy Gower Street.... *Tel 020/7636-5601 (800/333-3333 in the U.S.). Fax 020/7636-0532. www.radisson edwardian.com. 9-13 Bloomsbury St. WC1B 3QD. Tube: Tottenham Court Rd. 173 rooms. AE, DC, MC, V. $$–$$$$*
See Map 3 on p. 36, bullet 5.

Radisson Edwardian Mountbatten Hotel (p. 33, 35) COVENT GARDEN Sister to the Marlborough (see above), this hotel has a gimmicky theme: Everything pays homage to Lord Mountbatten. It's in an absolutely central Covent Garden location, secreted in one of the winding lanes. There are so many restaurants nearby, you won't need the French brasserie, but the bar's handy.... *Tel 0207/836-4300 (800/333-3333 in the U.S.). Fax 0207/ 240-3540. www.radissonedwardian.com. 20 Monmouth St. WC2H 9HD. Tube: Covent Garden. 151 rooms. AE, DC, MC, V. $$$$*
See Map 3 on p. 36, bullet 13.

St. Martin's Lane (p. 28, 29, 33) WEST END Ian Schrager and designer Philippe Starck transformed a 1960s office building next to the London Coliseum near Leicester Square into this oh-so-hip hangout. The decor is starkly Starckian, natch, with surreal touches in the lobby and elegantly minimalist, mostly white rooms that allow you to control color and mood (but don't touch any of those pretty amenities that you thought might be free). Asia de Cuba is the hotel's main restaurant, but there are two others, all quite swish with snotty people guarding the entrances.... *Tel 020/7300-5500. Fax 020/7300-5501. 45 St. Martin's Lane WC2N 4HX. Tube: Leicester Sq. 204 rooms. AE, DC, MC, V. $$$–$$$$$*

See Map 3 on p. 36, bullet 11.

The Savoy (p. 27, 28, 33, 34) WEST END There's something especially glamorous about this over-a-century-old Thames-side Victorian/Art Deco palace, the only London hotel with its own theater. As with all the Savoy Group hotels, it has handmade beds, most staff are from its world-renowned training school, and the shower heads are the size of hubcaps. The Savoy Grill is one of London's power-lunch places; the Restaurant and more casual Upstairs aren't at all bad, and the American Bar brought the martini to town.... *Tel 020/7836-4343 (800/637-2869 in the U.S.). Fax 020/7240-6040. www.savoy-group.com. Strand WC2R 0EU. Tube: Charing Cross. 233 rooms. AE, DC, MC, V. $$$–$$$$$*

See Map 3 on p. 36, bullet 17.

Sloane Hotel (p. 30, 31, 32, 35) CHELSEA Though you won't see price tags, everything here, from the 18th-century oaken teapot and the Edwardian silver-backed hairbrushes to the carved, canopied, four-poster bed is for sale; you can even buy the TV. This gimmick is saved from being tacky by the incredibly good taste of owner and antiques-auction-addict Xavier Colin. The decor is stunning, the young European staff disarming, the rooftop terrace charming, and the Chelsea location central. No restaurant, but there's 24-hour room service.... *Tel 020/7581-5757 (888/ 254-0637 in the U.S.). Fax 020/7584-1348. www. premierhotels. com. 29 Draycott Place SW3 2SH. Tube: Sloane Sq. 12 rooms. AE, DC, MC, V. $$$*

See Map 4 on p. 38, bullet 29.

Stafford (p. 27, 30, 32) ST. JAMES'S Sandwiched between the Ritz and Dukes is this little place in an 18th-century town house. It's remarkable for its barrel-vaulted wine-cellar private dining salon, and for the dozen secluded Carriage House rooms in back, converted from stables and overlooking a cobbled mews. Decor here and in the main hotel tries a little too hard to be British, with displays of firearms and silverware and some overbearing color schemes, but everyone means well and there is air-conditioning. The American Bar, its ceiling strung with toys, is a

useful martini hideaway, and there's an English restaurant....
*Tel 020/7493-0111. Fax 020/7493-7121. www.thestaffordhotel.
co.uk. St. James's Place SW1A 1NJ. Tube: Green Park. 80 rooms.
AE, DC, MC, V. $$$$–$$$$$*

See Map 3 on p. 36, bullet 9.

Sydney Hotel (p. 29, 30, 32, 35) SOUTH KENSINGTON Formerly
Sydney House, the Sydney is superchic but without pretensions.
This Chelsea boutique hotel was originally designed by young
Jean-Luc Aeby, who has an eye for the witty antique—more of a
flea-market than a Sotheby's sensibility. There's 24-hour room
service rather than a restaurant, and satellite TV in the rooms,
some of which are pretty small.... *Tel 020/7376-7711. Fax 020/
7376-4233. 9–11 Sydney St. SW3 6PU. Tube: South Kensington.
21 rooms. AE, MC, V. $$$*

See Map 4 on p. 38, bullet 23.

Thistle Hyde Park (p. 35) BAYSWATER One of the white palaces
that line Bayswater Road, this is the only one with any glitz. The
hybrid Victorian–Louis XV decor leans heavily to the rococo, in
lemon and rose and powder blue colors. The best rooms have
high ceilings and balconies overlooking Hyde Park. There's a
little-known restaurant/bar with a pretty conservatory facing the
park—great for breakfast, tea, or aperitifs.... *Tel 0870/333-
9110. Fax 0870/333-9210. www.thistlehotels.com/hydepark.
90-92 Lancaster Gate W2 3NR. Tube: Lancaster Gate. 54 rooms.
AE, DC, MC, V. $$$–$$$$$*

See Map 5 on p. 40, bullet 36.

Twenty Nevern Square (p. 28, 32, 33, 35) EARL'S COURT No one
blames you for wanting to avoid Earl's Court, but this elegant
boutique hotel on a pretty street of Victorian town houses might
make you change your mind. The decor is flagrantly stylish, uti-
lizing gorgeous natural fabrics and woods, and the overall feel is
blissfully contemporary. Bathrooms you'll never want to leave,
and a good restaurant, too.... *Tel 020/7565-9555. Fax 020/
7565-9444. www.twentynevernsquare.co.uk. Nevern Sq. SW5
9PD. Tube: Earl's Court. 20 rooms. AE, MC, V. $$–$$$*

See Map 4 on p. 38, bullet 18.

Uptown Reservations (p. 28, 31) A reputable B&B agency, with
fewer swanky uptown addresses than the Bulldog Club (see
above), but a much greater selection in different neighborhoods.
All homes have been inspected. See London as she is lived....
Tel 020/7351-3445. www.uptownres.co.uk. AE, MC, V. $$

DIN

ING

2

Map 7: London Orientation—Dining

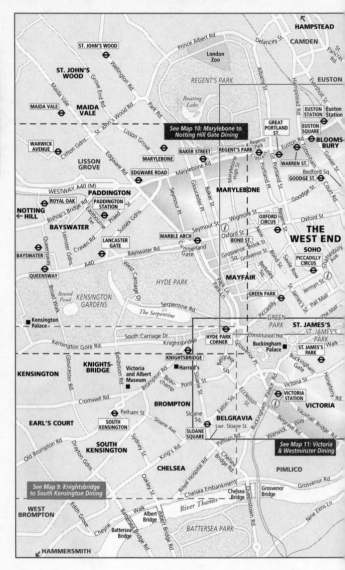

DINING

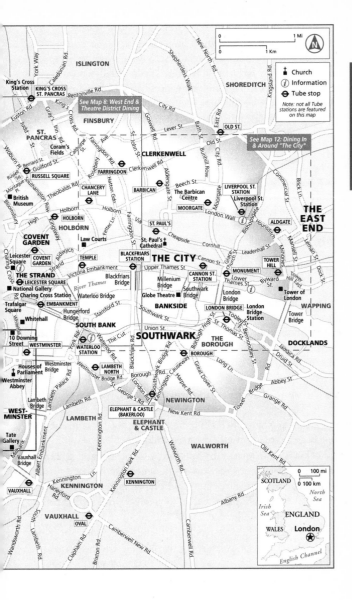

Basic Stuff

The true London cuisine is jellied eels, mashed potato, and an emerald green gravy known as liquor. If that doesn't whet your appetite, the better-known great British dish is fish and chips—white, flaky fish battered and deep-fried, served with big, fat fries shaken with salt and vinegar. Even more common is curry—so common, in fact, that chicken *tikka masala* is now unofficially considered the British national dish. Indian tandoor houses, a fixture on every high street in the British Isles, serve marinated, spiced dishes cooked in the clay tandoor oven, as well as other dishes mostly of Bangladeshi origin. South Indian vegetarian food can be found in London, too, along with the latest craze—*balti*, a gloppy curry named after the Pakistani word for the iron woklike *karahi* in which it is cooked.

Only in London

So, has there really been a restaurant explosion here? Yes. Not only is there a new place opening every day, but everyone is now a foodie. Newspapers have become mere excuses for pages and pages of gastroporn. Chefs like Jamie Oliver and Gary Rhodes are equally revered and detested and have achieved rock star status. Food really is the new rock 'n' roll for your average Brit on the street, mostly because for too long there weren't many choices and what was available was mostly greasy or fatty or relatively tasteless comfort food. *Ready Steady Cook,* a kitsch kitchen show, is the hit of TVland, closely followed by the venerable *Masterchef,* which stages cook-offs between real people, and it's a rare chef who lacks a media outlet for his (and they're mostly male) once strictly culinary ambitions.

The 1990s restaurant was an aircraft hangar: a huge, echoey, hard-edged, dress-up stage, where an Asian (mostly Thai) tinge to menus based around French bistro, or Italian, or pan-Mediterranean dishes began to yield to North African and Middle Eastern influence. Now the mood has shifted and small, artisanal, chef-owners' cafe-bistros are more the chic thing, Mittel Europa is usurping the Middle East, and sushi is the fast food *du choix* (of choice), with a peculiar proliferation of cafes where you pick your own nigiri and maki off a conveyor belt—which is *not* recommended, no matter how cutely *Jetsons*-like it may look.

As for beverages, you'll certainly find French wines, but every restaurant that isn't making a point of its Gallic roots also has New World wines, as well as German, Italian, and other

European (Spanish, Bulgarian, Portuguese) bottles on its list. English wine exists, but barely, and is usually wildly overpriced; beer is the British drink. Among the types of beer, bitter is less aerated, more hoppy, deeper, and, yes, more bitter than most American beers. Local brews include Fuller's, Young's, beers called things like Dogbolter and Rail Ale, from the Firkin division of Allied Breweries, and the ever-increasing numbers of microbrewed beers.

DINING

How to Dress
Unless otherwise noted in the index below, dress however you like. Only the swankiest dining rooms and a few French throwbacks bother with a dress code, although lunch can be a business-dressy affair, and there is less of a penchant for dressing down on all possible occasions than of old. The weather rules out shorts and tank tops nearly all the time, but if it ever gets hot enough to wear them to dinner, go ahead—London's heat waves are so rare that when they do occur, the city loses its collective mind, taste, and sense of decorum.

When to Eat
Conservative mealtimes are the rule: breakfast, 7:30 to 9:30am; lunch, 12:30 to 2:30pm (1pm is prime); dinner, 7 to 9:30pm. Afternoon tea is from 3:30 to 5:30pm, though hardly anyone takes it. It is *not* "high tea": High tea is a nursery meal (what Mary Poppins would have served the Barks children at Cherry Tree Lane), a cross between tea and dinner that's eaten around 6pm, or else it's the northern English term for dinner (you may hear a Yorkshireman asking for his tea way after 5:30pm). Lunch is often called dinner, and dinner is frequently known as supper. The upstart meal of brunch is always called brunch, and where it exists (mostly in Covent Garden and South Kensington), it's served noonish to 4:30-ish on weekends.

Getting the Right Table
Unless a restaurant doesn't accept reservations (noted below in the index), it's always a good idea to book a table in advance. In fact, it's often essential, especially in this week's dozen or so hot spots. A few places must be reserved weeks (River Café) or even months (Aubergine) ahead, unless you have an "in." The trick to this is knowing someone and/or being someone. The slowdown in the economy has meant that it's easier than it used to be to get into any restaurant you want. The big Conran joints of the

'90s, places like Quaglino's, used to require a booking weeks in advance, but now a couple of days will suffice. A few hotel concierges (e.g., the Metropolitan's) have table-conjuring ability in the trendy places; others get preferential treatment in local haunts (e.g., the Covent Garden—the Ivy; the Stafford or Dukes—Le Caprice; the Portobello—the Sugar Club).

The Lowdown

Book before you fly... London has become quite New York in this respect. Newspapers run op-eds about how irritating it is that you can't just show up without a reservation anymore. Of course, you still can in many a neighborhood dive, but these days—read my lips—*you should always call ahead.* The most popular places need advance planning-and-a-half. Top of the list now, as ever, are **Aubergine** and the **River Café,** and the little sister of the former, **L'Oranger,** has joined the several-weeks-ahead club, too. Those other gorgeous sister restaurants **Le Caprice** and **The Ivy** are perennial sellouts, with The Ivy taking the lead by a furlong. If you want a weekend, either call *now,* forget it, or be famous. Beyond the West End, **Moro** is small and a constant sellout, while two south of the river that require forethought are **OXO Restaurant & Brasserie,** especially during summer, and **Livebait.** Both are generally deemed a bit out of the way, while **Putney Bridge** also gets mobbed, but by local luminaries. In West London, always reserve for the **Sugar Club, Assaggi,** and **192,** and forget about **Wódka** on a weekend, unless you made that call. Weekends also find **Belgo Noord** and **Casale Franco** mobbed by north London locals, while weekday lunches are impossible at the **Savoy Grill** and **Orso**—same reason, different clientele.

Celebrate here... The hokey choice is the **OXO Restaurant & Brasserie,** but you'll have to splash out in the restaurant, because the weird, cadaverous lighting in the brasserie will ruin the mood. The ceiling, for some reason, is made out of slats that rotate at whim, displaying either navy, or turquoise, and letting in a bluish glare from above. **Quaglino's** was the watchword for a big night on the town in the '20s, then was resurrected by Sir Terence

Conran in the early '90s, when all London talked about it again. Now, though still nominally glamorous due to its size and its movie-star staircase, it's nothing but a feeding trough for herds (dwindling herds, since you can now get a table a couple of days in advance instead of having to wait for weeks). Drop in for a preprandial, just to check out the glam decor. The good Conran option is that terrace overlooking Tower Bridge, at **Le Pont de la Tour.** If you're pulling out all the stops, for something completely different, **Belgo Zuid** has stark concrete (carved with quotes from Rabelais) and is cheap and suitably raucous. For the daytime, **The Belvedere,** in Holland Park, is heavenly; or you could eat there early on a summer's evening before a performance at the park's open-air theater nearby. Champagne and oysters at **Green's Restaurant and Oyster Bar** is especially and seriously British, followed by tea and cake at **The Fountain** in Fortnum and Mason. For a precious lunch, perch on a love seat at **The Causerie** and have the waiters refresh your smorgasbord plate frequently. And from the sublime to the ridiculous, the Chinese restaurant **Elvis Gracelands Palace** is forever full of hen nights and birthdays, come to worship at the court of the King, aka owner and Elvis impersonator Paul Chan.

Suddenly starving in Covent Garden... There *seem* to be so many places to eat in this neighborhood, but few that are truly worthwhile. **Joe Allen** is good for any time, but impossible to locate: Walk down Exeter Street and when you think you're close, look for a small brass plaque and follow the staircase down. Right by the Covent Garden tube station is **Maxwell's,** also simple and cheap, but stick to the burgers and fries. The French food is fine at the brasserie **Le Palais du Jardin,** where the crowd is a good sign (not always the case around here). Small or big food is excellent, and very healthy, at the casual vegetarian spots **Neal's Yard Dining Room** and the decor-challenged **Food for Thought,** and there's always the **Prêt à Manger** at 77 St. Martin's Lane (head toward Trafalgar Sq.).

Caught in Portobello with low blood sugar... The **Brasserie du Marché** was made for this purpose. It's way up in the Golborne Road regions, past the Westway flea market, and a long, long way from the antiques market you came for, but it's a worthy destination, serving food with a French accent. Closer to the antiques stalls, if you want a cocktail for unwinding, crowded **Beach Blanket Babylon** is the place; its restaurant—fantastical-looking in its Antonio Gaudí-meets-the-Addams-Family style—serves good grilled meats and fish, salads, and pasta. The absolute, all-purpose, favorite dive of the area, however, is **192**. Whatever the time of day, there'll be hangers-out at this wine bar to the stars (or people who think they are). On the cheaper side, the **Sausage and Mash Café** serves lots of different sausages with a variety of flavored mash and gravies. Finger-licking good. Cheapest of all is the **Lisboa Patisserie** on Golborne Road. Sample the delicious deep-fried fish and prawn balls.

Most comforting... At the **Gay Hussar,** a long-lived Hungarian restaurant in Soho, bouncy banquettes envelop people wearing tweed jackets with leather elbow patches, who consume vast portions of cold cherry soup, goulash, and *paprikás töltött palacsinta* (chicken-veal-paprika pancakes). Knightsbridge's **Brasserie St. Quentin** is pure Paris, elegant yet unstuffy, handsome yet undesigned, serving wonderful unfashionable food without attitude. Lovely, friendly **Costas Grill,** on the other side of town in Notting Hill, is a comforting Greek taverna with a garden. A high class of nursery tea can be relived (or discovered) at **The Fountain,** in Fortnum & Mason, where auntly waitresses serve Elegant Rarebit (cheese on toast with bacon and tomato), ice cream with tiny jugs of hot butterscotch sauce, and pots of Earl Grey tea. Back west, this time in Shepherd's Bush, we find **Patio,** an excellent, inexpensive Polish place whose set meal includes vodka.

For grown-ups... When your parents dressed up and left you with the babysitter, such are the places you imagined they went. A sophisticated place, sober, but not stuffy, is **L'Oranger,** where spectacular food stands in for the pizzazz of London's louder restaurants. At **The Square,** diners dress expensively to partake of Philip Howard's inspired prix-fixe menus. You'd better be mature enough at **Clarke's** not to mind eating what you're given, because Sally C. sets the menus herself, based on the best of what's fresh today. Her well-heeled patrons are rarely disappointed. At **Alastair Little,** the minimal decor leaves you free to concentrate totally on your plate, where the excellent hybrid Modern Brit/Med/Pacific Rim cuisine features a lot of fish. The high-priced blue-and-yellow Chelsea salon that is **La Tante Claire** attracts grown-up and wealthy palates to the inventive cooking of chef Pierre Koffman. Burgers are tailored to restrained and genteel tastes at Covent Garden's **Christopher's.** The **Savoy Grill** exists for captains of industry, newspaper editors, and parliamentarians who eat only the most British foods—beef Wellington, liver and bacon, fish pie.

For kids... Kids are happy with the burgers at **Tootsies, Maxwell's,** and **Ed's Easy Diner,** and particularly like the 1950s styling, on-table jukeboxes, and extrovert waitstaff of the latter. If it's pizza they're longing for, the noisy American-style **Chicago Pizza Pie Factory** is ideal. **Marine Ices,** an ice-cream parlor near Camden Lock, and **Lauderdale House,** a park cafe next to Highgate Cemetery, seem to have been made for kids. Much higher on the culinary scale, **River Café** extends a surprisingly warm welcome to small people, though they'd better be budding gourmets. **The Fountain** at Fortnum & Mason is a useful good-behavior bribe: a dress-up and sit-tall place for ice-cream sundaes on special occasions.

Party hearties... The *patron* of **Wódka** brews his own stickily wicked cherry vodka, which—along with *ziborowa* and *krupnik,* and wines from everywhere but Poland—fuels many a private-room party. See the bachelors stagger out around midnight. An insidery but jolly atmosphere goes down in the restaurant itself, too. **Belgo Zuid** is the opposite of a serious salon, what with waiters dressed as medieval monks, and vast quantities of *moules-frites* and Belgian *kriek* beer. The noise level is high, as it is at **St. John,** which looks like a supercool school refectory with a buzz that invites good times. Strangers have been known to get very interactive around the grand piano in the frescoed upstairs room at South Kensington's tony, yet louche, **Star of India,** especially when owner Reza Mohammed is in an ebullient mood.

Pre- and post-theater... For West End theaterland, Japanese-y **Wagamama** is perfect for fast-fueling before curtain up, though it closes too early for after. *The* place for late-night after-the-curtain-calls dining is where the actors themselves go (in London as in New York), **Joe Allen...** unless you're the star, in which case you take your entourage only to **The Ivy.** You may not know what time the curtain falls on the play you're seeing, but they do, and will take your reservation accordingly. A bargain, speed-delivered pre-theater deal is offered from 6 to 7pm at that toniest of American transplants, **Christopher's.** On the other side of Charing Cross Road, in Soho, are several options that will feed you late at night. Get French-ish bistro food at **Café Bohème,** if you can squeeze in past the crowds of drinkers. **Melati** serves good Malaysian food and lacks any bar scene at all. One place to drink, eat, people-watch, and extend your evening almost as long as you like is the **Atlantic Bar and Grill,** with its eclectic menu and late-night weekend crowds. Less frenetic than that, the beautiful **Criterion,** across the street, serves until mid-night, and is easy to reach from any of the West End houses. So is **Mezzo,** but do you really want to pay the £5/$8.25 per person cover charge for music (in the restaurant after 10:30pm)? Up in Islington, the "Off–West End" Almeida Theatre has the divine, upscale pizzas of **Casale Franco,** in a hidden courtyard, though be warned that you're not allowed to order only the pizza, and there are no reservations, so come very early to make the play on time. If curry is your thing, **Soho Spice** (no relation to the girls) is spacious and convenient for West End shows.

Beautiful people... London, since it got swinging again, is a model's favorite city. You also get what you always got here: incredibly cool and interestingly dressed people posing for all they're worth. Apologies for the unavoidable past-the-"sell-by"-date list of their hangouts, which seem to change weekly: **Nobu,** the London version of Matsuhisa's New York and L.A. supersushi joints, is in the Metropolitan hotel, and is good for posing and off-loading serious amounts of money. Open all night, though fueled by caffeine instead of alcohol, is **Bar Italia.** All around it, Soho attracts youth and the best-looking gay men in town. Proper restaurants with tables full of pulchritude include

Aubergine, OXO Restaurant & Brasserie, Le Caprice, and **The Ivy. Daphne's** has the moneyed crowd whose clothes, at least, are good-looking. Both **Kensington Place** and **Wódka** attract professionally groomed fashion-biz characters.

Most romantique... Any place whose name translates into "the love apple" is probably conducive to amorous encounters, and so it is at **La Pomme d'Amour,** with its conservatory garden and classic but light French cuisine; even its Holland Park location, reminiscent of a Paris boulevard, is kinda cute. Nearby neighbor **The Belvedere** outdoes it for setting however, since it has one of the most gorgeous London locations, in Holland Park itself. In town, **Le Caprice** feels delicious and decadent, with its modern black-and-silver color scheme and its well-spaced, white-dressed tables. The service here tends to pamper diners, too. Ditto at **L'Oranger,** which has the sweetest courtyard tables in summer, as well as exquisite food. There's something illicit about Soho's **French House Dining Room,** hidden above the ever-crammed pub of the same name; it's lined with mirrors and photos of French boxers (fighters, not shorts) and upholstered in vermilion. It's the earlier success of Fergus Henderson and Margot Clayton, the pair responsible for **St. John,** so the food's great, too, in a hearty, naked way. Way north, **Lemonia** is a breath of the Aegean, lighter and leafier of decor than most London Greek places, and so authentic you'll imagine you're getting a suntan.

Britburgers... Oh, yes, there is such a thing, and there are a few good examples of the art of short-order cooking around town, most of them in Covent Garden, burger capital of London. Conveniently close to that tube stop is **Maxwell's,** the (relocated) place that brought the trendy burger to London in the 1970s. Between here and the Strand is tiny **Christopher's,** decidedly not a burger joint, but the downstairs cafe serves good burgers for less money, with less swank and swagger. Just around the corner, **Joe Allen,** as you'd expect from the twin brother of Joe's New York original, also turns out a near-perfect patty. The West London chain **Tootsies** is well worth remembering, too, and it has crinkle-cut fries to die for. That other great

American culinary import, Tex-Mex, is also popular. Two of the best places to get it are **Cactus,** with a South American spin, and **Exquisite,** which also serves pasta. Both are very reasonably priced and friendly.

Really old but still alive... This is usually a recommendation in the world of restaurants: They have to be doing *something* right to stay in business so long. London has fewer very venerable eating houses than you might expect in such a historic city, but the oldest of all, **Rules,** is *very* old. Founded in 1798, it's probably serving the same game-laden menu, give or take the odd fruit sauce and sprig of lemongrass. Younger by far, but showing tenacity, is the beautifully preserved Victorian **Manze's** by Tower Bridge, for the traditional dishes of jellied eels and pie and mash. **Clark & Sons** is another one; it's been there in Exmouth Market since 1930, but, tragically, the interior's been redone (See "Cockneys and East Enders," below, for more about London eels.) Some of London's loveliest places are those that persisted through decades of low profile, only to attain a sort of hipness again by accident. The **Gay Hussar,** in Soho, is one such—never in fashion and never out of it. **Bahn Thai,** nearby, was one of the pioneers of a cuisine that now challenges Indian as London's native nosh. **Brasserie St. Quentin**'s exact simulation of a Paris brasserie only improves with the patina of age.

Overrated... **Quaglino's** is glamorous and fun and very big, but it's not the culinary heaven the out-of-towners that pack it every night seem to think it is, and the service can be decidedly offhand. Something similar could be said for a couple of the other Conran juggernauts, although they continue to succeed mightily. **Mezzo** was the biggest until the **Bluebird** came along in 1997. The characteristic shared by all three is that their menus read deliciously, but their meals are curiously disappointing. People find them soulless—hardly surprising, given the scale. Opinion is divided over **St. John.** Some hate Fergus Henderson's style; scorn has been heaped on his appetizer of a bunch of carrots and a boiled egg on a plate, but many dishes are stunningly original without gimmick, like his signature salad of bone marrow and parsley. The food at the clamorous, table-hopping **Kensington Place** isn't what it used to be either.

Sometimes boring food-wise, you might say. Marco Pierre White's newer place, the restaurant at **Pharmacy,** is also overrated. The same is true at the equally overstyled **Mash** restaurant, run by previously Midas-like Oliver Peyton.

Auld London towne... **Rules** (see "Really old but still alive," above) is the auldest of all, serving deer and grouse to the gentry and the hoi polloi for 2 centuries. A handful of other places, often in the grand old hotels, serve once-reviled English food and serve it right. The **Savoy Grill** has two sides to its menu—literally: There's a French side and a British one, both good, but you're safe with the steak-and-kidney here. **Simpsons-in-the-Strand** is the master carver, where great trolleys bearing joints of roasted meat are wheeled to your table and served with spuds, gravy, and the correct accompaniments (Yorkshire pudding and horseradish for beef, mint sauce for lamb, applesauce for pork). This 1828 wood-paneled Edwardian also offers "pig's nose with parsley and onion sauce" for breakfast. The seafood soul of Britain is expressed beautifully at **Green's Restaurant and Oyster Bar,** another wood-paneled establishment, where native oysters (small and strong) or "big" ones precede Devon crab salad or, if you insist, something with meat. Finally, if your credit cards can take some pounding, don't forgo **The Connaught.** There's the (again) wood-paneled restaurant and the smaller green-and-gold grill, both serving perfect English food from a kitchen presided over by Frenchman Michel Bourdin for over 20 years.

Cockneys and East Enders... It's easily argued that this stuff is the real London cuisine: fish and chips, pie and mash, breakfast fry-ups, and mixed grills. When it's good, it's very, very good, and mostly very, very bad for you. Fish and chips—cod, plaice, or haddock deep-fried in batter and served with thick, slightly flabby french fries, golden tan outside, fluffy white inside—has been appropriated by trendy restaurateurs not just in England, but on the other side of the pond, too. London's best are found at **Geales** and the **Sea Shell,** and—if you like the dish—are worth a special trip. In Covent Garden you could do worse than the **Rock & Sole Plaice.** Even if you're squeamish about grease, you'll probably like the sound of fish 'n' chips better than the other London dish: eels, stewed or jellied, and served with emerald green "liquor," a kind of parsley broth. Pie and mash is more easily envisaged: ground beef with a pastry lid, and mashed potato—not creamed, not whipped, but mashed, and sliced like cake. **Manze's** is worth visiting for the beauty of the functional decor alone: the wooden, high-backed benches; ornate green, brown, and white ceramic tiles; sawdust-covered floor; and marble-topped wrought-iron tables haven't changed a bit since the Victorian era. Also little changed is the way business is conducted at Smithfield, the main meat market; after 8am, when the selling's over, the porters repair to the **Fox and Anchor** for the biggest British breakfast in town, black pudding (sausage made from boiled blood) and pints of bitter (there's a unique licensing situation here).

Vegging out... No city restaurant completely ignores the increasing ranks of people who don't eat things with faces, but some cater more than others. Among totally vegetarian restaurants, not too many enjoy gourmet ambience, however good the food. One unlikely exception is **The Place Below**—below, that is, a Christopher Wren church, in the crypt. Two nights a week, this wonderful cafe becomes a candlelit real restaurant, serving a divine set dinner. For lunch or tea, the spring blossom–canopied church courtyard of **The Wren at St. James's** is also a veggie haven. In Covent Garden are two places which, though the food is fresh and delicious, close early, presumably following the weird *idée fixe* that vegetarians don't eat out at night. **Food for Thought** has horrible clunky yellow pine decor and 1,000-watt lighting, whereas **Neal's Yard Dining Room** at least makes an attempt at ambience, with an on-view kitchen and natural light. A great way for vegetarians to feed is on the cuisine of South India, at **Diwana Bhel Poori** and other places along Drummond Street, not far from the British Museum.

Something fishy... **Alastair Little** has a special affinity for fish, always doing something interesting and pan-Pacific with it. Those Conran places **Quaglino's** and The **Bluebird** serve *plateaux de fruits de mer* that approximate the ur-*plateaux* of La Coupole and its ilk. So does that better Sir Terence palace, **Le Pont de la Tour.** Oysters are best at **Green's Restaurant and Oyster Bar;** at yet another Conran shop, the **Bibendum Oyster Bar;** and at **Daphne's,** where shellfish are still on the diets of the ladies who lunch. If a pint of beer and some *fruit de mer* near Portobello Road is your game, you could do a whole lot worse than the junior Conran establishment **The Cow,** another occasional celeb hangout. **Belgo Zuid,** living up to its Belgian provenance, has the most fun with mussels. Near Piccadilly Circus is a useful, relatively budget piscine emporium, **Cafe Fish.** It's no great gourmet shakes, but the fish is fresh, the execution reliable. Broiled fish is wonderful at the good Greek **Lemonia. Costas Grill** on a fine summer's night in the small garden is evocative of Greek-island vacations, if you drink enough retsina with your *psari.* The carp in aspic at **Wódka,** which may or may not be back on the menu, was very memorable. Sushi is still not worth bothering with in London on the whole, except for expense-account-only **Nobu.** In the Portobello zone, **Mediterraneo** is great for simple, uncultured fish done the Italian way, with loads of fresh herbs and a drizzle of olive oil. Actually, just about every good restaurant is friends with fish these days, but perhaps none more so than **Livebait.**

For oenophiles... Wine lists in London used to be all French, and mostly Bordeaux and Burgundy at that, but this is far from true now. New World wines from Australia, Chile, and, yes, even California, are ubiquitous, and you'll see Italian, German, and some Spanish wines, plus various eastern European bottles on many a list. All the grand dining salons fulfill the Important Wines requirement, of course, with only French on the list at **Le Gavroche;** mostly French, with a little German and Italian, at **The Connaught.** The requisite Places with Interesting Lists include **192,** which picks out seasonal selections on your behalf. If you're homesick for Californian wines, go straight to **Clarke's,** because Sally Clarke and her Cali cuisine share a special affinity for them. If wine's your thing but the budget is tight, you could do a lot worse than **The Wine Factory.** It offers simple but good pasta and pizza with wines sold at shop—rather than restaurant—prices (£10/$17 in a restaurant, £6/$9.90 here).

Neighborhood places where Londoners go... Every neighborhood these days has at least one restaurant loved by the locals, and worth a look by you, especially if you want a deeper view into this city's life. The **Brackenbury,** hidden in a backstreet in Hammersmith, is packed every night. Not only is its "new British" food always interesting, the atmosphere is warm and homey, and the service sweet. Putney, a families' and affluent media folks' village of big Edwardian houses upstream on the Thames, lacked a locus until the stunning, spaceshiplike, glass-walled **Putney Bridge** opened. Now *le tout* southwest London hangs at the bar, gazing at the tide. The food—by an ex–St. John man—is better than acceptable, if not worth the trek alone. On the other hand, the food at these two West London places certainly is worth crossing town for, and many people do just that, making reservations essential—especially at the **Sugar Club.** Once a humble above-the-pub dining room, **Assaggi** has become almost as much of a draw. Further west, upstairs at the **Star of India** has long been the open secret of Fulham dwellers and Chelseaites, plus a coterie of movie actors who know they can dine without gawpers when back in town. The totally unposh bit of West London by Olympia (exhibition center) has a tiny Persian restaurant row, on which **Yas** takes the *lavash* for the most friendly, reliable, bargain-rate, open-late (till 5am!) restaurant for miles. Back across the river, in the former wasteland between the Bridges Waterloo and Blackfriars, the fish place **Livebait** was such a hit, it sold itself and doubled its size, but is still selling every table every night. Another plainly decorated place, the Spanish/ Moorish cuisine–serving **Moro,** in the recently trendified Exmouth Market (in totally trendy Clerkenwell/ Farringdon), has probably had to expand by now, too, judging by the 2-week wait for a reservation.

Is this a pub or a restaurant?... The disappearance of the grungy British boozer from the streets of London has its bright side: namely, the emergence of the gastropub. In these, you can still imbibe only liquid sustenance, but hungrier, healthier people can eat really well at about a third of the price of a restaurant. The exception to the lower check part is **Assaggi,** which is really a separate restaurant, despite being above the Chepstow. Notting Hill has so many examples of this genre, the challenge is finding a pub that doesn't do food. **The Cow** is notable for its oysters-and-Guinness suppers in the bar downstairs, and for its cozy dining room upstairs, where a River Café alumna cooks. At Camden's **The Engineer,** there's a separate restaurant, too, serving Euro-Brit comfort food. Mercifully, this means you can reserve a table for bigger groups, though not in the garden—a summertime mob scene, especially Sunday evenings when the softball teams descend from nearby Regent's Park. The original gastropub, **The Eagle,** is still going strong—stronger than ever, actually, since its Farringdon neighborhood is now quite the hot spot, and its rustic southern European food has overtaken fish 'n' chips and curry as the basic local cuisine. An entirely residential corner of Hammersmith, near Ravenscourt Park, lacks any of Farringdon's gallery/shop/ design studio buzz, but boasts the incredibly successful food pub the **Anglesea Arms**—so successful that Dan Evans's hearty stews, risottos, salads, and fish take hours traveling from his kitchen to your mouth. By contrast to the pub-with-restaurant, some restaurants keep bars that have independent personalities: for instance, the vast **Atlantic Bar and Grill,** the Piccadilly Circus of late-night bars, located just off Piccadilly Circus itself. The food ranges from acceptable to good, but the reason to eat here is to secure a good table during rush hour. **192** is Notting Hill's social club, mobbed with barflies; although the food is good, the wine list (it's officially a wine bar) is even better. **Bar Italia,** in Soho, is a coffee bar, period—no alcohol, little food, much posing. Nearby, in Covent Garden, **Joe Allen** has a New York–style proper bar with bar stools, as this true Manhattan transfer should, and **Maxwell's** does those sugary blender cocktails for office workers. Riverside restaurants that give good bar are: **OXO, Le Pont de la Tour,** and **Putney Bridge**—all, obviously, best on a summer's night. Special mention in this category must go to the three **Belgo** restaurants (three and counting, that is). Belgian beer is the thing here, and the list includes more than a hundred. Beware the hangover.

Cheap 'n' cheerful... Fish and chips, pie and mash—these are always bargains, but there are other things to eat when belts are tight. Indian food, as we've noted, is the real British cuisine, and virtually any high street tandoori house will be good. For English diner–equivalent food, the **Chelsea Kitchen** has been there since Chelsea was the swinging center of the world, and it's still likeable. There's good French diner food, and a lovely, casual ambience at **L'Artiste Musclé,** the wine bar in picturesque Shepherd's Market, while Thai bargains are offered at **Ben's Thai,** above a big pub in untouristy Maida Vale. There's always a line for the noodles and "health dishes" and communal fun food of the frighteningly popular **Wagamama,** and any **Belgo** is a bargain if you stick to mussels and fries (which is what they do best). In Piccadilly, as central as can be, the spring blossom–canopied church courtyard of **The Wren at St. James's** is perfect for lunch or tea. All around town you'll see Paris-style brasseries, which can be useful, with their baguette sandwiches and goat's-cheese salads and Toulouse sausages. Better are the London versions of the Tokyo noodle shops, **Wagamama,** where a refueling of noodles, in or out of broth, is guaranteed fast, inexpensive, and surprisingly fresh and good. Lastly, and mostly, you'll get sick of the sight of sandwich monarch **Prêt à Manger** branches, but they're ubiquitous because they provide what we need: speedily, deliciously, and prettily (those industrial metal floors, that funky recycled paper packaging...).

Indian institutions... There are so many good neighborhood curry houses that they alone could fill this book, but these few are good examples of their genre: The **Star of India,** with superb—they call it evolved—cuisine, controlled hubbub, and fancy murals, is a psychedelic's dream. Nearby, **The Bombay Brasserie** offers perhaps the best Raj atmosphere at its Sunday lunchtime buffet (pith helmet optional). Over in the East End Bangladeshi community around Brick Lane, the same role is fulfilled by the **Nazrul,** whose waiters' jackets say on the pocket "Naz Rules," and which is almost embarrassingly inexpensive. Near Euston Station, **Diwana Bhel Poori** isn't much on ambience, but does great South Indian meals. Nearby, rock-bottom cost and complete immersion in another culture are available at the **Indian YMCA.** Also central, albeit not as dirt-cheap as the last three spots, is **Soho Spice,** a modern, well-designed restaurant with vibrantly colored walls, furniture, waiters' uniforms, and food; the tandoori salmon is highly recommended.

Best Asian... London has ambassadors from most Asian kitchens, and has had them for decades. First to arrive were the Cantonese; then Hong Kong chefs who wanted to remain part Brit; and the Chinese food scene is changing again. Dim sum here has a good reputation and the biggest, most ornate, and best-known place to partake of those unrecognizable steamed things on trolleys is **New World.** Among Chinatown Cantonese, **Fung Shing** is not only reliable, but prettier than most, in restful pale green. Malaysian food is not available everywhere, but its satays and noodle dishes are easy to eat, as Londoners have been doing for years at **Melati.** The *Tom yam koong* (very spicy shrimp soup), pad Thai (noodles with everything), green and red curries, and so on of Thailand have been thoroughly adopted in this town. Try Thai in Soho at **Sri Thai Soho** and **Bahn Thai,** or make an outing to far-flung Maida Vale and the nongourmet but pleasing **Ben's Thai.** Japanese is proliferating, but rarely well, except at **Nobu,** where the interpretation is personal to that international Matsuhisa man, but extremely pricey. Cheaper Japanese that is still highly edible can be found at **Misato,** in Soho. Pan-Asian is butting in everywhere, mostly as accents on menus (like at **Sugar Club** and **Putney Bridge**).

The rest of the world... The melting pot that is London offers many other ethnic culinary experiences. Moroccan and North African foods are everywhere. **Pasha,** the brainchild of posh restaurateur Mogens Tholstrup, is cleaning up at the pricier end of the market. For those without a platinum card, the less-established **Yima Café,** in Camden, is a good choice. The food of Eritrea is admirably re-created at a low, low cost in Brixton at **Asmara.** West African food in the East End is best represented by the Nigerian **Obalende Suya,** whose chicken *kirikiri* is reputedly "imprisoned for hours in notorious herbs and spices." Crossing the Atlantic, and moving northward to Archway, we start in **Sabor do Brasil,** a friendly little local favorite that offers national specialties; the English owner, whose

Brazilian wife runs the kitchen, will happily guide you through the menu. If Caribbean-style cuisine is what you crave, try **Bamboula,** a new place in Brixton. The menu is a little more experimental than in the more traditional local spots, but its staples—curried goat and the like—are still grade A. Unfortunately, while friendly, the service is as authentic as the food, so come prepared for a West Indian wait. Just chill out with a couple of rum punches and take it all as it comes.

The French connection... Time was, going to a London restaurant was a big night out, and the restaurant was Escoffier-French, with great batteries of flatware and wait-ers who said *"Et pour madame?"* and served the vegetables from the left. Now, of course, the Brits understand that French is not the only cuisine, even if France is still the most food-obsessed nation of Europe, and they understand this partly because there aren't so very many "genuinely" French restaurants left. **L'Artiste Musclé** may be the least pretentious, most basic (in a good way) French place in town. The check is also reasonable at Covent Garden's **Le Palais du Jardin,** a creditable simulated French brasserie. A step up in terms of food, price, and ambience is Portobello Road's **Brasserie du Marché,** where fab French food is delivered by pleasant staff—not very Franco-typical, you might argue. Going further up the scale, the *comme il faut* award for all-around French authenticity, lovability, and understated charm goes to the Knightsbridge **Brasserie St. Quentin,** with its beauteous, summery setting and reliable, slightly old-school cuisine. If you're going to lavish many pounds on the French meal-fairly-near-France of your life, do it at **La Tante Claire.** It never misses. Those who crave extra waiterly flourishes, a surfeit of very rich people, and even richer ingredients, favor **Le Gavroche,** where Michel Roux Jr.'s cuisine is as classical as you'll find.

Old Italian... Soho was originally the home of London's Italian community, and a few red-sauce survivors of the rent wars remain in this groovy, schmoozy neighborhood. Some I don't recommend, but you've gotta love **Pollo** for its grungy plastic-ivy, pine-paneled decor, and hordes of art-student club kids feeding on chicken cacciatore, ravioli in *brood* (broth), and cassata. While in Soho, don't forget to drop in at **Bar Italia,** which functioned for years as the Soho Italian community's center before being adopted forever by clubbers. It got an architect's redesign a few years ago, but much to the relief of old and new fans alike, it looks exactly the same. One venerable Italian place that has kept up with the times is **Bertorelli's,** where some of the kind waitresses have remained loyal through redecorations and chef changes and everything. They still offer the fabulous olive bread with big smiles.

Noov Italian... Actually, **Bertorelli's** has kept up so well, it belongs in this category, too, for the inventive but not over-challenging food of Maddalena Bonino. Queen of the sturdy southern style that replaced the creamy-ragù-giant-pepper-mill Italians is the **River Café.** Anyone who went there before 1994 will be surprised at the new lighter, bigger room, with its long mirrored bar; anyone who's never been there before will be surprised at the lack of any river view. Its prices, which used to seem outrageous, haven't risen much and now appear more reasonable in the big picture, especially for food of this quality. More central, and close to **Bertorelli's,** is Joe Allen's Italian cousin, **Orso,** also a carbon copy of the New York version. Astonishingly, it manages to attract a similar crowd to its NYC model, though London's has fewer thespians and more magazine editors. An edge of Portobello-land harbors **Assaggi,** which serves food of the River Café school, which is to say, the ingredients are the best available, and not too much mucked-about with. **Mediterraneo** is another, newer Portobello resident with simple, uncluttered food. **The Eagle** does rather play with its food, but then you should come here feeling downright greedy, to partake of the latest versions of Italian gypsy cuisine.

Best prix-fixe... The places presenting the most shocking checks are the hotel dining rooms, the big-star chefs, the haute French places, and permutations of same. But at any of these, big savings can be harvested over lunch—a lunch that could run for hours. **The Connaught, Bibendum,** and **La Tante Claire** all offer a three-course lunch for around £32 ($53). Some of those include coffee, but none the half-bottle of wine that **Le Gavroche** throws in for £39 ($64). **The Ivy**'s weekend set lunch is a steal, as is **L'Oranger's**

midday meal Monday through Saturday—£18 ($30) for two courses, £22 ($36) for three courses—not to mention its just-under-30-quid (under $50) dinner. At **Kensington Place,** fill in the missing weekday lunches for £15 ($24) for three courses. **Aubergine,** if you can get in at all, isn't so frighteningly priced if you go the £24 ($40) lunch route; there's also the seven-course £55 ($91) dinner to consider. **Alastair Little**'s three courses for £25 ($41) is looking more like a bargain as the prices edge up everywhere. All the Conran places do set meal deals. If you must do **Quaglino's,** do it pre-theater, with the 5:30 to 6:30pm £15 ($24) three-course menu; in Soho, **Mezzo** has a similar 6 to 7pm sitting on the Mezzanine floor (which is better anyway), for a bargain £7.95 ($13) for two courses. The **Bluebird**'s early-bird £12/£15 ($19/$24) menu is pointless without anywhere to go nearby (okay, there's the Royal Court), but the best of these prix fixes is at **Bibendum**— the only truly good place in the pantheon—where there's a £28 ($46) three-course lunch. **OXO**'s set lunch, at £24 ($39), for some reason, is the only way to afford the restaurant.

The great British breakfast... If your hotel only does Continental, repair for morning sustenance to any greasy-spoon caff you happen upon. Good luck—they're a dying breed. For under a fiver, you can order: bacon, egg (fried), sausage, black pudding, a slice (fried bread), beans (baked), mushrooms (fried or poached), tomatoes (grilled), and toast. If that's not enough, add kippers, liver, kidneys, or porridge (oatmeal). If you can't find a caff, head to **Simpsons-in-the-Strand,** which offers the works in Edwardian splendor from £12 ($19), actually anointing it "The Great British Breakfast," which is off-putting. The quality is not as high as it looks like it's going to be, but it does come with coffee, OJ, newspaper, and pastries. In St. James's is the best genteel purveyor of the traditional breakfast: **The Fountain.** Early risers (or night people) can try the **Fox and Anchor** pub, at its best very early when the meat porters from nearby Smithfield market are still there. On weekends your best bet is any one of "gastropubs" that are cutting their way through the forest of dingy old pubs in London. Dirty old carpets make way for stripped pine floors, and overstuffed leather sofas are replaced by, well, overstuffed leather sofas—but most are comfortable; they serve food by definition and many offer a fantastic week-end fry-up.

Tea for two... Let me say it again: The meal the British take around 4pm is *not* "high tea." Actually, you'd have trouble locating a single Londoner who takes tea at all, except for the hot beverage, which is still widely drunk pot after pot after pot. The British Empire no longer comes to a grind-ing halt at 4pm with all of England rushing for their cuppa. The English still like a cup of tea in the afternoon, but in workaday London that tea is often consumed at desks piled high with papers. A proper sit-down tea is reserved mainly for those ladies-who-lunch who like to follow lunch with fattening but delectable pastries in the late afternoon. Visitors are also fond of participating in this ritual. London is awash in coffee-bar chains, and while many have abandoned the time-honored custom of afternoon tea alto-gether, not all of them have. Some Londoners are return-ing to this quaint custom, and the city is experiencing a revival of tea-drinking. Everyone should indulge in a for-mal afternoon tea at least once while in London. It's a relaxing, drawn-out, civilized affair that usually consists of three courses, all elegantly served on delicate china: first, dainty finger sandwiches (usually filled with cucumber, egg, or salmon—with the crusts cut off, of course), then fresh-baked scones served with jam and deliciously deca-dent clotted cream (Devonshire cream), and then an array of bite-size sweets. All the while, an indulgent server keeps a pot of tea of your choice fresh at hand. Sometimes ports and aperitifs are on offer to accompany your final course. **The Savoy** does a lovely tea, with attentive, uniformed ser-vice and endless refills, not just of tea but of all the tiers of the cake stand, too. The timeless and elegant **Fountain,** which is behind Fortnum & Mason and belongs to it, serves its own blends of tea; it's quite suitable for dowagers and Little Lord Fauntleroys. For a more Continental tea, with palmiers and éclairs and mille-feuilles, try **Patisserie Valerie**'s original Soho branch and its outposts, or **Maison Bertaux** around the corner—these two stalwarts have gone head-to-head in the cake wars for decades, and still nobody wins, nobody loses. If in Hampstead, try the local teatime institution, the Hungarian **Louis Patisserie.**

Map 8: West End & Theatre District Dining

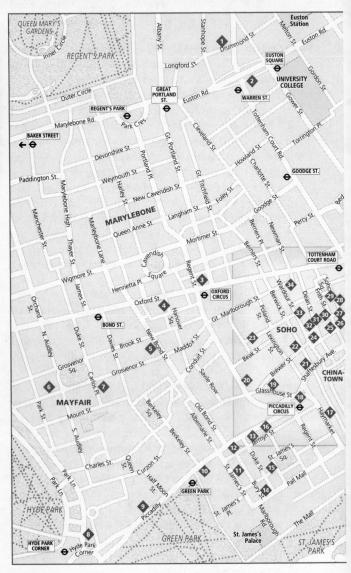

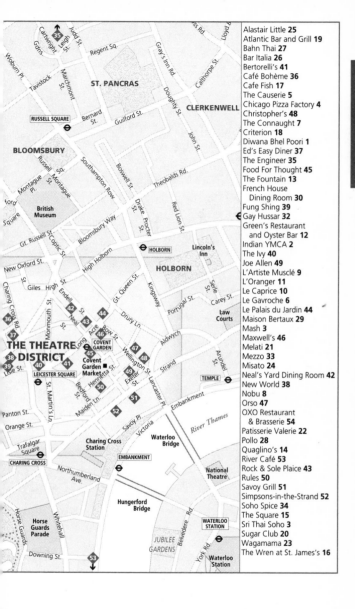

Alastair Little **25**
Atlantic Bar and Grill **19**
Bahn Thai **27**
Bar Italia **26**
Bertorelli's **41**
Café Bohème **36**
Cafe Fish **17**
The Causerie **5**
Chicago Pizza Factory **4**
Christopher's **48**
The Connaught **7**
Criterion **18**
Diwana Bhel Poori **1**
Ed's Easy Diner **37**
The Engineer **35**
Food For Thought **45**
The Fountain **13**
French House
   Dining Room **30**
Fung Shing **39**
Gay Hussar **32**
Green's Restaurant
   and Oyster Bar **12**
Indian YMCA **2**
The Ivy **40**
Joe Allen **49**
L'Artiste Musclé **9**
L'Oranger **11**
Le Caprice **10**
Le Gavroche **6**
Le Palais du Jardin **44**
Maison Bertaux **29**
Mash **3**
Maxwell's **46**
Melati **21**
Mezzo **33**
Misato **24**
Neal's Yard Dining Room **42**
New World **38**
Nobu **8**
Orso **47**
OXO Restaurant
   & Brasserie **54**
Patisserie Valerie **22**
Pollo **28**
Quaglino's **14**
River Café **53**
Rock & Sole Plaice **43**
Rules **50**
Savoy Grill **51**
Simpsons-in-the-Strand **52**
Soho Spice **34**
The Square **15**
Sri Thai Soho **3**
Sugar Club **20**
Wagamama **23**
The Wren at St. James's **16**

80

Map 9: Knightsbridge to South Kensington Dining

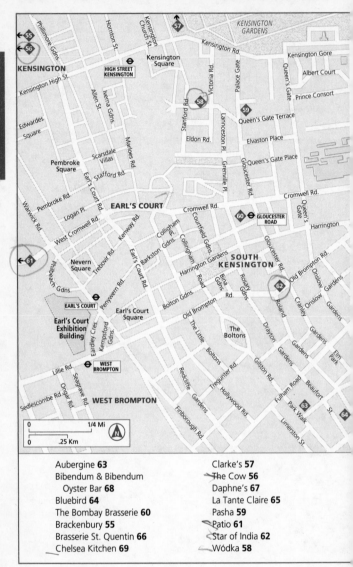

Aubergine **63**

Bibendum & Bibendum
  Oyster Bar **68**

Bluebird **64**

The Bombay Brasserie **60**

Brackenbury **55**

Brasserie St. Quentin **66**

Chelsea Kitchen **69**

Clarke's **57**

The Cow **56**

Daphne's **67**

La Tante Claire **65**

Pasha **59**

Patio **61**

Star of India **62**

Wódka **58**

DINING

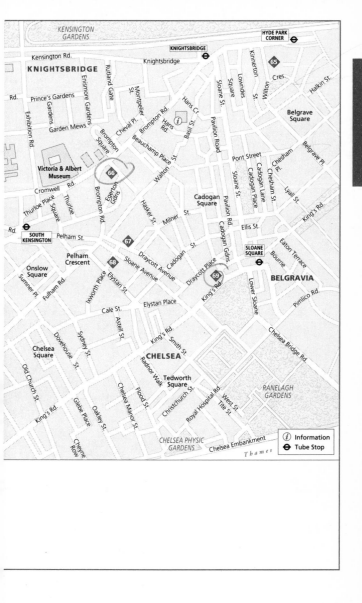

KENSINGTON GARDENS

HYDE PARK CORNER

KNIGHTSBRIDGE

Kensington Rd.

Knightsbridge

KNIGHTSBRIDGE

Prince's Gardens

Ennismore Gardens

Rutland Gate

Montpelier St.

Kinnerton

Lowndes Square

Wilton

Cres.

65

Halkin St.

Belgrave Square

Rd.

Exhibition Rd.

Garden Mews

Cheval Pl.

Brompton Rd.

Brompton Square

Beauchamp Place

Hans Rd.

Hans Cr.

Basil St.

Sloane St.

Pavilion Road

Sloane Square

Pont Street

Cadogan Lane

Chesham Pl.

Belgrave Pl.

Victoria & Albert Museum

66

Cromwell Rd.

Thurloe Place

Thurloe Square

Thurloe

Walton

Egerton Gdns.

Brompton Road

Hasker St.

Milner St.

Cadogan Square

Sloane St.

Cadogan Place

Chesham St.

Lyall St.

King's Rd.

SOUTH KENSINGTON

Rd.

Pelham St.

67

Draycott Avenue

Cadogan St.

Pavilion Rd.

Cadogan Gdns.

Ellis St.

SLOANE SQUARE

Eaton Terrace

Bourne

Onslow Square

Summer Pl.

Fulham Rd.

Pelham Crescent

Ixworth Place

68

Sloane Avenue

Elystan St.

Draycott Place

69

King's Rd.

Lower Sloane

BELGRAVIA

Cale St.

Elystan Place

Pimlico Rd.

Chelsea Square

Dovehouse St.

Sydney St.

Astell St.

King's Rd.

Smith St.

CHELSEA

Chelsea Bridge Rd.

Old Church St.

King's Rd.

Glebe Place

Oakley St.

Chelsea Manor St.

Flood St.

Radnor Walk

Christchurch St.

Tedworth Square

Royal Hospital Rd.

Tite St.

West St.

RANELAGH GARDENS

Cheyne Row

CHELSEA PHYSIC GARDENS

Chelsea Embankment

Thames

ⓘ Information
⊖ Tube Stop

Map 10: Marylebone to Notting Hill Gate Dining

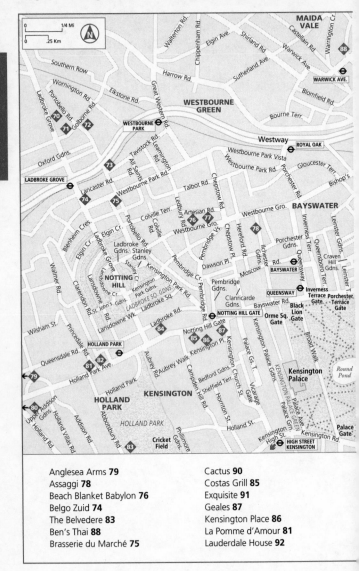

Anglesea Arms **79**
Assaggi **78**
Beach Blanket Babylon **76**
Belgo Zuid **74**
The Belvedere **83**
Ben's Thai **88**
Brasserie du Marché **75**

Cactus **90**
Costas Grill **85**
Exquisite **91**
Geales **87**
Kensington Place **86**
La Pomme d'Amour **81**
Lauderdale House **92**

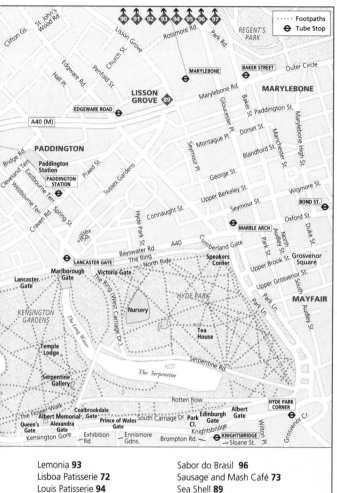

Lemonia **93**	Sabor do Brasil **96**
Lisboa Patisserie **72**	Sausage and Mash Café **73**
Louis Patisserie **94**	Sea Shell **89**
Marine Ices **95**	Tootsies **82**
Mediterraneo **70**	The Wine Factory **77**
192 **71**	Yas **80**
Pharmacy **84**	Yima Café **97**

Map 11: Westminster & Victoria Dining

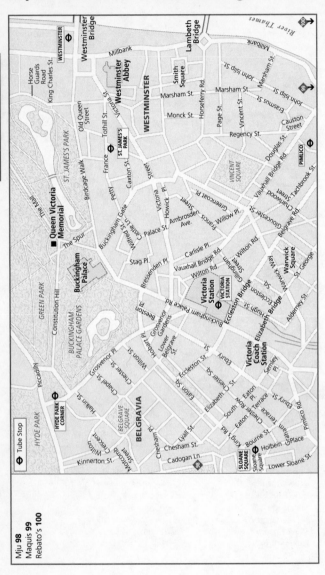

Mju **98**
Maquis **99**
Rebato's **100**

Map 12: Dining In and Around "The City"

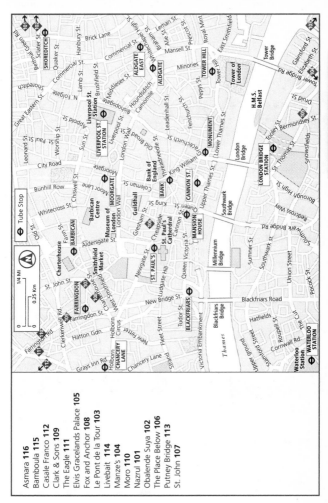

Asmara **116**
Bamboula **115**
Casale Franco **112**
Clark & Sons **109**
The Eagle **111**
Elvis Gracelands Palace **105**
Fox and Anchor **108**
Le Pont de la Tour **103**
Livebait **114**
Manze's **104**
Moro **110**
Nazrul **101**
Obalende Suya **102**
The Place Below **106**
Putney Bridge **113**
St. John **107**

DINING

The Index

$$$$$	over $66	over £40
$$$$	$41–$66	£25–£40
$$$	$30–$41	£18–£25
$$	$17–$30	£10–£18
$	under $17	under £10

(Per person for three courses and coffee, no wine)

Alastair Little (p. 63, 68, 76) SOHO *MODERN BRITISH* Chef/owner Little serves a hybrid modern Brit/Med/Pacific Rim cuisine to groovy foodies in this minimalist, none-too-comfortable Soho salon. Fish is prominent; menus change twice a day.... *Tel 020/ 7734-5183. 49 Frith St. W1. Tube: Leicester Sq. Reservations recommended. AE, DC, MC, V. $$$$*

See Map 8 on p. 78, bullet 25.

Anglesea Arms (p. 71) SHEPHERD'S BUSH *MODERN BRITISH* An old-fashioned pub with a blazing log fire became a blazing hit when 192 alum Dan Evans moved in to cook. Service is nowhere; waits eternal...is the salsify and truffle risotto worth it? Usually, yes.... *Tel 020/8749-1291. 35 Wingate Rd. W6. Tube: Ravenscourt Park. No reservations. MC, V. $$*

See Map 10 on p. 82, bullet 79.

Asmara (p. 73) BRIXTON *EAST AFRICAN* Well-established Eritrean (East African) restaurant. Try the traditional *messobs* (lamb and spinach). Service can be slow.... *Tel 020/7737-4144. 386 Coldharbour Lane, SW9. Tube: Brixton. AE, MC, V. $$*

See Map 12 on p. 85, bullet 116.

Assaggi (p. 60, 70, 71, 75) NOTTING HILL *SOUTHERN ITALIAN* Above a pared-down pub is this sun-filled restaurant hung with color-block canvases. The service, and the check, aren't remotely publike, but neither is the southern Italian food. Try the pasta "loaf" of eggplant, radicchio, fontina, and Gruyère.... *Tel 020/ 7792-5501. 39 Chepstow Place W2. Tube: Notting Hill. Reservations essential. DC, MC, V. $$$–$$$$*

See Map 10 on p. 82, bullet 78.

Atlantic Bar and Grill (p. 64, 71) WEST END *MODERN BRITISH* This late-night spot looks like a jazzed-up, parquet-floored ocean liner. Despite being the size of a small village, it gets packed most nights, and weekends are a zoo. Some food's good.... *Tel 020/7734-4888. 20 Glasshouse St. W1. Tube: Piccadilly Circus. Reservations essential weekends. AE, DC, MC, V. $$$$*

See Map 8 on p. 78, bullet 19.

Aubergine (p. 59, 60, 65, 76) CHELSEA *FRENCH* For years now, London's hottest reservation has been a table at former soccer star Gordon Ramsay's place. Apparently, his supermodern, audacious Frenchy style can't miss.... *Tel 020/7352-3449. 11 Park Walk SW10. Tube: Sloane Sq. Reserve months ahead. AE, DC, MC, V. $$$$–$$$$$*

See Map 9 on p. 80, bullet 63.

Bahn Thai (p. 66, 73) WEST END *THAI* A long-standing Soho Thai restaurant often called the best in town, with a menu several pages long. Soft-shell crab, duck with honey dipping sauce, and a decor of bamboo chairs and halogen spotlights.... *Tel 020/7437-8504. 21A Frith St. W1. Tube: Leicester Sq. Reservations essential for dinner. MC, V. $$$*

See Map 8 on p. 78, bullet 27.

Bamboula (p. 74) BRIXTON *AFRO-CARIBBEAN* New and unassuming Brixton Afro-Caribbean place with a slightly quirky menu. Try old faves like curried goat or "sudden-fried chicken."... *Tel 020/7737-6633. 12 Acre Lane SW2. Tube: Brixton. MC, V. $$*

See Map 12 on p. 85, bullet 115.

Bar Italia (p. 64, 71, 75) SOHO *ESPRESSO BAR* This Soho institution is the ur-espresso bar, always open, nearly always full of life, and lined with Rocky Marciano-abilia. Sandwiches, panettone, and unmemorable gelati are the meager food choices, but the espresso and cappuccino are good, if a bit pricey.... *Tel 020/7437-4520. 22 Frith St. W1. Tube: Leicester Sq. No reservations. AE, DC, MC, V (noon–3am only). $*

See Map 8 on p. 78, bullet 26.

Beach Blanket Babylon (p. 62) NOTTING HILL *MEDITERRANEAN* This outrageous-looking dungeonlike fantasy is the nearest thing to a singles bar you'll find in Notting Hill. Cross the drawbridge to the restaurant to pick up a meal here, too—Mediterranean is the style.... *Tel 020/7229-2907. 45 Ledbury Rd. W11. Tube: Notting Hill Gate. Reservations required for dinner. AE, MC, V. $$$–$$$$*

See Map 10 on p. 82, bullet 76.

Belgo Zuid (p. 61, 63, 69) LADBROKE GROVE *BELGIAN* New third restaurant in the Belgo chain. Giant pine, concrete, and steel-lined refectory-style dining hall with waiters dressed as monks(!). Order mussels and fries, *waterzooi* (fish stew), or wild-boar sausages.... *Tel 020/8982-8400. 124 Ladbroke Grove, W10. Tube: Ladbroke Grove. AE, DC, MC, V. $$–$$$. Branches:*

Belgo Centraal (Tel 020/7813-2233, 50 Earlham St. WC2, Tube: Covent Garden); **Belgo Noord** (Tel 020/8267-0718, 72 Chalk Farm Rd., Tube: Chalk Farm)

See Map 10 on p. 82, bullet 74.

The Belvedere (p. 61, 65) HOLLAND PARK *MODERN BRITISH* The beautiful midpark setting for this serene room of huge windows and white linens sometimes outstrips the Med-Brit menu (scallops with chives and gingers, tagliatelle of langoustines, garlic mash; Welsh rarebit; chocolate marquise).... Tel 020/7602-1238. Holland Park, off Abbotsbury Rd. W8. Tube: Holland Park. Reservations recommended weekends. AE, DC, MC, V. $$$$

See Map 10 on p. 82, bullet 83.

Ben's Thai (p. 72, 73) MAIDA VALE *THAI* A big, off-the-beaten-track, Art Nouveau pub harbors this wood-paneled dining room upstairs. There's better Thai food in town, but value and casual ambience this has got.... Tel 020/7266-3134. The Warrington Hotel, 93 Warrington Crescent W9. Tube: Warwick Ave. Reservations for dinner. MC, V. $$

See Map 10 on p. 82, bullet 88.

Bertorelli's (p. 75) COVENT GARDEN *MODERN BRITISH* It's been around forever, but you'd never know it from the fabulous modern decor (a 1997 refit), the great service, the friendly buzz, and the modish (but not too) menu—garganelli with green beans and cobb nuts; monkfish ragout; panna cotta.... Tel 020/7836-3969. 44A Floral St. WC2. Tube: Covent Garden. AE, DC, MC, V. $$$

See Map 8 on p. 78, bullet 41.

Bibendum (p. 75, 76) SOUTH KENSINGTON *FRENCH* This cherished French treat, beneath the stained-glass windows of the Michelin tire man (this was that company's HQ), is still on the money, with Matthew Harris at the stove.... Tel 0207/581-5817. Michelin House, 81 Fulham Rd. SW3. www.bibendum.co.uk. Tube: South Kensington. Reservations essential 2 weeks ahead. $$$$$

See Map 9 on p. 80, bullet 68.

Bibendum Oyster Bar (p. 69) SOUTH KENSINGTON *SEAFOOD* In the same exquisite, exuberantly tiled Art Nouveau building as the Bibendum restaurant (and the Conran Shop), eat plateaux de fruits de mer, crab or Caesar salads, as well as oysters, in great style.... Tel 020/7589-1480. Michelin House, 81 Fulham Rd. SW3. Tube: South Kensington. No reservations. AE, DC, MC, V. $$$

See Map 9 on p. 80, bullet 68.

Bluebird (p. 66, 68, 76) CHELSEA *MODERN BRITISH* The menu is annoying, the food is overpriced, and the waiters have plenty of attitude, but the formula works, and still they flock....Tel 020/7559-1000. www.conran.com. 350 King's Rd. SW3. Tube: Sloane Sq. AE, DC, MC, V. $$$$

See Map 9 on p. 80, bullet 64.

The Bombay Brasserie (p. 72) KENSINGTON *INDIAN* A slice of Raj in the restaurant attached to Bailey's Hotel. Cooking is not always up to snuff, given the high prices, but the Sunday lunch buffet remains incredibly popular.... *Tel 020/7370-4040. Courtfield Rd. SW7. Tube: Gloucester Rd. AE, DC, MC, V. $$$–$$$$*
See Map 9 on p. 80, bullet 60.

Brackenbury (p. 70) HAMMERSMITH *MODERN BRITISH* Take a cab to reach this secret Hammersmith pocket, where market availability dictates the menu—smoked herring with beetroot salad, mussel stew, onion-thyme tart, gooseberry and elderflower sorbet. Loud and friendly.... *Tel 020/8748-0107. 129–131 Brackenbury Rd. W6. Tube: Hammersmith. AE, DC, MC, V. $$$*
See Map 9 on p. 80, bullet 55.

Brasserie du Marché (p. 61, 74) LADBROKE GROVE *FRENCH* This big-windowed, wood-floored eatery does laid-back French food, like salmon tartare, duck magret, *saucisses de Toulouse*.... *Tel 020/8968-5828. 349 Portobello Rd. W10. Tube: Ladbroke Grove. AE, MC, V. $$$–$$$$*
See Map 10 on p. 82, bullet 75.

Brasserie St. Quentin (p. 62, 66, 74) KNIGHTSBRIDGE *FRENCH* A long-running, informal, classy French place. Prix fixes are a great deal.... *Tel 020/7589-8005. 243 Brompton Rd. SW3. Tube: Knightsbridge. AE, DC, MC, V. $$–$$$*
See Map 9 on p. 80, bullet 66.

Cactus (p. 66) BELSIZE PARK *TEX-MEX* Chalk Farm Tex-Mex with South American chefs. An all-you-can-eat buffet (£6.90/$11) pulls in lots of locals.... *Tel 020/7722-4112. 85A Haverstock Hill, NW3. Tube: Belsize Park or Chalk Farm. AE, MC, V. $$*
See Map 10 on p. 82, bullet 90.

Café Bohème (p. 64) WEST END *FRENCH* Most useful as a Soho rendezvous and after-hours drinking den, this Continental brasserie nevertheless has okay food, along the ciabatta-roast-veg-goat's-cheese-sandwich axis.... *Tel 020/7734-0623. 13 Old Compton St. W1. Tube: Leicester Sq. Reservations for dinner. AE, DC, MC, V. $$*
See Map 8 on p. 78, bullet 36.

Cafe Fish (p. 69) WEST END *SEAFOOD* With a menu divided into cooking methods (steamed, meunière, fried, grilled), this bustling West End spot does fish standards and has a fast, cheap, busy basement wine bar; from the creators of Livebait (see below).... *Tel 020/7930-3999. 39 Panton St. SW1. Tube: Piccadilly Circus. AE, MC, V. $$ (wine bar), $$$$ (restaurant)*
See Map 8 on p. 78, bullet 17.

Casale Franco (p. 60, 64) ISLINGTON *ITALIAN* Ask, or you'll never find the cobbled courtyard entrance to this Islington hangout famous for great pizza. It has a ridiculous no-pizza-*only* policy, no reservations, and a sometimes surly staff, but the brick-walled warehouse chic and the compulsory other food (calves' liver, polenta, salads) are fine.... *Tel 020/7226-8994. Behind 134–137 Upper St. N1. Tube: Highbury and Islington. No reservations. AE, MC, V. $$–$$$*

See Map 12 on p. 85, bullet 112.

The Causerie (p. 61) WEST END *MODERN BRITISH* How sweet it is to perch on delicate couches at low oval tables and be cosseted by charming French waiters as you load up at this 30-dish smorgasbord. An unexpected bargain in one of London's snottiest of grand hotels.... *Tel 020/7629-8860. Claridge's Hotel, Brook St. W1. Tube: Bond St. Jacket and tie required for men. AE, DC, MC, V. $$$*

See Map 8 on p. 78, bullet 5.

Chelsea Kitchen (p. 72) CHELSEA *BRITISH* Since Chelsea swung in the sixties, this has been its kitchen, filling up the proletariat with cheap, wholesome fodder, from egg and chips to beef stew with veggies, moussaka, chicken curry, and apple crumble and custard.... *Tel 020/7589-1330. 98 King's Rd. SW3. Tube: Sloane Sq. No reservations. No credit cards. $$*

See Map 9 on p. 80, bullet 69.

Chicago Pizza Pie Factory (p. 63) WEST END *PIZZA* Where deep-dish lives in London. Chicago pop radio blares and it's a fairly successful imitation of what you might find in the Windy City, right down to the eager service.... *Tel 020/7629-2669. 17 Hanover Sq. W1. Tube: Oxford Circus. Reservations essential for kids' Sun lunch. AE, MC, V. $$*

See Map 8 on p. 78, bullet 4.

Christopher's (p. 63, 64, 65) COVENT GARDEN *MODERN BRITISH* Upscale Hamptonsy-style dining transplanted to Covent Garden. Up the stone stair is a soaring mirrored space, where opera music fills the air and you can dine on plain broiled steak, chicken, and fish; creamed spinach or nutmeggy mashed potatoes; and salsas and salads. Brunch is best.... *Tel 020/7240-4222. 18 Wellington St. WC2. Tube: Covent Garden. AE, DC, MC, V. $$–$$$$*

See Map 8 on p. 78, bullet 48.

Clark & Sons (p. 66) FARRINGDON *FISH & CHIPS* Get the full monty of jellied eels, or pie with mash served from an ice-cream scoop, like school dinners. The character was renovated out of this shop, just as it was renovated into its groovy 'hood.... *Tel 020/7837-1974. 46 Exmouth Market EC1. Tube: Farringdon. Closed evenings. No credit cards. $*

See Map 12 on p. 85, bullet 109.

Clarke's (p. 62, 69) KENSINGTON *MODERN BRITISH* Chef-owner Sally C. trained in Paris and California, and duly displays both influences in food that's classically treated and tastes fresh.

Ingredients are respected so much that each night's menu is dictated by the best available; there's one set menu, whatever Sally has chosen, period.... *Tel 020/7221-9225. 124 Kensington Church St. W8. Tube: Notting Hill Gate. AE, DC, MC, V. $$$$–$$$$$*
See Map 9 on p. 80, bullet 57.

The Connaught (p. 67, 69, 75) WEST END *MODERN BRITISH* Recent turbulence in the dining room resulted in the departure of two chefs and the arrival of Angela Hartnett, a disciple of Gordon Ramsay, who now has her own menu; too early to pronounce it a success, but everything's been freshened up in this venerable establishment.... *Tel 020/7499-7070. Carlos Place W1. Tube: Green Park. Jacket and tie required for men. AE, DC, MC, V. $$$$*
See Map 8 on p. 78, bullet 7.

Costas Grill (p. 62, 69) NOTTING HILL *GREEK* A welcoming Greek taverna-diner that serves good Hellenic staples (homemade hummus with hot pita, moussaka). Garden's a polite word for the yard in back, but it's useful on a warm night.... *Tel 020/7229-3794. 14 Hillgate St. W8. Tube: Notting Hill Gate. Reservations for dinner. No credit cards. $*
See Map 10 on p. 82, bullet 85.

The Cow (p. 69, 71) WESTBOURNE PARK *MODERN BRITISH* Tom Conran's Dublin gastropub in Notting Hill, with oysters and soda bread as bar snacks, and a dining room upstairs, serving fresh sardines stuffed with lemon and pine nuts; chargrilled lamb with merguez; posh pizzas; gooseberry fool with shortbread.... *Tel 0207/221-5400. 89 Westbourne Park Rd. W2. Tube: Westbourne Park. AE, MC, V. $$$*
See Map 9 on p. 80, bullet 56.

Criterion (p. 64) WEST END *FRENCH* Byzantine splendor in Piccadilly Circus, another domain of Marco Pierre White. A grown-up atmosphere, a good percentage of beautiful people, and classical French dishes with interesting twists. The hangar-size place has a golden mosaic ceiling and cerulean drapes.... *Tel 020/7930-0488. 224 Piccadilly W1. Tube: Piccadilly Circus. AE, DC, MC, V. $$$$*
See Map 8 on p. 78, bullet 18.

Daphne's (p. 65, 69) CHELSEA *MEDITERRANEAN* Where the lady lunches: Big hair and gilt buttons are de rigueur after dark, when your baubles should be real. Food is from the Mediterranean hit parade (*fritto misto,* sea bass baked with fennel, an unctuous Caesar salad, and risotti); what really matters is which flagstone-floored conservatory you're seated in.... *Tel 020/7589-4257. 112 Draycott Ave. SW3. Tube: South Kensington. AE, DC, MC, V. $$$$–$$$$$*
See Map 9 on p. 80, bullet 67.

Diwana Bhel Poori (p. 68, 72) REGENT'S PARK *INDIAN* Staples of the South Indian menu include the *masala dosa* (a paper-thin

DINING

THE INDEX

rice/lentil flour pancake encircling spiced potato and green coconut chutney) and *bhel poori* mixtures (tortilla chip–like bits mixed with tamarind and coconut chutneys and spiced yogurt). It's delicious, enlivening food, served in a basic pine-table cafe.... *Tel 020/7387-5556. 121 Drummond St. NW1. Tube: Euston. No reservations. MC, V. $*

See Map 8 on p. 78, bullet 1.

The Eagle (p. 71, 75) FARRINGDON *MEDITERRANEAN* The first of the foodie pubs, still serving excellent rustic Mediterranean dishes, such as its famous marinated rump steak sandwich called *bife ana*. Beware of crowds at peak times.... *Tel 020/7837-1353. 159 Farringdon Rd. EC1. Tube: Farringdon. No credit cards. $$*

See Map 12 on p. 85, bullet 111.

Ed's Easy Diner (p. 63) WEST END *AMERICAN DINER* Some say this is a great burger, others accuse Ed of grease-mongering, but you also get a '50s decor with jukebox, cheese fries, kosher dogs, and peanut butter shakes.... *Tel 020/7434-4439. 12 Moor St. W1. Tube: Leicester Sq. MC, V. $*

See Map 8 on p. 78, bullet 37.

Elvis Gracelands Palace (p. 61) SOUTH BANK *CHINESE* Paul Chan is not the only Chinese restaurateur to perform Elvis impersonations, but he is the first and best. It's not famous for food, so make sure you book on a show night.... *Tel 020/7639-3961. 881 Old Kent Rd. SE15. Tube: Elephant and Castle, then 53, 172, or 173 bus. MC, V. $–$$$*

See Map 12 on p. 85, bullet 105.

The Engineer (p. 71) CHALK FARM *MODERN BRITISH* Sir Larry's daughter, Tamsin Olivier, is one of the hip young owners of this sitting room of a pub-resto, with its gorgeous garden and easy menus: roast chicken with scallion mash, wild mushroom and chestnut risotto, chocolate rum cake.... *Tel 0207/722-0950. 65 Gloucester Ave. NW1. Tube: Chalk Farm. MC, V. $$–$$$*

See Map 8 on p. 78, bullet 35.

Exquisite (p. 66) FINSBURY PARK *TEX-MEX* A wide selection of Tex-Mex at this not-exactly-inspirational restaurant. Good-size portions, though.... *Tel 020/7359-9529. 167 Blackstock Rd. N4. Tube: Finsbury Park. MC, V. $–$$*

See Map 10 on p. 82, bullet 91.

Food for Thought (p. 61, 68) COVENT GARDEN *VEGETARIAN* Meatless, microwaveless, nearly guiltless vegetarian happy food—happy because it's good, cheap, generous, and fresh. Thick slices of wholemeal bread, stir-fries, and maybe spinach-ricotta filo, followed by cakes and cookies.... *Tel 020/7836-0239. 31 Neal St. WC2. Tube: Covent Garden. No reservations. No credit cards. $*

See Map 8 on p. 78, bullet 45.

The Fountain (p. 61, 62, 63, 76, 77) WEST END *BRITISH* It's even more English than Mary Poppins, who would feel at home on the comfy chairs here. Order quaint food (things on toast, pies, and poached Dover sole) and/or Vesuvian sundaes oozing sauces and cream and fruit.... *Tel 020/7734-8040. Back of Fortnum & Mason, 181 Piccadilly W1 (entrance on Duke/Jermyn St.). Tube: Green Park. AE, DC, MC, V. $–$$*
See Map 8 on p. 78, bullet 13.

Fox and Anchor (p. 68, 76) FARRINGTON *BRITISH/PUB* This pub by the old Smithfield meat market serves a huge old-fashioned breakfast and big plates of meat. It opens at 7am, and has a unique license to serve alcohol with breakfast.... *Tel 020/7253-4838. 115 Charterhouse St. EC1. Tube: Farringdon. No reservations. MC, V. $*
See Map 12 on p. 85, bullet 108.

French House Dining Room (p. 65) SOHO *SCOTTISH-FRENCH* Above the Soho pub of the same name is a tiny dining salon, all red banquettes and mirror. It serves Scottish-French nursery food: crab and mayonnaise, giant lamb shanks, homemade cake, and ice cream.... *Tel 020/7437-2477. 49 Dean St. W1. Tube: Leicester Sq. MC, V. $$–$$$*
See Map 8 on p. 78, bullet 30.

Fung Shing (p. 73) SOHO *CHINESE* London's Chinatown, though improving, is not a patch on New York's or San Francisco's, but this cool green place has authentic dishes like salt-baked chicken, fried intestines, and stewed duck with yam.... *Tel 020/ 7437-1539. 15 Lisle St. WC2. Tube: Leicester Sq. AE, DC, MC, V. $$$*
See Map 8 on p. 78, bullet 39.

Gay Hussar (p. 62, 66) SOHO *HUNGARIAN* Rub elbows—literally, since the enveloping banquettes are shared—with old Labour politicians and other lefty intelligentsia at this beloved old Soho Hungarian. Eat big: "Heroic goose" is one dish; lots of cherry soup is slurped; cream and paprika favored ingredients.... *Tel 020/7437-0973. 2 Greek St. W1. Tube: Leicester Sq. AE, DC, MC, V. $$$*
See Map 8 on p. 78, bullet 32.

Geales (p. 67) NOTTING HILL *FISH & CHIPS* One of the best places to get ye famous British fish 'n' chips, it even has a restaurant attached (chippies are usually takeout only). Ordering anything else would defeat the object, but you could try a side of mushy peas.... *Tel 020/7727-7528. 2 Farmer St. W8. Tube: Notting Hill Gate. No reservations. AE, MC, V. $*
See Map 10 on p. 82, bullet 87.

Green's Restaurant and Oyster Bar (p. 61, 67, 69) MAYFAIR
BRITISH A manly set of wood-paneled rooms provides a sur-
prisingly sybaritic time among nobs and establishmentarians.
Quaff champagne from London's best list and feast on oysters,
grilled halibut, or calves' liver.... *Tel 020/7930-4566. 36 Duke St.
SW1. Tube: Green Park. Jacket and tie required for men. AE, DC,
MC, V. $$$$–$$$$$*

See Map 8 on p. 78, bullet 12.

Indian YMCA (p. 72) COVENT GARDEN *INDIAN* Imagine the dining
hall at Delhi University, only less humid. Get thoroughly, spicily
fed for very little; stand in line for a meal ticket first....
*Tel 020/7387-0411. 41 Fitzroy Sq. W1. Tube: Warren St. No reser-
vations. MC, V. $*

See Map 8 on p. 78, bullet 2.

The Ivy (p. 60, 64, 65, 75) COVENT GARDEN *MODERN BRITISH*
There is nothing wrong with the Ivy: no nastiness toward nobod-
ies, lots of eclectic dishes (blinis and caviar to shepherd's pie;
irresistible Desserts R Us), and, nearly every night, a glamorous
feeling that you're in the place where things happen. You are....
*Tel 020/ 7836-4751. 1 West St. WC2. Tube: Leicester Sq. Reserve
several days ahead. AE, DC, MC, V. $$$$*

See Map 8 on p. 78, bullet 40.

Joe Allen (p. 61, 64, 65, 71, 75) COVENT GARDEN *NORTH AMERI-
CAN* A London version of the original on Manhattan's 46th
Street Restaurant Row, from the brick walls to the corn muffin
with broiled chicken breast and salsa; from the cobb salad and
warm banana bread with caramel sauce to the theatrical flock
after curtain.... *Tel 020/7497-2148. 13 Exeter St. WC2. Tube:
Covent Garden. AE, MC, V. $$$*

See Map 8 on p. 78, bullet 49.

Kensington Place (p. 65, 66, 76) KENSINGTON *MODERN BRITISH*
Chef and newspaper columnist Rowley Leigh has had his turn as
flavor of the month, but now he's settled into being just hugely
liked by the legion of table-hopping regulars, who call this glass-
walled echo chamber "KP." Standards have fallen, alas, and the
food and service are both dodgy. Grilled foie gras on sweet-corn
pancakes is his signature appetizer.... *Tel 020/7727-3184.
201–209 Kensington Church St. W8. Tube: Notting Hill Gate. AE,
DC, MC, V. $$$*

See Map 10 on p. 82, bullet 86.

La Pomme d'Amour (p. 65) HOLLAND PARK *CLASSIC FRENCH*
As the name suggests, the ambience here is tooth-achingly
romantic. The interior is Provençal; the French food is classical-
lite and often sublime.... *Tel 020/7229-8532. 128 Holland Park
Ave. W11. Tube: Holland Park. Reservations essential on weekends. AE, MC, V. $$$*

See Map 10 on p. 82, bullet 81.

L'Artiste Musclé (p. 72, 74) MAYFAIR *FRENCH* A sweet little slice of provincial France in picturesque Mayfair, this simple wood-floored wine bar is best experienced from a sidewalk table in summer. Beef bourguignon is always on the menu.... *Tel 020/7493-6150. 1 Shepherd Market W1. Tube: Green Park. Reservations for 5 or more. SE, MC, V. $$$*

See Map 8 on p. 78, bullet 9.

La Tante Claire (p. 63, 74, 75) CHELSEA *FRENCH* Of all London's famous chefs, Gascon native Pierre Koffman is probably the most dedicated to his art; he's nearly always at his stove. If you're serious about food, this is the place.... *Tel 020/7823-2003. The Berkeley Hotel, Wilton Place SW1. Tube: Hyde Park Corner. Reservations essential. Jacket and tie required for men for dinner. AE, DC, MC, V. $$$$$*

See Map 9 on p. 80, bullet 65.

Lauderdale House (p. 63) CAMDEN *MODERN BRITISH* An exquisitely situated park cafe, with crafts stalls, an aviary, and Highgate Cemetery next door. There's more big food here than is usual in such places: lasagna, homemade quiches, and so on.... *Tel 020/8341-4807. Waterlow Park, Highgate Hill N6. Tube: Archway. No credit cards. $–$$*

See Map 10 on p. 82, bullet 92.

Le Caprice (p. 60, 65) ST. JAMES'S *FRENCH* Old London fave reopened by the classy Corbin-King duo is wonderful. Shiny '80s black furnishings (now looking a bit tired), sparkly lighting, and Japanese-y flowers set the scene for a round-the-world menu. Service is perfect.... *Tel 020/7629-2239. Arlington House, Arlington St. SW1. Tube: Green Park. Reservations essential. AE, DC, MC, V. $$$$*

See Map 8 on p. 78, bullet 10.

Le Gavroche (p. 69, 74, 75) WEST END *FRENCH-MEDITERRANEAN* Son of Albert, Michel Roux Jr. wears the toque in this dark green subterranean boîte, applying the highest classical traditions to family recipes, in a menu littered with foie gras, truffles, and lobster.... *Tel 020/7408-0881. 43 Upper Brook St. W1. Tube: Marble Arch. Jacket and tie required for men. Reservations essential. AE, DC, MC, V. $$$$$*

See Map 8 on p. 78, bullet 6.

Lemonia (p. 65, 69) CHALK FARM *GREEK* A big, beautiful, plant-filled, friendly pseudo-taverna on the street where the well-heeled locals go to get well fed. London Greeks are usually from Cyprus, and the personnel here are no exception.... *Tel 020/7586-7454. 89 Regent's Park Rd. NW1. Tube: Chalk Farm. MC, V. $$*

See Map 10 on p. 82, bullet 93.

Le Palais du Jardin (p. 61, 74) COVENT GARDEN *FRENCH* Wood-floored, halogen spotlit, this big brasserie is forever full because it's priced a notch below what it's worth. Volume can mar the service, and bits of the likeably hokey menu don't work, but there's always the shellfish stand.... *Tel 020/7379-5353. 136 Long Acre WC2. Tube: Covent Garden. MC, V. $$–$$$*
See Map 8 on p. 78, bullet 44.

Le Pont de la Tour (p. 61, 69, 71) BUTLERS WHARF *MODERN BRITISH* In Sir Terence Conran's "Gastrodrome" of converted-warehouse food emporia, just downstream from Tower Bridge. Salade niçoise or scallops with pancetta in the less swanky bar/grill is a relative bargain, but the shellfish is hard to resist. Kill for a terrace table in summer.... *Tel 020/7403-8403. www.conran. com. 36D Shad Thames, Butlers Wharf SE1. Tube: Tower Hill. Smart casual dress. Reservations essential. AE, DC, MC, V. $$$ (bar/grill), $$$$$ (restaurant)*
See Map 12 on p. 85, bullet 103.

Lisboa Patisserie (p. 62) NOTTING HILL *PORTUGUESE* One-shop Portuguese pit stop for Portobello shopping. Located on the hugely colorful Golborne Road. Try the *petiscos* (fried tidbits of prawn and fish). There are bakeries and delis next door.... *Tel 020/8968-5242. 57 Golborne Rd. W10. Tube: Ladbroke Grove. MC, V. $*
See Map 10 on p. 82, bullet 72.

Livebait (p. 60, 69, 70) SOUTH BANK *SEAFOOD* Adored by most, always packed, this tiled cafelike place serves plain grilled fish; he- or she-crabs; cockles and mussels; and fanciful inventions like pork, cod, and fennel pie in brioche crust. House-baked breads and some prawns arrive unbidden.... *Tel 020/7928-7211. 43 The Cut SE1. Tube: Waterloo. Reservations essential. AE, DC, MC, V. $$$*
See Map 12 on p. 85, bullet 114.

L'Oranger (p. 60, 62, 65, 75) ST. JAMES'S *FRENCH-ASIAN* This off-shoot of Aubergine is swanky yet friendly, romantic yet urbane. Marcus Wareing's fiendishly good Asian/French food—ravioli of duck confit in a consommé of cèpes, for example—reads well, eats even better.... *Tel 020/7839-3774. 5 St. James's St. SW1. Tube: Green Park. Smart casual dress. Reservations essential. AE, DC, MC, V. $$$$*
See Map 8 on p. 78, bullet 11.

Louis Patisserie (p. 77) HAMPSTEAD *HUNGARIAN PASTRY* Hampstead's traditional Sunday pastime is standing on line for the Hungarian pastries Louis Gat's been baking for over 35 years. Poppy-seed cake, baked cheesecake, and lousy coffee.... *Tel 020/7435-9908. 32 Heath St. NW3. Tube: Hampstead. MC, V. $*
See Map 10 on p. 82, bullet 94.

Maison Bertaux (p. 77) SOHO *FRENCH PATISSERIE* A little old Soho salon where you pick your pastry and have it brought to the plain upstairs room. It's in friendly rivalry with Patisserie Valerie (see below).... *Tel 020/7437-6007. 28 Greek St. W1. Tube: Leicester Sq. No credit cards. $*
See Map 8 on p. 78, bullet 29.

Manze's (p. 66, 68) SOUTH BANK *FISH & CHIPS* The most unspoiled pie-and-mash shop belongs to this eel dynasty.... *Tel 020/7407-2985. 87 Tower Bridge Rd. SE1. Tube: London Bridge. No credit cards. $*
See Map 12 on p. 85, bullet 104.

Marine Ices (p. 63) CAMDEN *ICE CREAM* Many flavors of ice cream and gelato are dispensed, along with sundaes and bombes, but you can also get a proper meal in this tiled and mirrored clean-cut parlor near Camden Lock market.... *Tel 020/ 7485-3132. 8 Haverstock Hill NW3. Tube: Chalk Farm. No credit cards. $*
See Map 10 on p. 82, bullet 95.

Mash (p. 62, 67) WEST END *MODERN BRITISH* Disappointing, over-styled restaurant/bar. Food is good, but portions are small.... *Tel 020/7637-5555. 19 Gt. Portland St. W1. Tube: Oxford Circus. AE, MC, V. $$$$*
See Map 8 on p. 78, bullet 3.

Maxwell's (p. 61, 63, 65, 71) COVENT GARDEN *BRITISH DINER* This place practically introduced the all-beef patty with correct fixings to London nearly a quarter-century ago. Avoid the Reuben sandwich.... *Tel 020/7836-0303. 8–9 James St. WC2. Tube: Covent Garden. AE, DC, MC, V. $$*
See Map 8 on p. 78, bullet 46.

Mediterraneo (p. 69, 75) NOTTING HILL *ITALIAN* Good, simple Italian cooking is what's on offer, with seafood a specialty. Grilled scallops and king prawns with rosemary oil is highly recommended.... *Tel 020/7792-3131. 37 Kensington Park Rd. W11. Tube: Ladbroke Grove. AE, MC, V. $$$$*
See Map 10 on p. 82, bullet 70.

Melati (p. 64, 73) SOHO *INDONESIAN* Pine-lined and brightly lit, this Indonesian is always full, as everyone in London returns to try to reach the bottom of the endless menu. *Tahu-telor* (bean-curd omelet) is juicy, savory, chewy; the bizarre desserts of avocado, colored syrup, fruit, beans, and ice are an acquired taste.... *Tel 020/7437-2745. 21 Great Windmill St. W1. Tube: Piccadilly Circus. AE, MC, V. $$*
See Map 8 on p. 78, bullet 21.

Mezzo (p. 64, 66, 76) SOHO *ASIAN* Conran's Soho giant is best for the first-floor mezzanine's bowls of Asian-ish, noodley, soupy food. Don't descend. The restaurant's overpriced, nonrelaxing,

loud, and mediocre, and there's a music charge if you're still there after 10:30.... *Tel 020/7314-4000. 100 Wardour St. W1. Tube: Leicester Sq. AE, DC, MC, V. $$ (mezzanine) $$$$ (restaurant)*
See Map 8 on p. 78, bullet 33.

Misato (p. 73) SOHO *JAPANESE* The best cheap Japanese in Chinatown. Bento and teriyaki are large, cheap, and reliable. Not much on atmosphere.... *Tel 020/7734-0808. 11 Wardour St. W1. Tube: Leicester Sq. No credit cards. $–$$$*
See Map 8 on p. 78, bullet 24.

Moro (p. 60, 61, 70) FARRINGDON *NORTH AFRICAN* River Café/ Eagle husband-and-wife chefs Sam and Sam Clark—yes, Sam and Sam—opened this instant hit in 1997. It's small, loud, casual, and serves Moorish-ish food, like crab *brik à l'oeuf* (a Tunisian deep-fried pastry); casseroles of rabbit; spiced lamb brochettes.... *Tel 020/7833-8336. 34–36 Exmouth Market EC1. Tube: Farringdon. Reservations essential. AE, DC, MC, V. $$–$$$*
See Map 12 on p. 85, bullet 110.

Nazrul (p. 72) BETHNAL *GREEN INDIAN* This very cheap, very basic BYOB Indian cafe in the Brick Lane Little Bangladesh is more a cross-cultural thrill than a gastronomic one. But generations of students have loved it, so join them if you're game.... *Tel 020/7247-2505. 130 Brick Lane E1. Tube: Aldgate East. No credit cards. $*
See Map 12 on p. 85, bullet 101.

Neal's Yard Dining Room (p. 61, 68) COVENT GARDEN *VEGETARI-AN* A burgeoning enclave of herbalists, masseurs, whole-food shops, and witchcraft-accessory stores, Neal's Yard is a Covent Garden must-see. This veggie cafe is a highlight, serving sampling platters of different world cuisines—African stews, Turkish mezze, Indian Thali.... *Tel 020/7379-0298. 14 Neal's Yard WC2. Tube: Covent Garden. No credit cards. $*
See Map 8 on p. 78, bullet 42.

New World (p. 73) SOHO *CANTONESE* Cantonese dim sum are best in this gigantic place where trolleys whiz by. At peak times, about 700 people, mainly Chinese, may be at their tables, clamoring for various little dishes of steamed goodies.... *Tel 020/ 7734-0396. 1 Gerrard Place W1. Tube: Leicester Sq. AE, DC, MC, V. $$*
See Map 8 on p. 78, bullet 38.

Nobu (p. 64, 69, 73) MAYFAIR *SUSHI/SASHIMI* Order *omakase* (chef's choice) or Matsuhisa's patented "new-style sashimi" (barely seared by hot, flavored oil) and be confused as to which city you're in. The blond-wood-on-white room is more L.A.

Matsuhisa than New York Nobu, but the crowd's the same.... *Tel 020/7447- 4747. Metropolitan Hotel, 19 Old Park Lane, W1. Tube: Hyde Park Corner. Reservations essential. AE, DC, MC, V. $$$$$*

See Map 8 on p. 78, bullet 8.

Obalende Suya (p. 73) SHORDITCH *NIGERIAN* East London Nigerian. Simple, cheap, and different—and worth the trek.... *Tel 0207/249-4905. 523 Kingsland Rd. E2. BR: Dalston Kingsland, then bus. MC, V. $$*

See Map 12 on p. 85, bullet 102.

192 (p. 60, 62, 69, 71) NOTTING HILL *MODERN BRITISH* A never-ending trend in Notting Hillbilly circles, this color-washed wine bar/ estaurant has a long and interesting wine list, fashionable salad ingredients (gremolata, Jerusalem artichokes), and a high-decibel crush of cuties.... *Tel 020/7229-0482. 192 Kensington Park Rd. W11. Tube: Ladbroke Grove. Reservations essential for dinner. MC, V. $$$–$$$$*

See Map 10 on p. 82, bullet 71.

Orso (p. 60, 75) COVENT GARDEN *ITALIAN* Joe Allen duplicated his Italian joint, Orso, from Restaurant Row, NYC, to rave reviews. The glossy clientele loves the salads, pastas, pizzas, and the basement, which looks like the Medici family dungeon.... *Tel 020/7240-5269. 27 Wellington St. WC2. Tube: Covent Garden. AE, MC, V. $$$*

See Map 8 on p. 78, bullet 47.

OXO Restaurant & Brasserie (p. 60, 65, 71, 76) SOUTH BANK *MODERN BRITISH* To partake of the glorious river view, do you 1) get a bank loan for the unnecessarily pricey restaurant, or 2) suffer the hideous blue light in the brasserie? Summer solves the dilemma, with terrace tables. Eat pretentiously and fairly well (acorn-fed black pig charcuterie, etc.) in either.... *Tel 020/7803-3888. Barge House St. SE1. Tube: Waterloo. Reservations essential. AE, DC, MC, V. $$$ (brasserie), $$$$$ (restaurant)*

See Map 8 on p. 78, bullet 54.

Pasha (p. 73) SOUTH KENSINGTON *MOROCCAN* High-class Moroccan nosh where the food quality does not match up to the price tag, and the service is snooty. Not recommended.... *Tel 020/7589-7969. 1 Gloucester Rd. SW7. Tube: Gloucester Rd. AE, DC, MC, V. $$$$*

See Map 9 on p. 80, bullet 59.

Patio (p. 62) SHEPHERD'S BUSH *POLISH* Cheaper than Wódka, with similar if less swanky fare. The set meal comes with vodka. The borscht is superb; the entrees are all very tasty. Excellent value.... *Tel 020/8743-5194. 5 Goldhawk Rd. W12. Tube: Goldhawk Rd./Shepherd's Bush. AE, DC, MC, V. $$*

See Map 9 on p. 80, bullet 61.

Patisserie Valerie (p. 77) SOHO *FRENCH PATISSERIE* The other essential Soho pastry shop, Valerie is older and bigger than Maison Bertaux. Choosing the better *pain au chocolat* of the two is a toss-up.... *Tel 020/7437-3466. 44 Old Compton St. W1. Tube: Leicester Sq. AE, MC, V. $*

See Map 8 on p. 78, bullet 22.

Pharmacy (p. 67) NOTTING HILL *MODERN BRITISH* Marco Pierre White's new kitchen was eagerly anticipated but not so well received. The food is good, but not good enough to inspire loyalty. The decor features endless works by boring bad boy artist Damien Hirst. It's okay, but all but the most trendy (and unimaginative) diners have fled.... *Tel 020/7221-2442. 150 Notting Hill Gate W11. Tube: Notting Hill Gate. AE, DC, MC, V. $$$$*

See Map 10 on p. 82, bullet 84.

The Place Below (p. 68) THE CITY *VEGETARIAN* You can do *wonders* with an old crypt when it's as pretty as this one. Here, below a Wren-designed church, you find Inventive vegetarian food and a useful lunching spot in the City.... *Tel 020/7329-0789. St. Mary-le-Bow, Cheapside EC5. Tube: St. Paul's. AE, MC, V. $–$$*

See Map 12 on p. 85, bullet 106.

Pollo (p. 74) SOHO *PIZZA/PASTA* In central Soho, on the Compton strip, here's another hangout for every student and club goer, and one they never outgrow. Good pasta, nothing fancy, long lines, shared Formica tables, great hubbub—you'll love it if you're in a budget mode.... *Tel 020/7734-5456. 20 Old Compton St. W1. Tube: Leicester Sq. No reservations. No credit cards. $*

See Map 8 on p. 78, bullet 28.

Prêt à Manger (p. 61, 72) EVERYWHERE *SANDWICHES* If you avoid these ubiquitous, PC, fast-food cafes because you're sick of the sight of them, you become eligible for the Stupid Visitor award. Excellent fresh sandwiches, good organic nosh.... *Everywhere. Any tube. No credit cards. $*

Putney Bridge (p. 60, 70, 71, 73) PUTNEY *MODERN BRITISH* A neighborhood alternative to OXO, this spectacular glass-walled ship of a riverside place is packed with well-heeled locals schmoozing at the bar or eating home-pickled herring with crispy bacon or roast mallard in red-wine sauce. Work up an appetite with a Thames towpath stroll.... *Tel 020/8780-1811. Embankment SW15. Tube: Putney Bridge. AE, DC, MC, V. $$$*

See Map 12 on p. 85, bullet 113.

Quaglino's (p. 60, 66, 68, 76) ST. JAMES'S *MODERN BRITISH* The food's okay—sea bass with mushrooms, chicken with smoked garlic—but it's way overpriced and the atmosphere is chilly, as Conran restaurants tend to be; spotty service and the buzz of the '90s is gone.... *Tel 020/7930-6767. www.conran.com. 16 Bury St. SW1. Tube: Green Park. Reservations essential. AE, DC, MC, V. $$$*
See Map 8 on p. 78, bullet 14.

River Café (p. 59, 60, 63, 71, 75) HAMMERSMITH *ITALIAN* This exceptional über-Italian salon began life as the staff canteen for Richard Rogers's architectural firm, and it's become the style-setting place to go for sublime pan-Italian cooking; try chargrilled peaches with Amaretto for dessert.... *Tel 020/7386-4200. Thames Wharf, Rainville Rd. W6. Tube: Hammersmith, then Bus 11. Reservations essential. AE, DC, MC, V. $$$$*
See Map 8 on p. 78, bullet 53.

Rock & Sole Plaice (p. 67) SOHO *FISH & CHIPS* The claim to fame of this punning place: It's the only true "chippy" in midtown and it's got sit-down tables. Stick to fish 'n' chips.... *Tel 020/7836-3785. 47 Endell St. WC2. Tube: Covent Garden. MC, V. $*
See Map 8 on p. 78, bullet 43.

Rules (p. 66, 67) COVENT GARDEN *BRITISH* London's oldest restaurant looks Edwardian, though it was founded in the Georgian age and renovated a moment ago. The menu features seasonal game. Most customers are, predictably, business-people or tourists.... *Tel 020/7836-5314. 35 Maiden Lane WC2. Tube: Covent Garden. AE, DC, MC, V. $$$$*
See Map 8 on p. 78, bullet 50.

Sabor do Brasil (p. 73) ARCHWAY *BRAZILIAN* Brazilian specialties of wholesome stews with beans and juicy meats are on the menu, but do ask for help if you need it.... *Tel 020/7263-9066. 36 Highgate Hill, N19. Tube: Archway. Reservations essential weekends. No credit cards. $$*
See Map 10 on p. 82, bullet 96.

St. John (p. 63, 65, 66) FARRINGDON *MODERN BRITISH* An amus-ingly spartan refectory of metal-shaded bulbs suspended from a soaring ceiling, iron rails, *white*. While getting noisily drunk on French wine, journalists and architects devour Fergus Henderson's in-your-face food.... *Tel 020/7251-0848. www.stjohnrestaurant. co.uk. 26 St. John St. EC1. Tube: Farringdon. AE, DC, MC, V. $$–$$$*
See Map 12 on p. 85, bullet 107.

Sausage and Mash Café (p. 62) LADBROKE GROVE *BRITISH* Wide variety of bangers, spuds, and sauces; fishie and veggie ones, too.... *Tel 020/8968-8898. 268 Portobello Rd. W10. Tube: Ladbroke Grove. MC, V. $–$$*
See Map 10 on p. 82, bullet 73.

Savoy Grill (p. 60, 63, 67) WEST END *BRITISH* Power lunch is staged weekdays. Service is avuncular and discreet. The whole place was undergoing a revamp at press time, so no telling if old standards will prevail.... *Tel 020/7836-4343. Strand WC2. Tube: Aldwych. Jacket and tie required for men. AE, DC, MC, V. $$$$$*
See Map 8 on p. 78, bullet 51.

Sea Shell (p. 67) MARYLEBONE *FISH & CHIPS* One of the best-known fish 'n' chips joints in town, and one traditionally favored by taxi drivers; find it a little ways off Marylebone Road.... *Tel 020/7224-9000. 49–51 Lisson Grove NW1. Tube: Marylebone. AE, MC, V. $*
See Map 10 on p. 82, bullet 89.

Simpsons-in-the-Strand (p. 67, 76) WEST END *BRITISH* Like eating on the set of a Merchant-Ivory period movie: heavy oak paneling, Edwardian glitz, roasted animals circulating on silver trolleys.... *Tel 020/7836-9112. 100 Strand WC2. Tube: Aldwych. Smart casual dress. Reservations essential. AE, DC, MC, V. $$$$*
See Map 8 on p. 78, bullet 52.

Soho Spice (p. 64, 73) SOHO *INDIAN* Imaginatively designed, upmarket curry house.... *Tel 020/7434-0808. 124–126 Wardour St. W1. Tube: Tottenham Court Rd. AE, MC, V. $$$*
See Map 8 on p. 78, bullet 34.

The Square (p. 62) WEST END *MODERN BRITISH* Philip Howard's inspired food is enhanced by perfect service. High-but-fair prix fixes attract the suit-and-tie, pearls-and-heels set.... *Tel 020/7495-7100. www.squarerestaurant.com. 6–10 Bruton St. W1. Tube: Bond St. Reservations required. AE, DC, MC, V. $$$$*
See Map 8 on p. 78, bullet 15.

Sri Thai Soho (p. 73) SOHO *THAI* An elegant dinner that happens to be Thai in central Soho.... *Tel 020/7434-3544. 16 Old Compton St. W1. Tube: Leicester Sq. AE, DC, MC, V. $$$*
See Map 8 on p. 78, bullet 3.

Star of India (p. 63, 70, 72) SOUTH KENSINGTON *INDIAN* Dine grandly upstairs on tandoori pheasant amid Romanesque frescoes and live opera arias.... *Tel 020/7373-2901. 154 Old Brompton Rd. SW5. Tube: Gloucester Rd. Smart casual dress. Reservations essential for dinner. AE, MC, V. $$$*
See Map 9 on p. 80, bullet 62.

Sugar Club (p. 60, 70, 73) WEST END *MED-ASIAN* The nondecor offers no distraction from Peter Gordon's clean Med-Asian cooking (seared salmon on soba noodles, etc.); memorable.... *Tel 020/7437-7776. 21 Warwick St. W1. Tube: Ladbroke Grove. Reservations essential. AE, DC, MC, V. $$$*
See Map 8 on p. 78, bullet 20.

Tootsies (p. 63, 65) HOLLAND PARK *DINER* Burgers in two sizes, served with crinkle-cut fries, big salads, and ice cream. Cheerful service in a place with vintage ads on brick walls.... *Tel 020/ 7229-8567. 120 Holland Park Ave. W11. Tube: Holland Park. No reservations. AE, MC, V. $*
See Map 10 on p. 82, bullet 82.

Wagamama (p. 64, 72) SOHO *JAPANESE* Excellent inexpensive noshing in giant nonsmoking environments modeled on Tokyo noodle shops. Japanese noodley-soupy dishes, along with "health dishes" and sake and beer, are dished out in vast quantity at high speed. There are branches all over the place.... *Tel 020/7292-0990. www.wagamam.com 10A Lexington St. W1. Tube: Leicester Sq. Tel 020/7323-9223. 4 Streatham St. WC1. Tube: Tottenham Court Rd. 26A Kensington High St. W8. 020/ 7376 1717. Tube: High St. Kensington. No reservations. AE, DC, MC, V. $$*
See Map 8 on p. 78, bullet 23.

The Wine Factory (p. 69) NOTTING HILL *PIZZA/PASTA* Pizza, pasta, and salads are good. The wine is excellent and extremely cheap (£5/$8.25 and up). For the boozy types among you.... *Tel 020/ 7229-1877. 294 Westbourne Grove W11. Tube: Notting Hill Gate. MC, V. $$$*
See Map 10 on p. 82, bullet 77.

Wódka (p. 60, 63, 65, 69) KENSINGTON *POLISH* Frequented by beau-monde types, this minimalist-looking but warm-feeling spot has founded a new genre: modern Polish.... *Tel 0207/937-6513. 12 St. Alban's Grove W8. Tube: Gloucester Rd. AE, DC, MC, V. $$$*
See Map 9 on p. 80, bullet 58.

The Wren at St. James's (p. 68, 72) ST. JAMES'S *VEGETARIAN* Cafe with an early (7pm) closing and pretty churchyard tables. Simple, vegetarian, and cheap dishes; great cakes and pastries.... *Tel 020/7437-9419. 35 Jermyn St. SW1. Tube: Piccadilly Circus. No reservations. No credit cards. $$*
See Map 8 on p. 78, bullet 16.

Yas (p. 70) WEST KENSINGTON *PERSIAN* Cute, friendly, red-walled Persian oasis, open very, very late.... *Tel 0207/603-9148. 7 Hammersmith Rd. W14. Tube: Olympia. AE, DC, MC, V. $$*
See Map 10 on p. 82, bullet 80.

Yima Café (p. 73) CAMDEN *MOROCCAN* Wacky design makes this cheap Moroccan joint a feast for the eyes as well as the stomach. No alcohol allowed.... *Tel 020/7267-1097. 95 Parkway, NW1. Tube: Camden Town. No credit cards. $$*
See Map 10 on p. 82, bullet 97.

DINING

THE INDEX

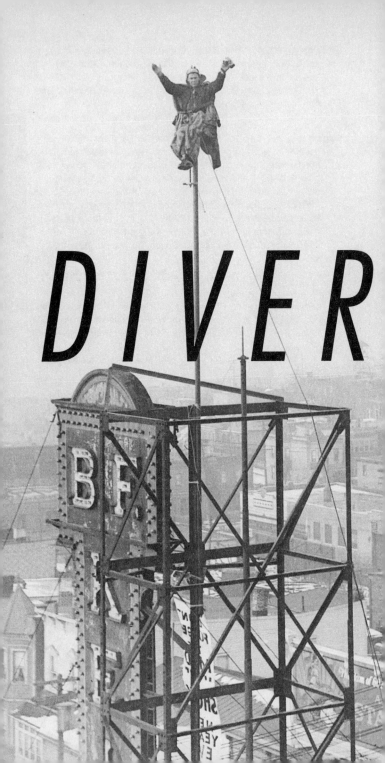

SIONS

3

Map 13: London Orientation—Diversions

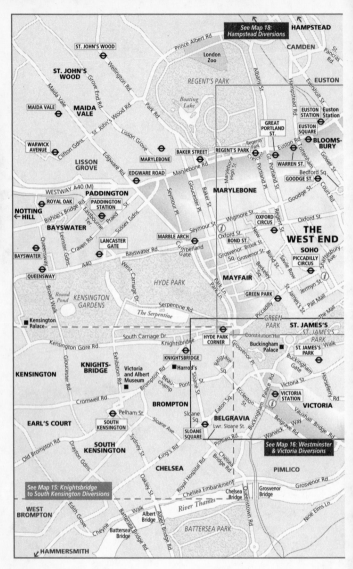

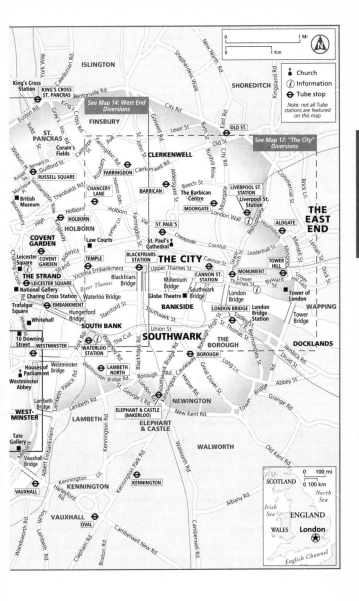

0 1 Mi

0 1 Km

✝ Church

ⓘ Information

⊖ Tube stop

Note: not all Tube stations are featured on this map

ISLINGTON

York Way

Caledonian Rd.

King's Cross Station

KING'S CROSS ST. PANCRAS

Pentonville Rd.

See Map 14: West End Diversions

Shepherdess Walk

New North Rd.

SHOREDITCH

City Rd.

King's land Rd.

East Rd.

OLD ST.

FINSBURY

Goswell Rd.

Lever St.

Bath St.

King's Cross Rd.

Euston Rd.

Gray's Inn Rd.

ST. PANCRAS

Judd St.

Woburn Pl.

St. Bernard's St.

Coram's Fields

Guilford St.

Cartlage

Farringdon Rd.

St. John St.

CLERKENWELL

Clerkenwell Rd.

Burhill Row

See Map 17: "The City" Diversions

Old St.

Commercial St.

Brick Ln.

Russell Square

RUSSELL SQUARE

Montague Pl.

Southampton Row

Theobalds Rd.

FARRINGDON

Hatton Gdn.

BARBICAN

Beech St.

Aldersgate St.

THE BARBICAN CENTRE

LIVERPOOL ST. STATION

Liverpool St. Station

Bishopsgate

Houndsditch

THE EAST END

British Museum

Bloomsbury

High Holborn

CHANCERY LANE

HOLBORN

Holborn

Holborn

Fetter Ln.

Farringdon St.

Via.

ST. PAUL'S

MOORGATE

London Wall

Moorgate

ⓘ

Cheapside

Cornhill

Leadenhall St.

ALDGATE

Leman St.

Mansell St.

Minories

Dock St.

COVENT GARDEN

Kingsway

Law Courts

Aldwych

TEMPLE

St. Paul's Cathedral

THE CITY

Cannon St.

Gracechurch St.

King William St.

TOWER HILL

Byward St.

Tower Hill

Tower Hill East

Leicester Square

COVENT GARDEN

ⓘ

LEICESTER SQUARE

Strand

THE STRAND

BLACKFRIARS STATION

Upper Thames St.

CANNON ST. STATION

MONUMENT

Lower Thames St.

Charing Cross Rd.

National Gallery

Charing Cross Station

Victoria Embankment

Blackfriars Bridge

River Thames

Millenium Bridge

Globe Theatre

Southwark Bridge

BANKSIDE

London Bridge

LONDON BRIDGE

Tooley St.

London Bridge Station

Tower of London

WAPPING

Tower Bridge

DOCKLANDS

Trafalgar Square

EMBANKMENT

Whitehall

Hungerford Bridge

Waterloo Bridge

Stamford St.

Southwark St.

Union St.

Borough High St.

St. Thomas St.

Bermondsey St.

Jamaica Rd.

10 Downing Street

WESTMINSTER

SOUTH BANK

The Cut

WATERLOO STATION

Westminster Bridge

Waterloo Rd.

Blackfriars Rd.

SOUTHWARK

Southwark Bridge Rd.

Kennington Causeway

THE BOROUGH

BOROUGH

Great Dover St.

Long Ln.

Tower Bridge Rd.

Druid St.

Abbey St.

Grange Rd.

Houses of Parliament

Westminster Abbey

Westminster

LAMBETH NORTH

Borough Rd.

London Rd.

St. George's Rd.

Harper Rd.

NEWINGTON

New Kent Rd.

Lambeth Bridge

Lambeth Palace Rd.

Lambeth Rd.

LAMBETH

ELEPHANT & CASTLE (BAKERLOO)

ELEPHANT & CASTLE

WEST-MINSTER

Tate Gallery

Albert Embankment

Kennington Rd.

Kennington Park Rd.

WALWORTH

Walworth Rd.

Old Kent Rd.

Vauxhall Bridge

Kennington Ln.

KENNINGTON

KENNINGTON

Albany Rd.

Harleyford Rd.

VAUXHALL

VAUXHALL

OVAL

Camberwell New Rd.

Brixton Rd.

Clapham Rd.

Camberwell New Rd.

Wandsworth Rd.

South Lambeth Rd.

0 100 mi

0 100 km

SCOTLAND

North Sea

Irish Sea

ENGLAND

WALES

London ★

English Channel

Basic Stuff

As with any big-city vacation, a London visit demands a strategy—maybe more so than most, because this city's so big and sprawling and there's so much to see. Decide what your priorities are. Does history turn you on? Is art your interest, or are you happiest just hanging? Time spent here is weather-dependent, too, since everything from the mood on the streets to the choice of activities changes in the rain. Fortunately, since rain can set in for 3 weeks without respite, there's plenty of scope for lousy weather.

Getting Your Bearings

The most important thing to do is to buy a copy of the pocket street atlas *London A to Z* (called simply "the A to Zed"—even Londoners themselves usually have one on hand). Buy it at the airport or at a newsagent in town (it's available everywhere) and navigating the city will become much easier. What follows here is a potted geography of London, containing the only parts of the *A to Z* you need to know.

West End: the center—you'd call this downtown. It's the younger of the two historic centers from which London grew, dating from 1050, when Edward the Confessor moved his court here and founded an abbey at **Westminster (SW1),** where the Houses of Parliament are. **St. James's (SW1),** now a posh area of shops and hotels, is named after the (Tudor) Court of St. James's; dignitaries are still said to be ambassadors to St. James.

Mayfair (W1) includes Bond Street and Oxford Street and most of the grand hotels. **Soho (W1),** east of Mayfair, is a small area packed with restaurants, bars (including gay bars), and nightclubs. **Covent Garden (WC2)** is the easternmost part of the West End, a target zone for shopping, museums, and restaurants. These last two areas also contain much of London's diverse theater scene—but don't dismiss what is staged at "fringe" venues in other districts.

In between Covent Garden and the City is the legal district, which contains the **Inns of Court (WC2),** the historic barristers' quarters and courts. **Holborn** (*"Hoe-*bn") borders this, an in-between area; **Bloomsbury (WC1)** is also here, with the British Museum and the University of London.

The City (EC2, EC4): The far older, Roman-founded center of town, dating from the first century A.D., it's still the financial center and still an autonomous entity. It is the City of London, with a capital *C,* aka "the Square Mile," although it isn't square. The Tower of London and St. Paul's Cathedral are here, also the Barbican (a concert-and-theater complex within one of the ugliest '70s redevelopment areas ever built) and the worth-seeing Museum of London. Plus a lot of churches designed by Christopher Wren, and a bunch of hideous skyscrapers from the 1980s, Norman Foster's just-opened "glass gherkin" rising among them.

West London: not West End. You'll spend a lot of time in neighborhoods like **Knightsbridge (SW3),** for Harrods, shopping, ladies lunching, and Hyde Park; and adjacent **South Kensington (SW5),** for the big museums (Science, Natural History, V&A). You'll probably spend less time in residential **Kensington (W8);** and **Chelsea (SW3, SW10),** though the former is worth visiting for its High Street Kensington shopping and the latter for King's Road shopping.

Notting Hill (W11) is the hip place for restaurants, gastropubs, and Portobello Market; it's bordered by residential **Holland Park (W11),** which has a park and restaurants. **Hammersmith (W6)** offers pleasant Thames-side walks and some restaurants.

The East End, where Cockneys come from (which makes it the true center, some say), is rough-and-tumble, with gentrified bits, and is definitely not touristy. Neighborhoods here include **Whitechapel (EC1)** and **Spitalfields (E1),** where you'll find art galleries, Georgian houses, and Petticoat Lane market. **Clerkenwell (EC1)** and **Farringdon (EC4)** are not really East End—they're trendy, with restaurants. In fact, Clerkenwell is so trendy, it's become a dining, shopping, drinking, hanging-out, art-gallery destination in itself. **Spitalfields,** too, has spawned a youthful art subculture that's fast dominating the neighborhood. Check them out.... **The Docklands (E14),** London's newest section, was reclaimed from industrial wasteland and old warehouses. A weird place with de Chirco–like empty urban landscapes is adjacent **Canary Wharf (E19),** a megabucks postmodern fake town containing Europe's tallest office tower, shops, and a concert hall. Don't make a special trip, though: The U.S. does this kind of development so much better.

North London: Here you'll find **Regent's Park (NW1),** which is not only a big green park that contains the zoo, but also the bordering streets, including **Marylebone,** with Madame Tussaud's. **Camden Town (NW1)** has the vast Camden Lock market; it's a grungy youth mecca. Mainly residential **Islington (N1),** which borders on Clerkenwell, has restaurants and the

Almeida Theatre. It's indicative of changing times that this arty area was the stamping ground of Labor Prime Minister Tony Blair, who sold his house for £615,000 ($1,014,750) when he came to power. (Margaret Thatcher hailed from suburban Grantham.) **Hampstead (NW3)** is a quaint, expensive hilltop village hemming a vast heath.

South of the River: This fast-evolving area first attracted Londoners to the **South Bank (SE1),** an arts complex that includes the National Theatre and Royal Festival Hall. Great views. **Bankside (SE1)** comes next, the site of the new Tate Modern, the OXO Tower and its surrounding activity, and the Globe Theatre.... **Butler's Wharf (SE1)** has the Design Museum, "Gastrodrome," and Tower Bridge; **Brixton (SW2)** is a funky neighborhood once synonymous with drugs and crime, now a byword for a rapidly increasing youth culture into music, art, and...well...drugs and crime. It must be said that SW2 is home to some great cheap eats and cool bars.

Getting from Here to There

London is usually described as being a good walking city, but you must add a coda to that: It's great to walk from, say, St. James's up Bond Street and across Regent Street to Soho, but it's a day's hike to go on foot from Chelsea to Regent's Park. London's a very big place. Also, the climate has not been exaggerated in folklore: You may find your entire stay is too damp and chilly to enjoy even a window-shopping stroll. However, using your trusty street atlas, *London A to Z,* walking is still the best way to see the details that make London a fun city.

Taking a bus costs less than the tube in money, but it can cost you much more time, especially during rush hour. The scarlet double-decker bus, however, is one of those features that screams "London," and when you're not in a hurry, the top deck provides the cheapest and best tour, especially for seeing residential nontourist neighborhoods. All you need to do is stay on the bus and when you've had enough, cross the street and take the same route back to where you started. Bus routes, of which there are some 300, are somewhat tough to decipher (pick up free maps at travel information centers). The bus stops are marked by concrete posts, each with a white or red sign on top and a rectangular one at eye level. A white sign means the bus stops automatically; at a red "Request" stop, you have to stick out your arm to flag a bus down. The rectangular sign shows the major stops on the route. Pay the conductor, or (usually) the driver/conductor, as you board; the fare if you're traveling anywhere within Central London is £1 ($1.65), otherwise 70 pence ($1.15). "N"-prefixed buses are Night Service buses. They run less frequently and cost £1.50 ($2.50). Thrifty night owls will also be glad to know that 1-day Travelcards are now valid on buses until 4:30am on the day after purchase.

The tube, aka the underground (but never called the subway), is far easier than the buses to negotiate—once you've decoded the system's rather beautiful, stylized map (unchanged since Harry Beck designed it in 1933), usually posted on station walls at just the points where you need to consult it. Get your own free map from any station, along with a booklet that explains the ticket price system. Fares are based on zones traveled. You can buy tickets for individual journeys, but at £1.60 ($2.65) a pop within Central London (up to £3.70/$6.10 for Zone 6), you'll save quite a bit by buying a **Travelcard.** The card works for buses and tubes (after 9:30am weekdays), and costs from £5.10 ($8.40) for a day within Central London. For £8 ($13), the **LT Card** covers all zones and is good for early risers because it's valid as long as the tubes are running—which is from 5am to about midnight. For buses only, a 1-day **bus pass** costs only £2 ($3.30), which makes it the most cost-effective way to travel London. Travelcards and bus passes are avail-

> **Pomp & Circumstance**
>
> *Your basic London ceremony is the **Changing of the Guard** at Buckingham Palace, which attracts throngs of visitors. The economy being what it is, they do it every day at 11:30am from April through early June and then every other day for the rest of the year (heavy rain stops it entirely). It may be a tourist cliché, but you cannot see a busby (the guards' fetching fur hats) anywhere else in the world. Another cliché of royal London is the **Crown Jewels,** housed in the Tower of London. Also at the Tower, and free, though you have to plan ahead, is the **Ceremony of the Keys,** a hilarious 10pm locking-up ritual that has used the same script and costumes every night for 700 years (for tickets, send a stamped, self-addressed envelope [British stamps] or International Reply Coupon, preferred dates, and names and addresses of others in your party to: Ceremony of the Keys, 2nd floor, HM Tower of London, London EC3N 4AB). "Halt! Who comes there?" demands the Sentry. "The Keys," answers the Chief Yeoman Warder. "Whose keys?" asks the Sentry. "Queen Elizabeth's keys," answers the CYW, whereupon the Sentry dispenses with grammar and announces: "Pass Queen Elizabeth's keys and all's well."*

DIVERSIONS

able from newsagents and at tube station windows and vending machines. You can also get weekly and monthly **Travelcards**

Money-Saving Passes

If you're coming to London to pubcrawl, forget doing it cheaply; but if you plan to visit a lot of museums, you can save money with the **London GoSee Card.** *It's valid for admission to many of London's major attractions, including Apsley House, Barbican Art Gallery, Shakespeare's Globe Theatre, and the Design Museum, plus a lot more. Validity ranges from 3 to 7 days. An adult 3-day card costs £16 ($26), and a 7-day card goes for £26 ($42). Families of two adults and up to four children can purchase a 3-day card for £32 ($51) or a 7-day card for £50 ($80). Cards are sold at British tourist information centers, London Transport centers, airports, and various attractions. For more details, call ✆ **800/223-6108** in the U.S. or ✆ **020/8995-4007** in the U.K., or try the website www.visitbritain.com.*

The **London Pass** *provides admission to 60 attractions in and around London, £5 worth of phone calls, "timed" admission at some attractions (bypassing the queues), plus free travel on public transport (buses, Tubes, and trains) and a pocket guidebook. It costs £26 ($42) for 1 day, £58 ($93) for 3 days, or £91 ($146) for 6 days (children pay £16/$26, £37/$59, or £50/$80). Visit the website at www.londonpass.com or call ✆ **870/242-9988.** Tip: Purchase the pass before you go because passes purchased in London do not include free transportation.*

(at tube stations, and requiring a photo), and the **Visitor Travelcard,** which you can buy only in the U.S. or Canada, for 3, 4, or 7 days ($31, $42, and $62, respectively). Basically it's the same as the all-zone LT Card, with a booklet of discount vouchers thrown in. Get it from your travel agent or **Rail Europe** (tel 877/257-2887 in the U.S.; 800/361-RAIL in Canada; www.raileurope.com).

You have to take a taxi (aka a "black cab," although they're not always black) at least once during your stay in London, just for the experience. Unlike taxi drivers in most cities, London cabbies have "the Knowledge"—they must pass an exhaustive exam to get their license, for which they memorize every single cul-de-sac, one-way system, and clever backstreet route in the entire metropolitan area. Many London cabbies are immensely proud of their encyclopedic memories and will regale you with information about the sights you pass; most will bore you senseless with some inane chitchat or other, anyway. Taxis have chuggy diesel-powered motors, doctored-up steering that enables them to make U-turns on a dime, and signs that say "Sit well back in your seat for safety and comfort." They cost £1.40 ($2.30) for the first 81.6 seconds or 378.6m (1,242 ft.), then 20p (30¢) for every 4.8 seconds or 189.3m

(621 ft.) until the fare display hits £11.20 ($18), when your 20p (30¢) will only buy you 126.2m (208 ft.) or 3.7 seconds. "But that is completely illogical, captain," we hear you cry. Yup. What can I say, they're British and they do things weird. Oh yeah, and they also add an incomprehensible surcharge of anything from 20p to £2 (30¢–$3.30) depending on luggage, number of passengers, pickup point, and so on. Don't try to understand; just pay up. What you end up paying is, of course, dependent on London's erratic traffic flow, but you'll be lucky to go anywhere for less than £8 ($13). While tipping is not obligatory—like in New York, for example—a meager 10% is always a good idea. A taxi is available when the yellow FOR HIRE sign on the roof is lit—though try an unlit one when desperate; sometimes they cruise without the light to skip drunks. Taxis have a way of not being there when you need them. When that happens, unlicensed minicabs come in handy. Minicabs belong to privately owned car services and must be ordered by phone or by stopping in at the office, since they can't be hailed on the street. The toll-free phone number (tel 0800/654-321) connects you with the nearest minicab operator—or look for a flashing orange light by the side of many of London's busier streets. Restaurants will usually call their pet service for you. Minicab fares may be about 20% lower than black cabs, but be prepared to bargain and give directions—although, before panic sets in, we should stress that most drivers carry a *London A to Z*, so a spot of map reading should be the only directions required.

The Lowdown

Is this your first time?... Where should you point your camera so that everyone knows you were in London? These places may be corny and crammed with visitors, but they are essential London sights. Start with the **Tower of London,** and to get an idea of the sheer age of this city, ogle the Beefeaters and the Crown Jewels. Next to that is the familiar silhouette of **Tower Bridge,** clad in Portland stone to make it seem as old as the neighboring Tower, though it is several centuries younger. Three more of the big sights are also strung along the banks of the Thames: **St. Paul's Cathedral, Westminster Abbey,** and the **Houses of Parliament.** The latter includes probably the most famous thing of all, the Clock Tower, better known as **Big**

Ben, although Ben himself is actually a bell housed in the tower, which is really named after St. Stephen. The adjacent Westminster Abbey was founded by Edward the Confessor in 1067 and was the structure around which London grew. St. Paul's, with its distinctive dome, is the great architect Sir Christopher Wren's masterpiece. If you had to choose only one museum, one art collection, and one park, you should make it the **British Museum,** the **National Gallery,** and **Hyde Park,** although you ought to also throw in one of the great Victorian museums of South Kensington—probably the **V&A,** which is almost never given its full title, the Victoria & Albert. It's not very cool to be fascinated by royalty, but, let's face it, we all are. Therefore you must look at the not especially beautiful **Buckingham Palace** (its fairly boring staterooms now open daily from July through September for a hefty fee) and catch the Changing of the Guard. Also, you'd better see the revamped and more pedestrian-friendly **Trafalgar Square,** containing **Nelson's Column,** another of those London landmarks you've seen in a million establishing shots in movies and on TV. And, of course, wend your way 'round **Piccadilly Circus** for a hit of neon and mostly sham-glam geared to tourists. Before you do any of this, though, you might want to catch a ride on the **British Airways London Eye,** a giant observation wheel that's been revolving across from the Houses of Parliament since 2000 and is so popular it will probably continue to revolve a few years more. It takes half an hour, and from the passenger pods you have incredible views over the entire city.

London's special moments... It's small things and details that arrest the attention and take the breath away, and these have done it for us: the **Holland Park peacocks'** bedtime, when the big blue birds flap into the trees, screeching in their special way, while the sun sets over the ruins of the Jacobean mansion. Sneaking in to swim the **Serpentine** in Hyde Park after midnight during a heat wave. Pacing the Glass Gallery walkway at the **V&A** on a day without school parties, or looking down on Waterhouse Way—the great hall at the **Natural History Museum**—when it's swarming with children on their way to have the bejesus scared out of them by the animatronic T-Rex in the dinosaur exhibit. **Trafalgar Square** at 2am in December (when the giant Norwegian fir tree's up and lit), waiting for a night bus. The romantic bleakness of the **Thames** during misty gray weather as you walk along the river from Westminster Bridge to Tower Bridge. Crossing one of the bridges at night, with the mighty river below and the city illuminated all around, can also bring out the eternal romance of London. And London's lovely when new segues into old, especially if you come upon an ancient thing when you weren't looking for it—like the **Temple of Mithras,** or parts of the **Roman walls** near the Museum of London. The very best London moments come out of just happening on odd little lanes and garden squares, mews and mansions, noticing details and watching life go on. If time is limited and you want the picturesque highly concentrated, try the **Inns of Court** and **Hampstead.**

Only in London... The most screamingly London activities have history, a special relationship with the weather, and are taken for granted by the locals. Qualifying on all counts is a **Thames boat trip,** starting at Westminster Pier, passing St. Paul's and the Tower on the left, the South Bank Centre on the right, and going under Tower Bridge to **Greenwich.** Disembark there and see the one and only **prime meridian,** from which all time is measured. Parks exist elsewhere, but few cities have palaces across the lawn. **St. James's Park** has two—the **Buckingham Palace** facade and the back of St. James's Palace, while **Kensington Gardens** and **Kew Gardens** have an eponymous palace apiece. For assessing the current state of eccentric English behavior, **Speaker's Corner** is the lodestone, though a visit to **Sir John Soane's Museum** illustrates how London-style unconventionality looks when taken to its natural conclusion. Number **18 Folgate Street** shows the same thing, but being the brainchild of an American, suggests that London may be more a state of mind than a collection of historic buildings. It's not meant to be grisly, but you can practically hear the screams at the **Old Operating Theatre,** a completely intact operating theater that presents a vivid picture of surgical before HMOs and anesthesia. And of course you've heard of the Bank of England, but have you heard of the **Bank of England Museum,** devoted to filthy lucre in all its British forms?

DIVERSIONS

What if it's raining?... And it probably will be (nobody lives in England for the climate). Museums are the obvious thing to do, especially now that so many of them are free, and the **British Museum** (with its fabulous new Great Court) is big enough—it has about 100 galleries—to keep you indoors all day. So is the **V&A,** but here you can do more than just look—this enterprising museum of decorative arts runs short drawing and painting courses attended by everyone from total beginners to art-school professors. Or you could just pig out at the V&A's Sunday morning brunch and read the papers. Take in the Glass Gallery first, because it's so full of reflected light, you'll forget the awful weather. Another hot ticket for a cold rainy day is the new **Saatchi Gallery** in County Hall next to Westminster Bridge, where you can view deliberately controversial contemporary works. Further down the Thames, in Bankside, the new **Tate Modern** is another great place to spend a few rainy hours, though it's heaving on weekends. Afterwards, have a coffee in the cafe and watch the rain on the Thames. Two art-laden houses in which to forget the gray clouds are that eccentric wonderland **Sir John Soane's Museum,** and the 18th-century version, the **Wallace Collection.** Satisfy a different sense during lunchtime concerts at the churches of **St. John's Smith Square** and **St. Martin-in-the-Fields.** (At the latter, descend to the crypt for the **London Brass Rubbing Centre** and fashion your own souvenir.) For some unpredictable and occasionally ghoulish live theater, drop in on a trial at the **Old Bailey,** the principal criminal courts of the land. If you must shop, the department stores are obviously good, but better still are the **Piccadilly Arcades** (see the Shopping chapter), which predate the oldest mall by about 150 years and are rather more posh. Have afternoon tea nearby, because it's always best in the rain.

That pre-eminent London sleuth Sherlock Holmes didn't ever actually live at 221B Baker Street—it's the Abbey National Building Society's offices now—but there is a hokey **Sherlock Holmes Museum** that has appropriated the famous address, though it's really at number 237.

When the sun shines... Anything you do in London on a warm, sunny day is enhanced at least 100%, since everyone's idiotically happy (this doesn't apply to heat waves, when complaints soon set in), but a **Thames boat trip** is the best of all. Take one downriver from Westminster to the Tower, or to **Greenwich,** but think twice before committing to a long (about 3-hour) upstream trip to **Hampton Court Palace** or **Richmond** since there are great stretches of nothing to look at. The **Regent's Canal** is fun, whether on foot or by canal barge; the prettiest parts are between **Camden Lock** (by the markets) and **Regent's Park,** and at **Little Venice,** an expensive, little-visited area of big white houses. The **Canal Café Theatre** (see the Entertainment chapter) can be your destination, or maybe you're here on the first weekend in May for the water festival called **Canalway Cavalcade,** a celebration with boat pageants, crafts stalls, and a teddy bears' picnic (Blomfield Rd., Little Venice, W9). The **London Zoo** is where everyone with children congregates on sunny days. Avoid it. Go instead to the recently renovated **Ham House** in Richmond, with its great 17th-century gardens, or to the exquisite **Chelsea Physic Garden,** both in neighborhoods that cry out for aimless strolling. Or stay in **Regent's Park** and buy tickets for Shakespeare (usually one of the comedies) at the open-air theater. Another open-air theater is secreted in exquisite **Holland Park,** on a stage fashioned from the ruins of a Jacobean mansion blitzed in the Blitz. It stages opera and dance, all to the sound of peacocks screeching. For a theatrical experience without script, go to **Speaker's Corner,** by Marble Arch, where anyone is welcome to stand on a soapbox and hold forth. You may be lucky enough to catch a memorable loony—sunny days attract them.

The oldest things... London's very oldest thing has nothing to do with London, or with the person it's named after. It is the Egyptian obelisk by Victoria Embankment, **Cleopatra's Needle,** and it's around 3,500 years old. Younger, but still ancient, are two of the **British Museum**'s best treasures, the 4th-century **Mausoleum of Halicarnassus,** one of the Wonders of the Ancient World, and the controversial **Parthenon Sculptures** (called the Elgin Marbles in less PC times), carved in Athens in about 440 B.C. They should now go back to Greece, say the Greeks (and many Brits). Only about 200 years younger than Cleopatra's Needle is the **Sarcophagus of Seti I,** which the fun-loving architect of the Bank of England, Sir

John Soane, bought for a song and installed in the basement of his house, now **Sir John Soane's Museum.** As for indigenous things, you can see parts of London's **Roman walls** in and around the **Museum of London,** as well as the 3rd-century A.D. **Temple of Mithras,** which was unearthed about 50 years ago. It's a little strip of history, although there's nothing but a boring set of foundations to look at. A better example of ancient/modern juxtaposition is the rose window of **Winchester House,** palace of the Bishops of Winchester until 1626, built into the St. Mary Overie Dock development adjacent to the bishops' old jail, now a museum called **The Clink.** Down in the law enclave, on High Holborn, you'll find London's oldest (1586) Elizabethan black-and-white half-timbered building, the **Staple Inn,** where wool traders were lodged and their commodity weighed and traded. Times have changed; now it's Ye Olde Smoke Shoppe. The oldest part of the famously old **Tower of London** is the **White Tower,** which was the tallest building in London on its completion in 1097. Westminster Abbey, with tombs of those arch-rivals Queen Elizabeth I and Mary Queen of Scots, dates mostly from the 13th and 14th centuries, though there's been a church on the site for at least a thousand years. Meanwhile, the oldest operating theater in Britain—appropriately called the **Old Operating Theatre and Herb Garret**—is tucked away on the South Bank; it dates from 1822 and was discovered completely intact a few years ago after being walled up and forgotten.

The newest... The **Museum in Docklands,** London's newest museum, opened in 2003 but probably isn't the sort of place to draw a general-interest tourist pressed for time, though it's got some interesting stuff. Just as new is the **Saatchi Gallery,** which moved its controversial stable of self-publicizing contemporary art to a high-visibility location in County Hall next to Westminster Bridge (above the London Aquarium). Two new galleries have opened in **Somerset House,** a 1,000-room civil palace on the Strand that has been tarted up for the public with a lovely courtyard fountain (the courtyard becomes a skating rink in the winter) and a summer-only river-terrace cafe: The **Gilbert Collection** is a cornucopia of snuff boxes and valuable objets d'art, and the **Hermitage Rooms** show off on-loan treasures from the strapped-for-cash Hermitage Museum in St. Petersburg. A new, improved **Queen's Gallery** at Buckingham Palace reopened in 2002 during QEII's Golden Jubilee; it's even got a coffee shop. The **Tate Modern,** housed in the old Bankside power station, is high on everyone's must-see list; it's no longer new, but newish, having opened in 2000, and it's connected to the St. Paul's area by the sleek new **Millennium Bridge,** a pedestrian walkway designed by Lord Norman Foster, everyone's architectural darling. He also designed London's newest skyscraper, the **Swiss-Re Tower,** an unmistakable glass gherkin of a building on St. Mary's Axe in the City, and the just-opened **London City Hall,** a super-green building shaped like a wasp's behind beside Tower Bridge. **Shakespeare's Globe Theatre** is newish in one sense (it's about 5 years old), but it's also London's oldest stage: a reconstruction of the Bard's "wooden O" on its original site (give or take a few meters), using original materials and building techniques. Erected for the duddish millennium celebrations, the **British Airways London Eye** is a 135m-high (450 ft.) observation wheel that offers 30-minute "flights" on the south bank of the Thames. It was supposed to have a built-in shelf life but has proved to be so popular that it will probably continue to revolve for a couple of years more. The twin pedestrian walkways alongside **Hungerford Bridge** make walking to the South Bank Centre from Embankment a real pleasure. On the latte front, Starbucks has opened coffee bars on nearly every street in Central London.

Architectural highs and lows... The tallest building now is Cesar Pelli's 50-story tower at 1 Canada Square, the centerpiece of London's weirdest square mile, **Canary Wharf.** Modeled on an American downtown, this business district was reclaimed from slums as part of the 1980s redevelopment of the Docklands, but it never really fit in or took off; it makes for a really offbeat de Chirico–esque outing, from deserted mall to riverside pub. The newest train line in town, the **Jubilee line** extension, is the way to get there. Or see it all from the **Docklands Light Railway (DLR).** The new **British Library** opened in 1997 after a decade of design traumas were solved and decanted its 18-million-odd books into an orange-brick edifice by King's Cross Station. Many dislike the building intensely and say it reminds them of a supermarket, but the exhibition galleries show off **a magnificent horde of original manuscripts.** A building that's become for some inexplicable reason an instant architectural totem is the sinisterly ugly **Lloyd's Building;** Sir Richard Rogers was the culprit responsible for this graceless, unwelcoming, pseudo-science-fictionish behemoth. Everyone's current darling is Lord Norman Foster, whose pickle-shaped, 40-story **Swiss-Re Tower** can be seen rising in the City, and whose environmentally aware **London City Hall,** shaped like a wasp's behind (or a fencing helmet, depending on whom you talk to) stands next to Tower Bridge on the South Bank. Foster's **Millennium Bridge,** which had to be closed twice due to structural problems before it actually opened (pedestrians couldn't walk on it because of the bounce) spans the Thames between the **Tate Modern** (a reworking of the old Bankside Power Station).

Go out of your way for... If it's royal residences you're after, you can't get a better one than **Hampton Court Palace,** closely associated with that most colorful and obese king, 'Enery the Eighth, of the six wives and the gout problem, who moved in in 1525. The last monarch to call it home was poor George III—he of *The Madness of King George* fame—who decamped to Kew to go mad in relative peace. See one of the world's best privet mazes, the restored Tudor kitchens, the Great Hall, the Banqueting House, and—what you can't see at Buckingham Palace—the State Apartments, all in a beauteous Thames-side setting. It'll take the whole day, being 32km (20 miles) out of London, further still than Richmond. Ah, Richmond. **Richmond Park** is quite the wildest in London (well, near London), complete with herds of deer; you can go horseback riding there, or biking, or use it as an excuse for a few pints at the Cricketers, which is like a real village pub. There also are two stately homes almost facing one another on opposite banks of the Thames: **Ham House** and **Marble Hill House.** At the opposite end of town, and not too much of a trek if you're staying in the West End, is **Hampstead,** a pricey village high on a hill, with quaint cottages and Georgian mansions, expensive boutiques, **Keats House** and the Everyman Cinema, branches of the Gap and McDonald's (how the residents hate that), and surprisingly bad restaurants. Hampsteadites are represented in Parliament by the Oscar-winning former actress Glenda

Jackson, which should give you an idea of the tone up there. Some of the best things are the other wild park, **Hampstead Heath,** all rolling hills and dells and ancient woods, which leads to **Kenwood House,** worth seeing for two reasons: the Iveagh Bequest of paintings (Gainsborough, Rembrandt, Turner, Van Dyck, and Vermeer) and summer concerts at the open-air bowl—with tea at the cafe an important adjunct. The best and oldest necropolis in London is barely known by Londoners themselves: It's the 31-hectare (77-acre) **Kensal Green Cemetery,** where you can descend to the catacombs guided by fanatic local historians dressed in black, who also point out the last resting places of novelists Thackeray, Trollope, and Wilkie Collins.

Inspiring spires... You don't have to be a believer to love London's churches. Many of the most loved are the work of the great architect so closely associated with London, Sir Christopher Wren, who rebuilt 51 of the 87 churches destroyed in the Great Fire of 1666. Twenty-five remain, plus, of course, his masterpiece, **St. Paul's Cathedral.** We'll leave it to other guides to do the exhaustive Wren tour, but here are a couple

DIVERSIONS

The Wren Style

One of the great geniuses of his age, Sir Christopher Wren (1632-1723) was a professor of astronomy at Oxford before becoming an architect. After the Great Fire of London in 1666, Wren was chosen to rebuild the devastated city and its many churches, including **St. Paul's,** on which work began in 1675. His designs had great originality, and he became known for his spatial effects and his impressive fusion of classical and baroque. He believed in classical stability and repose, yet he liked to enliven his churches with baroque whimsy and fantasy.

In our view, his crowning glory is the **dome over St. Paul's,** which is celebrated for the beauty of it's proportions. Surely Michelangelo would have patted Wren on the back. If, during his stay in France, Wren stole an idea or two from the Invalides in Paris, so what? We'll never tell.

Nothing better represents the Wren style than the **facade of St. Paul's,** for which he combined classical columns, reminiscent of Greek temples, with baroque decorations and adornments. Regrettably, the town plan that Wren conceived for rebuilding London was rejected, and the city was reconstructed piecemeal. Could you imagine what London would look like if Wren had been turned loose? Surely Prince Charles would praise the architecture of London rather than denouncing it.

from the Wren stable. The usefully central **St. James's Piccadilly** was his last (1684) and his favorite; its spire, hit by the WWII blitz, is now fiberglass. Learn to read the tarot, or hear a Handel recital there—the acoustics are angelic. **St. James's Garlickhythe** (with **St. Michael Queenhithe** and **Holy Trinity-the-Less,** to give it its full name) also has recitals, Tuesday lunchtimes, under Wren's highest ceiling (apart from St. Paul's). It's a handy stop en route to Shakespeare's Globe across the river and the adjacent **Southwark Cathedral** (more recitals there). A lesser building than Westminster Abbey, Southwark Cathedral is London's second-oldest church, with parts of its 12th-century self still intact. Shakespeare worshipped here, and his brother Edmund is buried here. It's also the only church with its own pizza cafe. The Cafe-in-the-Crypt at **St. Martin-in-the-Fields** is pretty good, too, and the church itself is fab. The music program at St. Martin-in-the-Fields is the best, apart from the June music fes-tival at an exquisite church hardly anyone visits: Sir Nicholas Hawksmoor's 1728 **Christ Church Spitalfields.** Admittedly, it will hardly ever be open, until restoration is finished in the next few years, but go see the gorgeous colonnaded portico on a Brick Lane outing.

Their Majesties live here... After her death, Diana's former home, **Kensington Palace,** became a prime place of pilgrimage. (It was Princess Margaret's London address, too, but nobody really cared much when she died in 2002.) K.P. hasn't harbored a monarch since Victoria decamped from here to Buckingham Palace at her accession (1837); its none-too-successful run as primary royal residence started with the Bill and Hill of English monarchs, William and Mary (1689–1702). William fell off his horse and died of pleurisy; Mary succumbed to smallpox; Queen Anne suffered a fatal apoplectic fit due to overeating; so did George I (he OD'd on melons); and poor George II met the most ignominious Kensington Palace end—he burst a blood vessel while on the royal commode. But by far the most embarrassing monarch was "Farmer George," George III, the mad one. He succumbed to lunacy and died at **Kew Palace,** the most intimate and domestic and the least visited of all London's palaces, though lots of visitors stroll around its gardens. I've already accused **Buckingham Palace** of being the most boring of royal residences, but it does have the best gardens in London and since you probably won't manage to wrangle an invitation to one of HRH's garden parties, the only way to see them is to buy the exorbitantly priced ticket to the palace during its summer opening. The queen is in, by the way, when the royal standard is hoisted, and is never there (God forbid) when the place is open to tourists. You can't see the current HRH's living quarters, but you can see her horses and coaches at the **Royal Mews.** And you can see treasures she holds in trust for the nation at the newly revamped **Queen's Gallery.** Previous palaces are much more fun than Buckingham: I've already mentioned the **Tower of London** and **Hampton Court Palace,** but I haven't said a word about another piece of Henry VIII's real estate, **St. James's Palace,** the sweetest and smallest of all, and the one to which visiting dignitaries are still sent. The catch is that it's a completely private palace and all you can see is its red-brick Tudor facade and some side views. The present queen, by the way, has nothing to do with the **Queen's House** in Greenwich, which was designed by the great Inigo Jones for James I's queen, Anne of Denmark. The first classical building in Britain, it is important and exquisite. Inigo Jones was also responsible for all that remains of yet another of Henry VIII's palaces (and the one he died in), **Banqueting House,** the only surviving bit of the labyrinthine Whitehall Palace, which burned to the ground in 1698. **Windsor Castle** nearly burned down, too, in 1992. You'll need an entire day for the excursion to this place, reputed to be Elizabeth II's favorite of her modest homes and now all back in working order, thanks to funding by...you. Right, 'nuff palaces.

Modern art... Art lives. It starts in the national collections, continues in galleries mounting exhibitions of new work, and culminates in commercial spaces, avant-garde *boîtes,* and independent dealerships. The **Tate Britain** holds by far the most important and extensive modern collection of British artists in London (though works on display date back to 1500). They were constantly rehanging the stuff around to give it all a fair show...until they built a whole new museum, the fabulous **Tate Modern,** in Bankside on the South Bank. It's near **Shakespeare's Globe Theatre** and is one of London's busiest attractions; the works here are international in scope. The **Hayward Gallery** in the South Bank Centre is also a major public space, with changing shows favoring sculpture and installation. Neither is especially known for taking risks, though the Tate causes an occasional outcry when it buys a controversial work (most infamously when it invested in Carl André's *Bricks*—a block of bricks). For controversy a la mode, you have to visit the new home of the **Saatchi Gallery** in County Hall, where all those self-publicizing and occasionally repellent works by Saatchi's current in-crowd are displayed. These are the pieces that were shown at the "Sensation" show in Brooklyn and caused New York Mayor Rudy Giuliani to threaten closure (which, of course, only increased attendance). The **ICA** and the smaller but creatively curated **Serpentine Gallery** are close to the cutting edge, too, and so is the **White Cube** gallery in Hoxton Square. If you're heading eastward, the **Whitechapel Gallery** is always worth the trek, with major shows, lecture series, and a good cafe. Among the other newer outlying spaces, **Gasworks** is worth checking out for exciting artists not yet sanctified by the establishment. But if you want one neighborhood for unplanned, aimless gallery-hopping, then head to Notting Hill, where many tiny independent galleries around Portobello Road have led to a little scene like New York's SoHo. Way the hell out in the East End (combine it with the White Cube, the Whitechapel, and the **Lux Cinema,** which promotes art-house films and young filmmakers), the radical **Camerawork** is a standout for photography. Convenient to Covent Garden is the consistently excellent **Photographers' Gallery,** while the **Barbican Centre,** the **National Portrait Gallery,** and the foyer of the **Royal Festival Hall** often feature photography exhibits. For a somewhat surreal look at surrealism, you might want to check out the newish **Dalí Universe** exhibition on the South Bank, but don't put it high on your list of priorities unless you love him.

The old masters... The world does not need another guide to the **National Gallery,** so I'll just point you in that direction and leave you to it. The adjacent **National Portrait Gallery** is not to be sniffed at, though it's smaller and has many obscure faces among the familiar ones. In this museum, who is represented is of more interest than how, and so some of the work is egregiously bad. That can't be said for the **Royal Academy of Arts,** housed in the imposing Burlington House, and center of the British art establishment—except during the annual Summer Exhibition, which consists of thousands of works, many unsolicited and chosen by committee in "auditions." In the newly refurbed and quite wonderful Somerset House, you find the wonderful **Courtauld Institute Gallery,** which still has the most impressive Impressionists and Postimpressionists, plus the odd Rubens (speaking of which, don't miss the Rubens ceiling at **Banqueting House**). For viewing pleasure and fewer crowds, try the exquisite **Wallace Collection,** where the Fragonards, Bouchers, and Canalettos are displayed *in situ,* as if the marquesses of Hertford who collected them were about to stroll by. Ditto the small, eccentric collection of paintings, starring several from Hogarth's bawdy "Rake's Progress" series, at **Sir John Soane's Museum,** with countless statues and architectural fragments and *objets* bursting the walls of this amazing house. Soane also designed what was London's first public art gallery, the practically perfect **Dulwich Picture Gallery,** little changed since its 1811 opening, right down to its parkland surroundings; it's a mere 12-minute train ride from Victoria for Tiepolo, Canaletto, Gainsborough, Rembrandt, Van Dyck, Poussin...and all for free on Fridays. In leafy Hampstead, lovely **Kenwood House** is also free; inside you can ponder some astounding works left to the nation by Lord Iveagh in 1927, including a Rembrandt self-portrait and Vermeer's *The Guitar Player.* There are some vast old-master paintings in **Apsley House,** and usually some are on view in the **Queen's Gallery** at Buckingham Palace.

Art alfresco... Avert your eyes when passing the paintings hung along the sidewalks on Sundays at Green Park's Piccadilly border and the Bayswater Road edge of Hyde Park, unless you like paintings on velvet and watercolors of big-eyed kittens and weeping clowns. But do keep an eye out for the ubiquitous statues on London streets. A random sampling: Hubert le Sueur's equestrian *Charles I* (on Trafalgar Sq. near Whitehall), re-erected by his son, Charles II, nearly on the spot of his father's execution; *Oliver Cromwell,* who was responsible for that execution; Rodin's *The Burghers of Calais* (nearby, in the Victoria Tower Gardens); and a 600-year-old—though nobody's quite sure of the exact date—*Alfred the Great* (Trinity Church Sq. SE1). **Kensington Gardens** has three famous sculptures: a rather splendid bronze horse and rider titled *Physical Energy;* a whimsical bronze *Peter Pan,* near the home of his creator, J. M. Barrie; and another children's favorite, the *Elfin Oak,* carved from a tree. The following are more obscure: *William Huskisson,* the first man to be killed by a train, confusingly dressed in a toga (Pimlico Gardens); the pretty blue column of the *Thames Water Surge Shaft* kinetic water barometer—functional art at its finest and most fun (Shepherd's Bush Roundabout W11); the granite Bedouin tent *Tomb of Sir Richard Burton* (the Victorian explorer, not the actor).

Won't bore the kids... That *Elfin Oak* statue stands just outside a much-loved playground in **Kensington Gardens.** There's also the newish **Princess Diana Memorial Playground** in the northwestern corner of Kensington Gardens. You'll find playgrounds in most parks, but the appropriately named **Holland Park Adventure Playground** is among the best. More touristy things that children like include the **London Zoo,** though it isn't much different from any other zoo; the **Royal Mews,** with its horses and ornate coaches; and the **Tower of London,** especially the gory parts. An expensive ticket, but worth the investment for older or tougher children, is the **London Dungeon,** a sort of extrapolation of the Tower's aforementioned gory bits crossed with Madame Tussaud's. Skip overpriced **Madame Tussaud's** and go next door instead, into the **London Planetarium,** with its laser shows and new star projector. You'll find it better than the **Pepsi Trocadero**'s plasticky high-tech shows, but the kids may disagree. In similar vein, try steering them straight past the scary **Namco Station,** which sits outside the London Aquarium's shop, its horrible lights blinking, disco music on a loop, video games bleeping. Ugh to London's least welcome new thing. The **London Aquarium,** by contrast, is more appealing, though Sea World alumni will scoff and the basement locale can feel claustrophobic and tacky. It's small scale, but it takes you deep into its watery world. The museums to pick are: the **Natural History Museum** (especially the animatronic T-Rex—although it may scare the little ones—and the Creepy-Crawlies Gallery), and the next-door **Science Museum** (the computer and outer-space stuff is brilliant). Also a hit are the **London Transport Museum,** where you can climb all over old double-deckers and tube cars, and the far-off **Horniman Museum,** with its bee colony and musical-instrument collection. Smaller kids will prefer the V&A's **Museum of Childhood at Bethnal Green;** it's way out in the East End but worth the trek because it has the world's biggest toy collection, including loads of fabulous dollhouses. If that's too far for you, try the quirky, labyrinthine **Pollocks Toy Museum. Greenwich** makes a great day out. Arrive by boat, and save the *Cutty Sark* for last, because it's the children's favorite, though kids also like seeing the **prime meridian,** from which the world's time is measured, at the **Old Royal Observatory**—you can stand with one foot in each hemisphere. You can do a canal day, too, taking a **Canal Barge Trip** from Little Venice to the zoo. You may be in luck and find the **Puppet Theatre Barge** is in town. Although the **Theatre Museum** in Covent Garden is pretty boring, they do hands-on stage makeup and costume demonstrations that kids love.

Photo ops... Essential tourist shots start with Trafalgar Square's **Nelson's Column,** which is the official center of London, or at least of the tourists around its now-pigeonless base. The rest of the shots you'd expect: the **clock tower** of the Houses of Parliament, which everyone mistakenly calls Big Ben (Big Ben is the largest bell inside), **Westminster Abbey,** and **Westminster Bridge** you can buy on postcards. Well, okay, shoot Big Ben from the walkway in front of the London Aquarium because you'll probably be there in any case. If the sun isn't too glaring or the day too gray, you can snap a bunch of aerial views of the city from the **British Airways London Eye** observation wheel. But then why not look for something more subtle? The **Chelsea**

Pensioners who live in Wren's **Royal Hospital,** a stunning Palladian retirement home for ex-soldiers, are just as picturesque as the **Beefeaters** in their red-and-gold frock coats; then whiz over to the **Monument,** Wren's memorial to the Great Fire. Run up the 311 steps and snap a view from the top. In late May, bring lots of color stock to capture the great tumbling banks of rhododendrons in **Kensington Gardens, Holland Park** (where you can maybe get a peacock in, too), and **Kew Gardens.** Get out a zoom lens for the facade of the **Natural History Museum,** with its intricate arches of fauna—extinct creatures to the right, living ones to the left. If, like John Lennon, you've wondered how many holes it takes to fill Royal Albert Hall, take a shot of this curious circular, domed Victorian building just off Kensington Gardens, then point your camera across the street toward the **Albert Memorial,** that ridiculously ornate love token from Victoria to her prematurely dead consort, now sparkling in new gold leaf after a decade of restoration. Forget nearby Harrods and go instead to **Fortnum & Mason** (see the Shopping chapter) and get a shot of one of the city's sweetest clocks, featuring automata of the founders shaking hands on the hour.

A day of romance... You must also take a **walk**—perhaps **along the banks of the Thames** around Embankment, or on the south side along Bankside, going as far east as Tower Bridge and timing things to end up at **Le Pont de la Tour** (see the Dining chapter) for cocktail hour and oysters from the raw bar. Any park is also good, especially in summer after dark, and there's something very appealing about London's squares, with trees in the middle and maybe a row of Georgian houses around it. Try 18th-century **Kensington Square** (take Derry or Young streets off Kensington High St.), or the even older—laid out around 1670—**St. James's Square,** from which you could explore the wonderful perfumers and shaving accoutrement emporia and shirt shops of Jermyn Street. Drop in to the **National Gallery** and restrict yourself to the romantic works, like Velasquez's *The Toilet of Venus* (you'll recognize her when you see her), Constable's *The Hay Wain* (so bucolic), and perhaps some Canalettos, then on to the **Tate Britain** for the splendid Turners and pre-Raphaelites. An evening stroll in **Hampstead** might segue into a show at the Everyman, one of London's last repertory cinemas and a sweet old-fashioned place. Alternatively, spend all day at the **Porchester Baths,** having massages and sweating in the steam rooms.

For gardeners... Serious horticulturalists should seriously consider coming to London in late May for the **Chelsea Flower Show,** one of the world's foremost flower shows and so pricey you may gasp or fall into a swoon. Failing that, try to be in London during the summer, when all the parks have flower beds stuffed full of color. In **Regent's Park,** St. Mary's Rose Garden is scented and formal, while **Holland Park** has its Dutch Garden, where the first dahlias in England grew in the late 18th century. With 60,000 plant species, **Kew Gardens** has something flowering in every season, and it also has the pair of spectacular 19th-century greenhouses, the Palm House and its corollary the Temperate House, which boasts the world's biggest greenhouse plant—a Chilean wine palm rooted in 1846. An even bigger greenhouse than those two is the 1987 Princess of Wales Conservatory, with its 10 separate climates. **Columbia Road Flower Market** (see the Shopping chapter) has just the one English climate, but you can fantasize planting your ideal English garden among the overflowing, blooming stalls and buy horticultural accoutrements to take home. Garden historians should under no circumstances miss **Ham House,** with its meticulously restored 17th-century grounds; they should also allow time to get to **Hampton Court Palace** for the Elizabethan Knot Garden, the Great Vine, the maze, and the topiary—not to mention the only flower show that rivals Chelsea. Speaking of which, the **Chelsea Physic Garden** is exquisite and educational in equal measure—medicinal plants are grown here alongside the country's oldest rock garden. There's one more stop on the itinerary: the **Museum of Garden History,** housed in a deconsecrated church and featuring another 17th-century knot garden for those who failed to get to Hampton Court.

DIVERSIONS

For the impecunious... Get on a bus, climb the stairs to the top deck, show your Travelcard, and sit back for the least expensive grandstand tour in the land. Good bus routes include the **94** or **12,** for Hyde Park on the north side, Oxford and Regent streets, Piccadilly Circus, Trafalgar Square, and more; the **11** for Chelsea through to Knightsbridge, the City via Westminster; the **74** for the South Ken museums through Hyde Park Corner past Lord's cricket ground to the zoo; and the **29** from Victoria or Piccadilly Circus through Bloomsbury and the British Museum to Camden Lock. Bus maps are free from major tube stations. Or else you could splash out and board a sightseeing bus. Outside the Green Park tube stop is the best place to get one. They travel around "the sights," allowing you to hop on and off at will. I'm happy to report that admission to the greatest museums in town is now free, free, free: The **British Museum,** the **National Gallery,** the **National Portrait Gallery, Tate Britain, Tate Modern,** the **V&A,** the **Natural History Museum,** the **Science Museum,** the **Museum of London,** and scads more won't cost you a penny. If it's late June, look in *Time Out* magazine for news of the student degree shows, where you get the chance to buy work straight from the hands of art-schoolers at ridiculously low prices. **Lunchtime classical recitals** in churches are another great delight of London to look up in the listings, and most are free or bargains. Hang around **Covent Garden** to see the buskers perform, too—if it's summer, the piazza may even feature a particularly juicy opera production beamed onto giant screens, courtesy of the Royal Opera House. **Street markets** (see the Shopping chapter) are probably the best free shows of all, though; those and just walking. Traveling by foot is especially entertaining because you will get lost and you will find yourself in the mewses and alleys and streetlets with which London is crammed.

Go east... There's a strong argument that the East End is the true London, following the truism that a real Cockney must be born within the sound of Bow Bells (at St. Mary-le-Bow church). *Eastenders,* the *Melrose Place* of England, is set here in the fictional, but recognizable, Albert Square. And this is Jack the Ripper land (take a Ripper walking tour if you must—there are loads of them). The neighborhoods of the east are gritty, so don't expect a smooth tourist patina.

The major museum, the **Museum of Childhood at Bethnal Green,** an outpost of the V&A, is a good excuse to head east, especially with kids in tow. There are several city farms nearby for them, too—**Spitalfields City Farm** has the works: sheep, goats, cows, horses, pony rides, and summer barbecues. Ask about the horse-and-cart local-history tour. Instead of Tobacco Dock, which sounds fab with its pirate ships and crafts fairs but turns out to be one of the most depressing malls you've ever seen, go to **Spitalfields Market** (see the Shopping chapter), where there are great sports facilities and a little opera house, a farmers market and good crafts shops. It's near Hawksmoor's **Christ Church Spitalfields,** which you should probably not make a special trip to see, since it's usually closed, but do check the concert schedule and watch for the two music festivals because both are real treats. Last but not least is one of London's most surprising and evocative museums, the **Geffrye Museum,** which contains a series of period rooms done with a Hollywood movie–scale attention to detail and authenticity. Unlike the stately homes you normally have access to, these interiors are domestic, so you get a powerful sense of how people lived. It's really out of the way but worth it if your interests tend at all toward popular and cultural history. Easier to reach (right next to the tube) is the **Whitechapel Gallery,** most certainly worth a special trip for anyone with an eye for the big-name and up-and-coming artists of now (plus it's got a pretty good cafe). From there, stroll down to the **Whitechapel Bell Foundry** to see the birthplace of the Liberty Bell (yes, that one) and Big Ben. You can't go into the actual foundry, but you can buy a hand bell and look at a cute little exhibit. The classic thing to do around here is to spend Sunday at the markets. Chief among them are the adjacent **Brick Lane** and **Petticoat Lane,** and **Columbia Road Flower Market** (see the Shopping chapter for details). The last one is not much use for souvenirs, but it's full of local color and then some, and some of the shops that open only on market day (Sun) are also well worth a gander. Number **18 Folgate Street** was the home of eccentric California-born Dennis Sever, who shared it with a ghostly fictional family named Jervis, who "lived" in the house from 1754 to 1914; on Monday evenings, a guide leads the audience on a silent tour of the house to appreciate its style but above all to conjure up the atmosphere of Olde Worlde London. The Georgian house in Spitalfields is in perfect period style, outdoing the Geffrye Museum in authenticity, since Sever actually lived here, without electricity but with a butler in 18th-century livery.

The deep south... Ignore any South of the River snobbery and lame jokes you encounter (don't forget your passport, and so on)—there really is life across the Thames. In fact, it's one of the hottest happening areas of the city just now, with new development all over the place. Walk from Westminster Bridge to Tower Bridge and you'll see what I mean. Catch one of the summer shows on the open-air stage of **Shakespeare's Globe Theatre.** Its neighbor is the all-new, all-fabulous **Tate Modern,** sister to the Tate Britain in Pimlico. There's a rather vibrant emerging arts scene in the cheaper, bigger spaces south of the river— check gallery listings in *Time Out* under "Alternative Spaces." After gallery-hopping, you could head to **Tower Bridge Experience** (check out the new Norman Foster– designed **London City Hall** next to the bridge), or lunch in one of the **"Gastrodrome"** restaurants, or visit the **Design Museum,** or the warship **HMS** *Belfast,* or the *Golden Hinde,* an exact replica of the ship Sir Francis Drake used to circumnavigate the globe. There's also the somewhat creepy **Old Operating Theatre and Herb Garret** in the church of St. Thomas, a place once attached to St. Thomas's Hospital. Back upstream, the **South Bank Centre** is still vibrant and fun, fun, fun, after all these years—London's biggest arts complex, housed in a set of Brutalist-style buildings by Denis Lasdun (about to be covered in Richard Rogers's glass canopy, if the funding comes through) that have weathered into classic London landmarks. Don't ignore **Southwark Cathedral,** between the Globe and the Royal National Theatre, as most people do. And **Battersea Park** is a charmingly different sort of place that will show you the echt atmosphere of South London like no museum can. Battersea is metamorphosing into the new Chelsea, with bars, shops, restaurants, and very, very young residents and their 4x4-driving preppy parents—hence the nickname "Nappy Valley" for the area along the south side of the park.

Street scenes... Brixton is the center of Caribbean culture in London and a magnet for the young and hip, though it helps to have a local to show you around. **Notting Hill** is the posher version, and even hipper. It's *the* place, with galleries, restaurants, gewgaw shops, antiques shops, and clothes shops, all clustered around the hub of **Portobello Road Market** (see the Shopping chapter) and the formerly Rasta ganja-dealing, now restaurant- and cafe-laden **All Saints Road.** You may hear people refer to this area as West Eleven, which is simply its post code. The 3-day **Notting Hill Carnival,** held over the August Bank Holiday weekend, is the biggest carnival in the Northern Hemisphere and the ultimate London street party; West Indian culture rules here, but it's eclectic. It once had a reputation for trouble, but the worst you'll have to deal with anymore is the crush of thousands of revelers. **Camden Town** is way less groovy and cool, being more populated with high-school kids and wannabes than are the Portobello environs, but it's not dissimilar. A million miles more touristy, and also dead central, is **Covent Garden.** Every single visitor to London swarms to the piazza, especially in summer, and actually, it's not too bad there—with its cobbled streets and picturesque converted market building, it's just a big ole mall. Nearby is **Leicester Square,** home of large movie houses and a backpackers' mecca. In London, which tends to close down early, it's nice to see so much life at night, and Leicester Square never gets too quiet. Next to that is **Soho** (see the Nightlife chapter).

Unwinding... When it's all been too, too much, try these relaxing diversions. London's best and finest-looking yoga school is the **Notting Hill Gate Life Centre,** where a very bendy staff teaches various levels mainly of the energetic Vinyasa technique. Iyengar devotees should try the **Maida Vale Institute of Iyengar Yoga.** Head to **Bodywise** for a one-on-one refresher if you're already started on the Alexander Technique—others can get massaged (whether *reiki-ed, shiatsued,* or *cranio-sacral-ed*) at this East End holistic health center. If you're a fan of that other conscious body-realignment therapy, Pilates, the **Belsize Studio** won't disappoint.

Map 14: West End Diversions

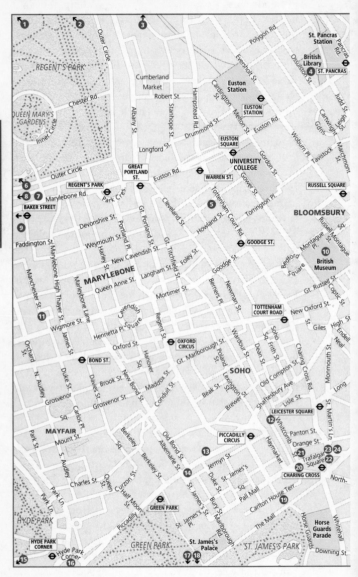

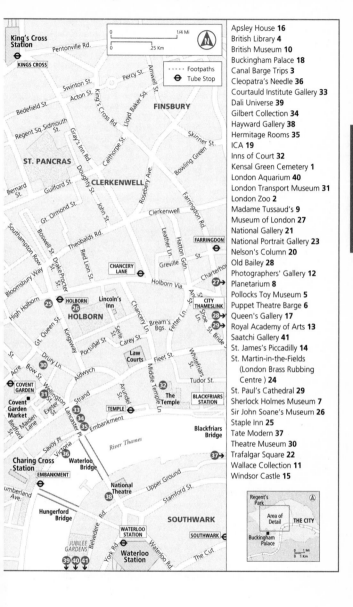

Apsley House **16**
British Library **4**
British Museum **10**
Buckingham Palace **18**
Canal Barge Trips **3**
Cleopatra's Needle **36**
Courtauld Institute Gallery **33**
Dali Universe **39**
Gilbert Collection **34**
Hayward Gallery **38**
Hermitage Rooms **35**
ICA **19**
Inns of Court **32**
Kensal Green Cemetery **1**
London Aquarium **40**
London Transport Museum **31**
London Zoo **2**
Madame Tussaud's **9**
Museum of London **27**
National Gallery **21**
National Portrait Gallery **23**
Nelson's Column **20**
Old Bailey **28**
Photographers' Gallery **12**
Planetarium **8**
Pollocks Toy Museum **5**
Puppet Theatre Barge **6**
Queen's Gallery **17**
Royal Academy of Arts **13**
Saatchi Gallery **41**
St. James's Piccadilly **14**
St. Martin-in-the-Fields
  (London Brass Rubbing
  Centre) **24**
St. Paul's Cathedral **29**
Sherlock Holmes Museum **7**
Sir John Soane's Museum **26**
Staple Inn **25**
Tate Modern **37**
Theatre Museum **30**
Trafalgar Square **22**
Wallace Collection **11**
Windsor Castle **15**

DIVERSIONS

Map 15: Knightsbridge to South Kensington Diversions

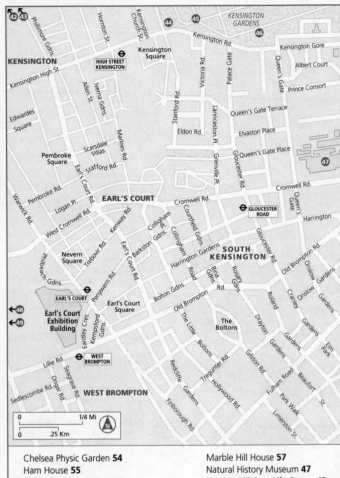

Chelsea Physic Garden **54**
Ham House **55**
Hampton Court Palace **56**
Kensington Gardens **46**
Kensington Palace **44**
Kew Gardens **48**
Kew Palace **49**
Maida Vale Institute of Iyengar Yoga **42**

Marble Hill House **57**
Natural History Museum **47**
Notting Hill Gate Life Centre **43**
Royal Hospital **53**
Science Museum **50**
Serpentine Gallery **45**
Speaker's Corner **52**
Victoria and Albert Museum **51**

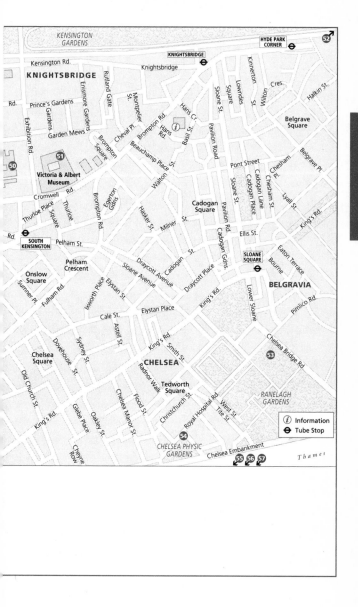

Map 16: Westminster & Victoria Diversions

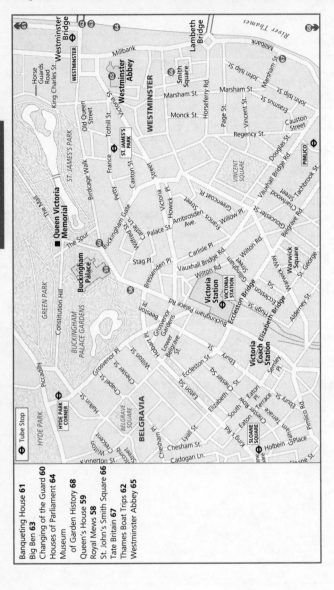

Map 17: "The City" Diversions

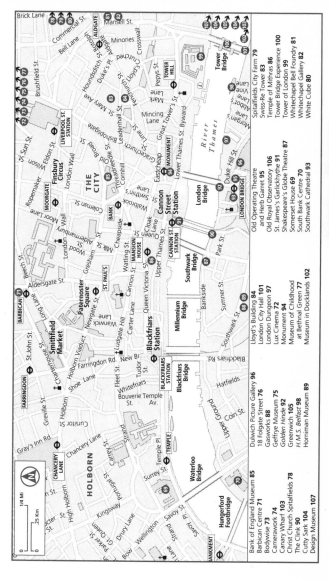

DIVERSIONS

Bank of England Museum 85
Barbican Centre 71
Bodywise 73
Camerawork 74
Canary Wharf 103
Christ Church Spitalfields 78
The Clink 90
Cutty Sark 104
Design Museum 107

Dulwich Picture Gallery 96
18 Folgate Street 76
Gasworks 88
Geffrye Museum 75
Golden Hinde 92
Greenwich 105
H.M.S. Belfast 98
Horniman Museum 89

Lloyd's Building 84
London City Hall 101
London Dungeon 97
Lux Cinema 72
Monument 94
Museum of Childhood
at Bethnal Green 77
Museum in Docklands 102

Old Operating Theatre
and Herb Garret 95
Old Royal Observatory 106
St. James's Garlickhythe 91
Shakespeare's Globe Theatre 87
Somerset House 69
South Bank Centre 70
Southwark Cathedral 93

Spitalfields City Farm 79
Swiss-Re Tower 83
Temple of Mithras 86
Tower Bridge Experience 100
Tower of London 99
Whitechapel Bell Foundry 81
Whitechapel Gallery 82
White Cube 80

Map 18: Hampstead Diversions

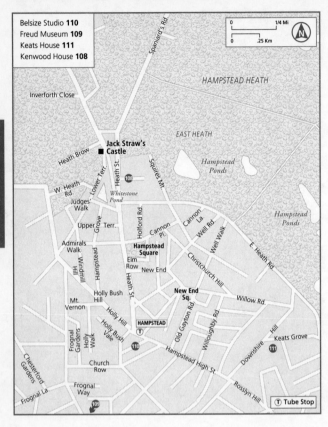

Belsize Studio **110**
Freud Museum **109**
Keats House **111**
Kenwood House **108**

DIVERSIONS

HAMPSTEAD HEATH

EAST HEATH

Inverforth Close

Jack Straw's Castle

Heath Brow

Hampstead Ponds

Spaniard's Rd.

Squires Mt.

Heath St.

Lower Terr.

W. Heath Rd.

Whitestone Pond

108

Judges' Walk

Upper Terr.

Grove

Holford Rd.

Cannon Pl.

Cannon La.

Well Rd.

Well Walk

Hampstead Ponds

E. Heath Rd.

Admirals Walk

Windmill Hill

Hampstead

Hampstead Square

Elm Row

New End

Christchurch Hill

Mt. Vernon

Holly Bush Hill

Heath St.

New End Sq.

Willow Rd.

Holly Hill

Old Gayton Rd.

Willoughby Rd.

HAMPSTEAD
T

Holly Bush Vale

110

Downshire Hill

Keats Grove

111

Frognal Gardens

Holly Walk

Church Row

Hampstead High St.

Rosslyn Hill

Chesterford Gardens

Frognal La.

Frognal Way

109

T Tube Stop

The Index

Apsley House (p. 125) WEST END The duke of Wellington was presented with this magnificent neoclassical mansion (completed in 1778) for his military prowess and it still contains his collections of art and silver. A rare chance to see the mostly unaltered interior of a private London town house.... *Tel 020/7499-5676. Hyde Park Corner W1. Tube: Hyde Park Corner. Open Tues–Sun 11am–5pm. Admission charged.*
See Map 14 on p. 134, bullet 16.

Bank of England Museum (p. 115) THE CITY We all know money makes the world go 'round, especially in expensive London, and this museum unabashedly devoted to capitalism shows you how.... *Tel 020/7601-5545. Bartholomew Lane EC2. Tube: Bank. Open Mon–Fri 10am–5pm. Admission free.*
See Map 17 on p. 139, bullet 85.

Banqueting House (p. 120, 123, 125) WEST END Inigo Jones (1573–1652) designed this Palladian hall, all that remains of Henry VIII's Whitehall Palace, which burned down in 1698. Charles I commissioned the Rubens ceiling in tribute to his father, James I.... *Tel 020/7839-3787. Westminster Embankment. Tube: Charing Cross. Open Mon–Sat 10am–5pm. Closed Easter, Dec 24–Jan 1, and at short notice for government functions (call first). Admission charged.*
See Map 16 on p. 138, bullet 61.

Barbican Centre (p. 124) THE CITY This mega–arts complex is famed for being ugly and labyrinthine, but it's useful for the gallery, the theaters—this is one of the London homes of the Royal Shakespeare Company—and the concert halls.... *Tel 0207/638-8891 (box office). www.barbican.org.uk. Silk St. EC2. Tube: Moorgate/Barbican. Open Mon–Sat 9am–11pm, Sun noon–11pm. Call or check the website for a list of events, times, and fees.*
See Map 17 on p. 139, bullet 71.

Belsize Studio (p. 133) BELSIZE PARK The Pilates body-alignment therapy is taught and practiced here.... *Tel 020/7431-6223. 5 McCrone Mews, Belsize Lane NW3. Tube: Belsize Park. Call for hours and fees.*
See Map 18 on p. 140, bullet 110.

Big Ben (p. 113, 127, 131) WESTMINSTER The nickname for the bell contained in St. Stephen's Clock Tower of the Houses of Parliament, often erroneously applied to the clock and tower as well. You can go on a tour, but you need a proven interest in horology (the science of measuring time) and a 3-month lead time.... *At the Houses of Parliament. Tube: Westminster. Admission free.*

See Map 16 on p. 138, bullet 63.

Bodywise (p. 133) BETHNAL GREEN A holistic health center in the East End offers various massages, yoga, osteopathy, homeopathy, and other therapies, and classes in the Alexander Technique.... *Tel 020/8981-6938. 119 Roman Rd., Bethnal Green E2. Tube: Bethnal Green. Call for hours and fees.*

See Map 17 on p. 139, bullet 73.

British Library (p. 119) ST. PANCRAS The new home of every book that's ever been published in England has a series of exhibition galleries open to the public and displaying famous documents (Magna Carta), handwritten novels (*Jane Eyre*), plays (Shakespeare's First Folio), and musical scores (Handel to Beatles); also audio recordings of authors like Virginia Woolf and T. S. Eliot reading.... *Tel 020/7412-7332. Euston Rd. NW1. Tube: King's Cross/St. Pancras. Open Mon and Wed–Fri 9:30am–6pm, Tues 9:30am–8pm, Sat 9:30am–5pm, Sun 11am–5pm. Admission free.*

See Map 14 on p. 134, bullet 4.

British Museum (p. 108, 114, 116, 117, 130) BLOOMSBURY The national collection of man-made objects from all over the world— some as old as humankind—fills 4km (2.5 miles) of galleries. Highlights are the Egyptian Rooms, including the Rosetta Stone and many mummies, and the Parthenon Sculptures, plus the spectacular new Great Court.... *Tel 020/7636-1555. Great Russell St. WC1. Tube: Russell Sq. Open Mon 9am–5pm, Tues–Wed 9am–8pm, Thurs–Sat 9am–9pm, Sun 9am–8pm. Closed Good Friday, Christmas, Jan 1. Admission free.*

See Map 14 on p. 134, bullet 10.

Buckingham Palace (p. 114, 115, 119, 120, 122, 123, 125) ST. JAMES'S The staterooms in the queen's London home are open to visitors for a limited period each summer. A great moneymaking scheme for one of the world's richest women, something of a rip-off and a bore for the rest of us. You can check out the Royal Mews, the Queen's Gallery, and the Changing of the Guard (see entries below) if you've lost your invitation to the palace.... *Tel 020/7839-1377. Buckingham Palace Rd. SW1. Tube: Green Park. Open Aug–Sept daily 9:30am–4:15pm (ticket office opens 9am). Admission charged.*

See Map 14 on p. 134, bullet 18.

Camerawork (p. 124) BETHNAL GREEN An East End gallery with a political conscience, it shows the latest in "lens-based media."... *Tel 0208/980-6256. 121 Roman Rd., Bethnal Green E2. Tube: Bethnal Green. Open Thurs–Sat 1–6pm, Sun noon–5pm. Admission free.*
See Map 17 on p. 139, bullet 74.

Canal Barge Trips (p. 117, 127) REGENT'S PARK/CAMDEN Cruise the Grand Union and Regent's canals by barge, from Little Venice or Camden Lock to the zoo.... *Jason's Trip, Tel 020/7286-3428, www.jasons.co.uk. London Waterbus Co., Tel 020/7482-2660. Both operate daily April–Oct; Sat–Sun Nov–March; call for details.*
See Map 14 on p. 134, bullet 3.

Canary Wharf (p. 109, 119) CANARY WHARF Futuristic new business district fashioned from a once-decrepit loop of the Thames called the Isle of Dogs.... *Tel 020/7418-2000 (general information), 020/7418-2783 (arts and events). Cabot Place E14. Tube: Canary Wharf. Admission free.*
See Map 17 on p. 139, bullet 103.

Changing of the Guard (p. 114) ST. JAMES'S Assigned to the queen as her personal guard, the Foot Guards of the Household Division of the Army change places in a colorful photo op that takes places in front of Buckingham Palace. If you miss this one, you can see something not quite as grand in front of Horse Guards in Whitehall at 11am (10am Sun).... *Tel 020/7839-1377. Buckingham Palace Rd. SW1. Tube: Green Park. Ceremony takes place daily April to early June 11:30am, alternate days thereafter. Admission free.*
See Map 16 on p. 138, bullet 60.

Chelsea Physic Garden (p. 117, 129) CHELSEA An exquisite and educational garden of medicinal plants, herbs, shrubs, and flowers, including England's first rock garden, dating from 1673.... *Tel 020/7352-5646. 66 Royal Hospital Rd. SW3. Tube: Sloane Sq., and Bus 11, 19, or 22. Open April–Oct Wed noon–5pm and Sun 2–6pm (during Chelsea Flower Show, daily noon–5pm). Admission charged.*
See Map 15 on p. 136, bullet 54.

Christ Church Spitalfields (p. 122, 131) SPITALFIELDS Nicholas Hawksmoor's 1729 masterpiece is one of only six London churches by the great associate of Wren's. The Spitalfield's Festival puts on classical concerts in June and December.... *Tel 020/7247-7202 (rectory), 020/7377-1362 (festival information). Commercial St. E1. Tube: Liverpool St. Free admission, concerts.*
See Map 17 on p. 139, bullet 78.

Cleopatra's Needle (p. 117) WEST END This granite obelisk, dating from about 1475 B.C., was given to the British by the viceroy of Egypt (named Mohammed Ali) in 1819.... *Victoria Embankment Gardens. Tube: Embankment. Admission free.*

See Map 14 on p. 134, bullet 36.

The Clink (p. 118) SOUTH BANK The jail of the bishops of Winchester's palace is now a black-walled prison museum, including a history of prostitution in the "Southwark Stews" and a reconstruction of a 1690 debtors' cell complete with Rat Man (a man who eats rats).... *Tel 020/7378-1558. 1 Clink St. SE1. Tube: London Bridge. Open daily 10am–6pm; summer 10am–9pm. Closed Christmas, Jan 1. Admission charged.*

See Map 17 on p. 139, bullet 90.

Courtauld Institute Gallery (p. 125) WEST END Impressionists and Postimpressionists star in this Somerset House gallery, with plenty of old masters to back them up.... *Tel 020/7848-2526. Strand WC2. Tube: Holborn. Open daily 10am–6pm. Closed Easter, Christmas, Jan 1. Admission charged.*

See Map 14 on p. 134, bullet 33.

Cutty Sark (p. 127) GREENWICH One of the Greenwich delights, this handsome tea clipper is evocative of the seafaring life and has a wicked collection of figureheads.... *Tel 020/8858-3445. Cutty Sark stop on Docklands Light Railway. Open daily 10am–5pm. Closed Easter, Christmas, Jan 1. Admission charged.*

See Map 17 on p. 139, bullet 104.

Dalí Universe (p. 124) SOUTH BANK To enjoy this Dalí-rama you have to believe the Spanish surrealist was such a genius that everything he did was brilliant and that it looks good against black walls. Underwhelming.... *Tel 020/7620-2720. County Hall, Riverside Building, Southbank SE1. Tube: Westminster or Waterloo. Open daily 10am–5:30pm. Admission charged.*

See Map 14 on p. 134, bullet 39.

Design Museum (p. 110, 132) BUTLER'S WHARF A temple to domestic and small-scale commercial design, from Corbusier chairs to the Coke bottle, this south-of-the-river museum (across Tower Bridge) always has special exhibitions on tap.... *Tel 020/ 7403-6933. Butler's Wharf SE1. Tube: Tower Hill. Open daily 10am– 5:45pm. Admission charged.*

See Map 17 on p. 139, bullet 107.

Dulwich Picture Gallery (p. 125) DULWICH Reopened in May 2000 after extensive renovation. Britain's first purposefully built art gallery, designed by Sir John Soane, has some 300 works on display, all old masters.... *Tel 020/8693-5254. Gallery Rd. SE21. BR: West or North Dulwich. Open Tues–Fri*

10am–5pm, weekends and holidays 11am–5pm. Free on Fri. Admission charged.

See Map 17 on p. 139, bullet 96.

18 Folgate Street (p. 115, 131) THE CITY Every Monday evening a small group is allowed in to view this meticulously authentic early-18th-century house created by American artist Dennis Severs; each room is a "still-life drama" pertaining to the life of a family of Huguenot weavers from 1754 to 1914.... *Tel 020/7247-4013. 18 Folgate St. E1. Tube: Liverpool St. Open Mon; time varies according to hour of dusk. Booking is required. Admission charged.*

See Map 17 on p. 139, bullet 76.

Gasworks (p. 124) SOUTH BANK One of South London's alternative gallery spaces.... *Tel 020/7582-6848. 155 Vauxhall St. SE11. Tube: Oval. Open Wed–Sun noon–6pm. Admission free.*

See Map 17 on p. 139, bullet 88.

Geffrye Museum (p. 131, 132) SHOREDITCH In a row of 18th-century almshouses, this perfect museum re-creates the sitting rooms of England's urban middle classes from 1600 to 2000.... *Tel 020/7739-9893. Kingsland Rd. E2. Tube: Liverpool St. Open Tues–Sat 10am–5pm, Sun and bank holidays noon–5pm. Admission free.*

See Map 17 on p. 139, bullet 75.

Gilbert Collection (p. 118) WEST END A collection of gold and silver snuffboxes (ah-*choo!*), portrait miniatures, and mosaics donated to the nation in 1996 forms the basis of this intriguing addition to the Somerset House galleries.... *Tel 020/7420-9400. Somerset House, Strand WC2. Tube: Temple. Open daily 10am–6pm. Admission charged.*

See Map 14 on p. 134, bullet 34.

Golden Hinde (p. 132) SOUTH BANK An explorable full-scale reproduction of Sir Francis Drake's 16th-century flagship that circumnavigated the globe; this one did the same before being parked here.... *Tel 08700/118-700. St. Mary Overie Dock, Cathedral St. SE1. Tube: London Bridge. Open daily but at varying times so call first. Admission charged.*

See Map 17 on p. 139, bullet 92.

Greenwich (p. 115, 117, 123, 127) This riverside town has many attractions, most of them free, some of them UNESCO World Heritage sites—the Cutty Sark (see above); the Royal Naval College; and the National Maritime Museum, Queen's House, and Old Royal Observatory (see below). Get there via boat (see Thames boat trips, below), tube (Jubilee Line to Greenwich) or the Docklands Light Railway (Island Gardens stop).

See Map 17 on p. 139, bullet 105.

DIVERSIONS

THE INDEX

Ham House (p. 117, 120, 129) RICHMOND This Stuart stately home, dating from about 1610, has 17th-century furniture and gardens; it's recently been restored.... *Tel 020/8940-1950. Ham St., Richmond, Surrey. Tube: Richmond. Open April–Oct 1–5pm (closed Thurs–Fri). Gardens only 11am–4pm. Admission charged.*

See Map 15 on p. 136, bullet 55.

Hampton Court Palace (p. 117, 120, 123, 129) EAST MOLESEY, SURREY Henry VIII's stunning Thames-side palace satisfies every royal fantasy—see everything from the King's Apartments to the Tudor kitchens, and maybe a royal ghost. The 1714 yew maze is famous.... *Tel 0870/752-7777. East Molesey, Surrey. BR: Hampton Court. Open April–Oct Mon 10:15am–6pm, Tues–Sun 9:30am–6pm; Nov–March Mon 10:15am–4:30pm, Tues–Sun 9:30am–4:30pm. Closed Dec 24–26, Jan 1. Admission charged.*

See Map 15 on p. 136, bullet 56.

Hayward Gallery (p. 124) SOUTH BANK The art department of the South Bank Centre stages about five exhibitions of modern work per year.... *Tel 020/7260-4242. Belvedere Rd. SE1. Tube: Waterloo. Open Thurs–Mon 10am–6pm, Tues–Wed 10am–8pm. Closed between exhibitions. Admission charged.*

See Map 14 on p. 134, bullet 38.

Hermitage Rooms (p. 118) WEST END Desperate to raise cash now that's it's gone capitalistic, Russia's Hermitage Museum has been selling franchises of itself all over Europe like so many Kentucky Fried Chicken outlets, only with art. The goods on display are from the fabulous Hermitage collections and the shows change periodically.... *Tel 020/7845-4600. Somerset House, Strand WC2. Tube: Temple. Open daily 10am–6pm. Admission charged.*

See Map 14 on p. 134, bullet 35.

HMS *Belfast* (p. 132) SOUTH BANK Built in 1938, this huge navy cruiser was used in World War II and is now berthed between Tower Bridge and London Bridge. You can poke around all seven decks and even "experience" a re-created battle.... *Tel 020/7940-6300. Morgan's Lane, Tooley St. SE1. Tube: London Bridge. Open Mar 1–Oct 31 10am–6pm, Nov 1–Feb 28 10am–5pm. Admission charged.*

See Map 17 on p. 139, bullet 98.

Horniman Museum (p. 127) FOREST HILL An anthropological museum of great charm, best known for its bee colony and its 1,500 musical instruments.... *Tel 020/8699-1872. 100 London Rd. SE23. BR: Forest Hill. Open Mon–Sat 10:30am–5:30pm, Sun 2–5:30pm. Free admission.*

See Map 17 on p. 139, bullet 89.

Houses of Parliament (p. 108, 113, 114, 127) WESTMINSTER "The mother of all parliaments" takes place in Charles Barry and Augustus Pugin's mid-19th-century neo-Gothic pile, complete with the famous Clock Tower housing Big Ben. It's possible to visit both the House of Commons and the House of Lords in session, but the lines are long; better to take one of the tours now offered during the summer recess.... *Tel 020/7219-3000 (House of Commons), 020/7219-3107 (House of Lords). Bridge St. and Parliament Sq. SW1. Tube: Westminster. Open (Commons) Mon–Wed 2:30–10:30pm, Thurs 11:30am–7pm, Fri 9:30am–3pm. Closed Easter week, May 1, July–Oct (tours available), 3 weeks at Christmas. Admission free.*
See Map 16 on p. 138, bullet 64.

ICA (p. 124) ST. JAMES'S The Institute of Contemporary Arts is secreted in a Nash terrace on the pink road and houses much arts action, with galleries, two small movie theaters, a theater, and a cafe/bar.... *Tel 020/7930-3647. The Mall, SW1. Tube: Charing Cross. Gallery open daily noon–7:30pm (Fri until 9pm). Admission charged.*
See Map 14 on p. 134, bullet 19.

Inns of Court (p. 108, 115) HOLBORN Legal London is still centered around the four Inns of Court: Gray's Inn, Lincoln's Inn, Middle Temple, and Inner Temple, the earliest part of which is the 12th-century Temple Church (not open to the public).... *Tel 020/7936-6000. The Strand WC2, Temple EC1. Tube: Chancery Lane, Temple, or Chancery Lane. Open (law courts) Mon–Fri 9am–4:30pm. Admission free.*
See Map 14 on p. 134, bullet 32.

Keats House (p. 120) HAMPSTEAD The poet lived 2 years of his short life here in handsome Hampstead; today it also houses the Keats archives.... *Tel 020/7435-2062. Keats Grove NW3. Tube: Hampstead. Open April–Oct Tues–Sun noon–5pm (Nov–March, call for opening times). Admission free.*
See Map 18 on p. 140, bullet 111.

Kensal Green Cemetery (p. 121) KENSAL GREEN London's oldest necropolis (from 1833) is atmospheric and beautiful to behold; it contains the remains of Wilkie Collins, Thackeray, Trollope, and other great Victorians.... *Tel 020/8969-0152; 020/7402-2749 for tours. Harrow Rd. W10. Tube: Kensal Green. Open Mon–Sat 9am–5:30pm, Sun 10am–5:30pm; tours Sun 2pm. Donation requested.*
See Map 14 on p. 134, bullet 1.

Kensington Palace (p. 122) KENSINGTON The state apartments contain the possessions of the Stuart and Hanoverian monarchs who called it home, the rather fabulous Ceremonial Dress Collection (important tips on how to dress for court), and frocks worn by Her Maj and Diana, who lived in one of the palace wings.... *Tel 020/7937-7079. The Broad Walk, Kensington Gardens W8. Tube: High St. Kensington. Open daily 10am–5pm. Admission charged.*

See Map 15 on p. 136, bullet 44.

Kenwood House (p. 121, 125) HAMPSTEAD HOUSE A Robert Adam masterpiece, this neoclassical villa on a heavenly hillside near Hampstead Heath holds the Iveagh Bequest, which has some important paintings, and the glittering Hull Grundy Jewelry Collection. The lakeside concert bowl opens in summertime.... *Tel 020/8348-1286. Hampstead Lane NW3. Tube: Archway or Golders Green, and bust 210. Open daily April–Sept 10am–6pm; Oct 10am–5pm; Nov–March 10am–4pm (opens 10:30am Wed and Fri year-round). Closed Dec 24–25. Admission free.*

See Map 18 on p. 140, bullet 108.

Kew Gardens (p. 115, 128, 129) KEW The 300-acre Royal Botanic Gardens grow 40,000 kinds of plants and feature a visitor center, Victorian greenhouses, an 18th-century ornamental pagoda, and lots more, all of which makes this a perfect day trip.... *Tel 020/8332-5000. Tube: Kew Gardens. Open daily 9:30–dusk. Closed Christmas and Jan 1. Admission charged.*

See Map 15 on p. 136, bullet 48.

Kew Palace (p. 122) KEW There's even a royal palace in the gardens—the littlest and most picturesque one of all, where King George III lost his marbles.... *Tel 020/8332-5000. Tube: Kew Gardens. Open April–Oct Sat–Sun 11am–5:30pm. Admission charged.*

See Map 15 on p. 136, bullet 49.

Lloyd's Building (p. 120) THE CITY One of London's most unappealing and sinister-looking modern buildings, this 1986 inside-out glass-and-steel tower, headquarters of the venerable Lloyd's of London, is the handiwork of Sir Richard Rogers (architect of Paris's Pompidou).... *Tel 020/7327-1000. 1 Lime St. EC1. Tube: Monument. Closed to visitors.*

See Map 17 on p. 139, bullet 84.

London Aquarium (p. 118, 126, 127) SOUTH BANK For Londoners, it's an especially surreal experience to penetrate the bowels of the former County Hall (one-time seat of the Greater London Council abolished by Thatcher) to find...fish! There aren't any really big ones, but there are luminous jellyfish, strokeable rays, unstrokable piranhas, a deep Atlantic pool of hound sharks and conger eel—all set out on a downward spiral with marine sound effects and eerie subaqueous light.... *Tel 020/7967-8000. County Hall, Westminster Bridge Rd. SE1. Tube: Westminster. Open daily 10am–6pm. Admission charged.*

See Map 14 on p. 134, bullet 40.

London Brass Rubbing Centre (p. 116) WEST END The crypt of St. Martin-in-the-Fields provides paper, metallic waxes, and instructions on how to rub your own replica of historic brasses.... *Tel 020/7437-6023. Trafalgar Sq. W1. Tube: Charing Cross or Leicester Sq. Open Mon–Sat 10am–6pm, Sun noon–6pm. Closed Easter, Christmas, Jan 1. Charge for rubbing varies.*

London City Hall (p. 119, 120, 132) SOUTH BANK The mayor of London (a newly created elected office not to be confused with the ceremonial lord mayor) and the London Assembly meet in this spherical glass Thames-side building designed by Lord Norman Foster and completed in 2002. *Tel 020/7983-4000. The Queen's Walk SE1. Tube: Tower Hill. Open to visitors Mon–Fri 8am–8pm. Admission free.*
See Map 17 on p. 139, bullet 101.

London Dungeon (p. 126) SOUTH BANK Ghastly and gory exhibits of torture and treachery, mostly from the Middle Ages, appeal greatly to horrid children. Complete with the "Jack the Ripper Experience."... *Tel 020/7403-7221. 28–34 Tooley St. SE1. Tube: London Bridge. Open daily April–Sept 10am–6:30pm; Oct–March 10am–5:30pm. Closed Christmas. Admission charged.*
See Map 17 on p. 139, bullet 97.

London Transport Museum (p. 127) COVENT GARDEN Better than it sounds, this has lots of hands-on stuff that kids like, and a fascinating collection of horse-drawn omnibuses, ancient buses, and early tube cars.... *Tel 020/7565-7299. The Piazza, Covent Garden WC2. Tube: Covent Garden. Open Sat–Thurs 10am–6pm, Fri 11am–6pm. Closed Dec 24–26. Admission charged.*
See Map 14 on p. 134, bullet 31.

London Zoo (p. 117, 126) REGENT'S PARK About 8,000 creatures great and small call this home. You can get real close to the big cats, watch the penguins feeding, and ride a camel—all the usual stuff, but in a pretty setting.... *Tel 020/7722-3333. Regent's Park NW1. Tube: Camden Town. Open daily March–Oct 10am–5:30pm; Nov–Feb 10am–4pm. Closed Christmas. Admission charged.*
See Map 14 on p. 134, bullet 2.

Lux Cinema (p. 124) SHOREDITCH This 120-seat cinema shows obscure films, hosts festivals, and showcases new talent; it also includes the first electronic art gallery in the United Kingdom and impressive projections.... *Tel 020/7684-0201. 2–4 Hoxton Sq. N1. Tube: Old St. Admission charged.*
See Map 17 on p. 139, bullet 72.

Madame Tussaud's (p. 109, 126) MARYLEBONE A Frenchwoman learned to make waxwork people by fashioning death masks of aristocrats beheaded during the French Revolution, then inflicted this museum of the frozen famous on London. Expect to stand

DIVERSIONS

THE INDEX

in line forever and see waxen effigies of important world leaders like Naomi Campbell and Pierce Brosnan.... *Tel 020/7935-6861. Marylebone Rd. NW1. Tube: Baker St. Open daily 9am, 9:30am, or 10am–5:30pm (opening time changes seasonally). Closed Christmas. Admission charged.*

See Map 14 on p. 134, bullet 9.

Maida Vale Institute of Iyengar Yoga (p. 133) MAIDA VALE For Iyengar yoga classes, just as the name promises.... *Tel 020/ 7624-3080. 223a Randolph Ave. W9. Tube: Maida Vale. Call for hours and fees.*

See Map 15 on p. 136, bullet 42.

Marble Hill House (p. 120) RICHMOND Built in the Palladian style for George II's mistress, Henrietta Howard, this Thames-side villa, nearly opposite Ham House, offers summertime concerts and teas in the Coach House.... *Tel 020/8892-5115. Richmond Rd., Twickenham. Tube: Richmond. Open April–Sept Wed–Sun 10am–6pm; Oct Wed–Sun 10am–4pm. Closed Christmas. Admission charged.*

See Map 15 on p. 136, bullet 57.

Monument (p. 128) THE CITY Christopher Wren's tower commemorates the terrible destruction wrought by the Great Fire of 1666. Climb the 311 steps for an iron-caged view of the City.... *Tel 020/7626-2717. Monument St. EC3. Tube: Monument. Open daily 10am–5:40pm. Admission charged.*

See Map 17 on p. 139, bullet 94.

Museum in Docklands (p. 118) DOCKLANDS Housed in an early-19th-century warehouse at East India Quay, London's newest museum (it opened in May 2003) unlocks the history of London's river, port, and people with a wealth of objects that provide glimpses of the people who have come and gone from the Docks over the last 2,000 years.... *Tel 0870/444-3857. No. 1 Warehouse West India Quay, Hertsmere Rd. E14. DLR: West India Quay. Admission charged.*

See Map 17 on p. 139, bullet 102.

Museum of Childhood at Bethnal Green (p. 127, 131) BETHNAL GREEN The V&A's outpost focuses on all things small, from dollhouses to teddy bears, illustrating the history of play.... *Tel 0208/980-2415. Cambridge Heath Rd. E2. Tube: Bethnal Green. Open Sat–Thurs 10am–5:50pm. Closed May 1, Christmas, Jan 1. Admission free.*

See Map 17 on p. 139, bullet 77.

Museum of Garden History (p. 129) LAMBETH The Tradescant Trust, named after great botanist John Tradescant (1570–1638), runs this museum in a deconsecrated church, complete with a 17th-century knot garden and the tomb of Captain Bligh of the Bounty.... *Tel 020/7401-8865. St. Mary-at-Lambeth, Lambeth Palace Rd. SE1. Tube: Lambeth North. Open daily 10:30am–5pm. Admission free.*

See Map 16 on p. 138, bullet 68.

Museum of London (p. 109, 115, 118, 130) THE CITY This chronologically arranged museum with some beautiful new galleries gives the background to what you have and haven't seen outside. Highlights include prehistoric, Roman, and medieval artifacts and the incredible gilded coach used by the lord mayor of London.... *Tel 020/7600-3699. 150 London Wall EC2. Tube: St. Paul's. Open Mon–Sat 10am–5:50pm, Sun noon–5:50pm. Closed Christmas, Jan 1. Admission free.*

See Map 14 on p. 134, bullet 27.

National Gallery (p. 114, 125, 128, 130) WEST END The national collection of art is suitably impressive, full of familiar masterpieces. The Sainsbury Wing contains the early Renaissance collection, but the whole place spans 700 years, up to 1920.... *Tel 020/7747-2869. Trafalgar Sq. WC2. Tube: Charing Cross. Open daily 10am–6pm (Wed until 9pm). Closed Easter, May 1, Dec 24–26, Jan 1. Admission free.*

See Map 14 on p. 134, bullet 21.

National Portrait Gallery (p. 124, 125, 130) WEST END Next to the National Gallery, this intimate and likeable museum, recently renovated, features portraits of the famous and the forgotten from medieval times to now.... *Tel 020/7306-0055. St. Martin's Place WC2. Tube: Charing Cross. Open Sat–Wed 10am–6pm, Thurs–Fri 10am–9pm. Closed Easter, Dec 24–26, Jan 1. Admission free.*

See Map 14 on p. 134, bullet 23.

Natural History Museum (p. 114, 127, 128, 130) SOUTH KENSINGTON Almost as big as the world it depicts, this is one of the best museums around, with its many renovated galleries and terrifying T-Rex.... *Tel 020/7942-5000. Cromwell Rd. SW7. Tube: South Kensington. Open Mon–Sat 10am–5:50pm, Sun and holidays 11am–5:50pm. Closed Dec 23–26. Admission free.*

See Map 15 on p. 136, bullet 47.

Nelson's Column (p. 114, 127) WEST END The touristic center of London is this 44m (145-ft.) granite column from which E. H. Baily's 1843 statue of Admiral Lord Nelson keeps watch.... *Trafalgar Sq. Tube: Charing Cross. Admission free.*

See Map 14 on p. 134, bullet 20.

Notting Hill Gate Life Centre (p. 133) NOTTING HILL Classes in Vinyasa yoga, Pilates, and tai chi offer a way to relax here.... *Tel 020/7221-4602. 15 Edge St. W8. Tube: Notting Hill Gate. Call for hours and fees.*

See Map 15 on p. 136, bullet 43.

DIVERSIONS

THE INDEX

Old Bailey (p. 116) THE CITY Crowned by a gilded statue of Justice, this incarnation of England's Central Criminal Court was built in 1907 on the site of notorious Newgate Prison.... *Tel 020/7248-3277. Public gallery entrance at Newgate St. EC4. Tube: St. Paul's. Public gallery open Mon–Fri 10:30am–1pm and 2–4pm. No children under 14. Admission free.*
See Map 14 on p. 134, bullet 28.

Old Operating Theatre and Herb Garret (p. 115, 118, 132) SOUTH BANK Britain's oldest operating theater, dating from 1822, features a wooden operating table, saws, and other "state-of-the-art" medical equipment that will make your knees go weak. Students watched medical procedures on patients whose only anesthetic was a bottle of booze and a blindfold. All that's missing is the blood and the screams.... *Tel 020/7955-4791. 9A St. Thomas St. SE1. Tube: London Bridge. Open daily 10:30–5pm. Closed Dec 15–Jan 5. Admission charged.*
See Map 17 on p. 139, bullet 95.

Old Royal Observatory (p. 127) GREENWICH This 1675 Wren-designed observatory in Greenwich calls itself "the place where time begins," because Greenwich mean time is measured from here and the prime meridian, which bisects the world, is right beneath your feet. Inside there's a collection of 18th-century chronometers and astronomical instruments.... *Tel 020/8312-6608. Greenwich Park SE10. DLR: Island Gardens. Open daily 10am–5pm (until 6pm in summer). Closed Christmas. Admission free.*
See Map 17 on p. 139, bullet 106.

Photographers' Gallery (p. 124) WEST END Conveniently central place to see top shows of 20th-century photographic art.... *Tel 020/7831-1772. 5 Great Newport St. WC2. Tube: Leicester Sq. Open Mon–Sat 11am–6pm, Sun noon–6pm. Admission free.*
See Map 14 on p. 134, bullet 12.

Planetarium (p. 126) MARYLEBONE You'll see better stars here than next door at Madame Tussaud's. There are outer-space exhibits, too.... *Tel 020/7935-6861. Marylebone Rd. NW1. Tube: Baker St. Open daily 9am–5:30pm, shows every 30 minutes from 10 or 10:30am. Closed Christmas. Admission charged.*
See Map 14 on p. 134, bullet 8.

Pollocks Toy Museum (p. 127) BLOOMSBURY A pair of 19th-century houses is crammed to the beams with every conceivable Victorian toy.... *Tel 020/7636-3452. 41 Whitfield St. W1. tube: Goodge St. Open Mon–Sat 10am–5pm. Admission charged.*
See Map 14 on p. 134, bullet 5.

Puppet Theatre Barge (p. 127) MARYLEBONE When it's open (usually until early June), this Little Venice floating marionette show is a treat for toddlers, with fairy tales, rhymes, and songs....

Tel 020/7249-6876. Blomfield Rd. W9. Tube: Warwick Ave. Call for times. Admission charged.

See Map 14 on p. 134, bullet 6.

Queen's Gallery (p. 119, 123, 125) ST. JAMES'S QEII formally reopened "her" refurbed and enlarged gallery in 2002 during her Golden Jubilee year. The new galleries display royal goodies from the humongous royal collections, including paintings, *objets,* and photos from the Royal Archives at Windsor. There's even a Royal coffee shop.... *Tel 020/7321-2233. Buckingham Palace Rd. SW1. Tube: Victoria. Admission charged.*

See Map 14 on p. 134, bullet 17.

Queen's House (p. 123) GREENWICH The first classical house in England, designed by Inigo Jones in 1616 for the Stuart Queen Anne of Denmark, is one of the delights of Greenwich; it was used as a model for the White House in Washington, D.C.... *Tel 020/8312-6608. Romney Rd., Greenwich Park. DLR: Island Gardens. Open daily 10am–5pm. Closed Christmas, Jan 1. Admission free.*

See Map 16 on p. 138, bullet 59.

Royal Academy of Arts (p. 125) WEST END Eighteenth-century Burlington House is the venue for whatever major art show is in town, plus the vast and unruly Summer Exhibition.... *Tel 020/7300-8000. Piccadilly W1. Tube: Piccadilly Circus. Open Sat–Thurs 10am–6pm, Fri 10am–8:30pm. Admission charged.*

See Map 14 on p. 134, bullet 13.

Royal Hospital (p. 128) CHELSEA The retirement home Charles II founded for his best soldiers, designed by Wren, still houses some 400 quaintly costumed ex-servicemen, "Chelsea Pensioners." Parts are open to the public, more when it's Chelsea Flower Show time.... *Tel 020/7730-0161. Royal Hospital Rd. SW3. Tube: Sloane Sq., and Bus 211 or 239. Open Mon–Sat 10am–1pm, daily 2–4pm (closed Sun Oct–March). Closed national-al holidays. Admission free.*

See Map 15 on p. 136, bullet 53.

Royal Mews (p. 123, 126) ST. JAMES'S Not all the queen's horses are here, but many are, alongside her ceremonial fairy-tale coaches and carriages.... *Tel 020/7839-1377. Buckingham Palace Rd. SW1. Tube: Victoria. Open March–July daily 10am–4; Aug–Sept daily 10am–5pm. Admission charged.*

See Map 16 on p. 138, bullet 58.

Saatchi Gallery (p. 116, 118, 124) SOUTH BANK All the sensa-tionalistic, self-publicizing young Turks of the British art scene are snapped up by the self-publicizing older Turk, advertising and media maven Charles Saatchi, to be shown off in this brand-new gallery created within County Hall.... *Tel 020/7825-2363. County*

DIVERSIONS

THE INDEX

Hall, Southbank SE1. Tube: Westminster. Open Sun–Thurs 10am–6pm, Fri–Sat 10am–10pm. Admission charged.

See Map 14 on p. 134, bullet 41.

St. James's Garlickhythe (p. 122) THE CITY One of Wren's City churches, notable for its concerts.... *Tel 0207/236-1719. Garlick Hill EC4. Tube: Mansion House. Concerts: Call to confirm. Admission free.*

See Map 17 on p. 139, bullet 91.

St. James's Piccadilly (p. 122) WEST END Another Wren church with a concert program, this one is improbably supplemented by various new-agey events, plus a crafts market and a cafe.... *Tel 020/7387-0441. Piccadilly. Tube: Piccadilly Circus. Call for hours. Admission free; call for details.*

See Map 14 on p. 134, bullet 14.

St. John's Smith Square (p. 116) WESTMINSTER Yet another church with concerts, this one deconsecrated and next to Conservative Party headquarters.... *Tel 020/7222-1061. Smith Sq. Tube: Westminster. Admission and hours vary; call for details. Admission charged.*

See Map 16 on p. 138, bullet 66.

St. Martin-in-the-Fields (p. 116, 122) WEST END Not another one? Yes, but this one's the granddaddy of all churches-with-music, being the home of the famous music ensemble, the Academy of St. Martin-in-the-Fields. This is where you can hear Bach and Mozart by candlelight and enjoy free noontime concerts. The James Gibbs church is well worth visiting in its own right.... *Tel 020/7930-0089, 020/7839-8362 (box office). Trafalgar Sq. W1. Tube: Charing Cross. Open Mon–Sat 10am–6pm, Sun noon–6pm. Concerts Mon, Tues, Fri noon, Thurs–Sat 7:30pm. Admission varies for evening concerts; call for details. Admission charged.*

See Map 14 on p. 134, bullet 24.

St. Paul's Cathedral (p. 109, 113, 121) THE CITY Wren's undoubted masterpiece (and final resting place) is instantly recognizable as one of the defining buildings of the London skyline. It's on everyone's must-see list, though the vast interior is really rather dull. Bring a friend and check out the Whispering Gallery and its supernatural acoustics.... *Tel 020/7266-8348. St. Paul's Churchyard, Ludgate Hill EC4. Tube: St. Paul's. Open for sightseeing Mon–Sat 8:30am–4pm. Admission charged.*

See Map 14 on p. 134, bullet 29.

Science Museum (p. 127, 130) SOUTH KENSINGTON Neighbor of the Natural History Museum, this is similarly popular with kids who love the interactive stuff, the cool Space Gallery and Flight Lab. But there's plenty of stuff here for adults, too, including lots of historic vehicles and thingamabobs, plus a giant IMAX.... *Tel 020/7942-4454. Exhibition Rd. SW7. Tube: South Kensington.*

Open daily 10am–6pm. Admission free to museum; admission charged for IMAX.

See Map 15 on p. 136, bullet 50.

Serpentine Gallery (p. 124) KENSINGTON In the middle of Kensington Gardens is this space for avant-garde, modern shows.... *Tel 020/7298-1515. Tube: Lancaster Gate. Open daily 10am–6pm. Closed between exhibitions. Admission free.*

See Map 15 on p. 136, bullet 45.

Shakespeare's Globe Theatre (p. 110, 119, 122, 124, 132) SOUTH BANK On the South Bank, in an area that was once London's Times Square for entertainment (theater, bear-baiting, prostitution), the Globe Theatre where Shakespeare's plays were performed has been re-created near its original site. There are tours, an exhibition on Elizabethan theater, and summer performances (you can sit on an authentic bum-numbing bench) of the Bard's immortal works.... *Tel 020/7902-1500. New Globe Walk, Bankside SE1. Tube: Mansion House. Open for tours and exhibition Oct–April 10am–5pm; May–Sept 9am–noon. Closed Christmas. Performances May–Sept. Admission charged.*

See Map 17 on p. 139, bullet 87.

Sherlock Holmes Museum (p. 116) MARYLEBONE A hokey tourist trap cashes in on the fictional detective, but it's probably magnetic to addicts for the address alone.... *Tel 020/7935-8866. "221B" Baker St. Tube: Baker St. Open daily 9–6. Closed Christmas.*

See Map 14 on page 134, bullet 7.

Sir John Soane's Museum (p. 115, 116, 118, 125) HOLBORN One of London's most memorable museum experiences, the architect (1753–1837) of the Bank of England's house is full of ancient sculpture, mad perspectives, juicy colors, and art, art, art. It makes you smile; view by candlelight first Tuesday of the month.... *Tel 020/7405-2107. 13 Lincoln's Inn Fields WC2. Tube: Holborn. Open Tues–Sat 10am–5pm (6am–9pm first Tues of month). Closed Christmas, Jan 1, bank holidays. Admission free.*

See Map 14 on page 134, bullet 26.

Somerset House (p. 118, 125) WEST END Somerset House is an enormous late-18th-century palace that was used for civil administration until it was transformed into a brilliant new public space with a beautiful courtyard (dancing fountains), a terrific riverside terrace cafe (summer), and new gallery space (see entries for the Courtauld Institute Gallery, the Gilbert Collection, and the Hermitage Rooms).... *Tel 020/7845-4600. Strand WC2. Tube: Temple or Charing Cross. Free admission to courtyard/cafe; admission varies for museums.*

See Map 17 on p. 139, bullet 69.

DIVERSIONS

THE INDEX

South Bank Centre (p. 115, 119, 124, 132) SOUTH BANK Home of the Royal National Theatre, the National Film Theatre, the Hayward Gallery, Royal Festival Hall, and other concert halls.... You're bound to end up here at least once. See the Entertainment chapter for more details.... *Tel 020/7960-4242. South Bank SE1. Tube: Embankment. Prices vary for plays, concerts, and exhibitions.*

See Map 17 on p. 139, bullet 70.

Southwark Cathedral (p. 122, 132) SOUTHWARK London's second oldest church, after Westminster Abbey, is where Chaucer and Shakespeare worshipped, Shakespeare's brother Edmund is buried, and the founder of Harvard College was baptized. Look out for lunchtime concerts, usually Monday and Tuesday.... *Tel 020/7367-6700. Montague Close SE1. Tube: London Bridge. Admission free.*

See Map 17 on p. 139, bullet 93.

Speaker's Corner (p. 115, 117) WEST END On Sunday afternoons, the northeast corner of Hyde Park welcomes anyone with anything to say and a soapbox to stand on; no swearing allowed.... *Tube: Marble Arch.*

See Map 15 on p. 136, bullet 52.

Spitalfields City Farm (p. 131) SPITALFIELDS As it sounds, this is a farm in the middle of the East End, complete with cows, sheep, goats, and ducks, pony rides for kids, and summer barbecues.... *Tel 020/7247-8762. Weaver St. E1. Tube: Shoreditch. Open Tues–Sun 10:30am–5pm. Admission free.*

See Map 17 on p. 139, bullet 79.

Staple Inn (p. 118) HOLBORN Central London's oldest surviving Tudor (1586) half-timbered house was once the wool staple, where that commodity was weighed and traded.... *High Holborn. Tube: Holborn.*

See Map 14 on p. 134, bullet 25.

Swiss-Re Tower (p. 119, 120) THE CITY Called the "glass gherkin" (or dildo, depending on whom you're talking to), Lord Norman Foster's newest City skyscraper is a 40-story, glass-clad, environmentally friendly office tower shaped like a pickle. It was just being completed as I wrote this, so there's no phone number and no info on public access, though there's supposed to be a rooftop observation floor. *30 St. Mary Axe EC3. Tube: Liverpool St.*

See Map 17 on p. 139, bullet 83.

Tate Britain (p. 123, 129, 130, 132) PIMLICO Here you'll find the national collection of British painting from 1500 to now, including works by the mad genius William Blake, loads of pre-Raphaelites, the fabulous Turner collection, some oddball Stanley Spencers, and plenty more.... *Tel 020/7887-8000. Millbank SW1. Tube: Pimlico. Open daily 10am–5:50pm. Closed Christmas. Admission free.*

See Map 16 on p. 138, bullet 67.

Tate Modern (p. 110, 116, 119, 120, 124, 130, 132) SOUTH BANK Located in the former Bankside power station, the Tate Modern opened in 2000 and is still the hottest gallery in town; come here for international 20th-century-and-newer art.... *Tel 020/ 7887-8000. 25 Sumner St., Bankside SE1. Tube: Southwark. Open Sun–Thurs 10am–6pm, Fri–Sat 10am–10pm. Closed Dec 24–26. Admission free except for special exhibitions.*
See Map 14 on p. 134, bullet 37.

Temple of Mithras (p. 115, 118) THE CITY Roman soldiers stationed in Britannia in the 3rd and 4th centuries worshiped Mithras, the Persian god of light, instead of Christ, and these meager foundation walls unearthed in 1954 are the remains of one of their churches.... *Queen Victoria St. Tube: Mansion House. Admission free.*
See Map 17 on p. 139, bullet 86.

Thames boat trips (p. 115, 117) Daily from April to October and on weekends the rest of the year, boats operated by many different companies ply the Thames, most departing from Westminster Pier or Embankment Pier. Destinations downstream are the Tower of London, Greenwich, and the Thames Barrier, while the longer upstream trips end up at Richmond, Kew, and Hampton Court.... *Call for schedules. Westminster Pier to: Greenwich and Thames Barrier, Tel 020/7930-1616; the Tower, Tel 020/7740-0400; Kew Gardens, Richmond, and Hampton Court Palace, Tel 020/7930-4721; www.wpsa.co.uk.*
See Map 16 on p. 138, bullet 62.

Theatre Museum (p. 127) COVENT GARDEN It's the repository of the National Collections of the Performing Arts but it's oddly boring, unless you're into the artifacts (playbills, photos, model sets). Kids love the demonstrations of stage makeup and costuming, though.... *Tel 020/945-4700. Russell St. WC2. Tube: Covent Garden. Open Tues–Sun 10am–6pm. Admission free.*
See Map 14 on p. 134, bullet 30.

Tower Bridge Experience (p. 132) THE CITY You can cross Tower Bridge for free, or you can pay to go inside and "experience" the inner workings. Harry, an animatronic Victorian bridge worker, tells the story of the famous drawbridge, complete with the architect's ghost and a miniature music-hall show. Fab walkway views, too.... *Tel 020/7403-3761. North Pier, Tower Bridge SE1. Tube: Tower Hill. Open daily 9:30am–6pm. Closed Christmas. Admission charged.*
See Map 17 on p. 139, bullet 100.

Tower of London (p. 109, 113, 118, 123, 126) THE CITY A prime must-see sight, where London's history is oldest, bloodiest, and most fascinating. The 900-year-old Tower has the Beefeaters, countless firearms and suits of armor, and, of course, the eye-popping crown jewels.... *Tel 0870/756-6060. Tower Hill EC3.*

DIVERSIONS

THE INDEX

Tube: Tower Hill. Open Mon–Sat 9am–6pm, Sun 10am–6pm (closes 5pm Nov–Feb). Closed Dec 24–26, Jan 1. Admission charged.
See Map 17 on p. 139, bullet 99.

Trafalgar Square (p. 114, 127, 130) WEST END The touristic center of London has just been connected to the National Gallery, making it more pedestrian friendly. The pigeons are gone but Nelson's Column still stands and so does the giant Christmas tree in December (a yearly gift from Norway for sheltering the Norwegian royal family during World War II).... *Tube: Charing Cross. Admission free.*
See Map 14 on p. 134, bullet 22.

Victoria and Albert Museum (p. 114) SOUTH KENSINGTON The V&A is the national shrine of the decorative arts, with everything from the Shakespeare-immortalized Great Bed of Ware to last year's Lacroix and Comme outfits in the famous dress collection. Don't miss the new British Galleries and the glittering Glass Gallery.... *Tel 020/7942-2000. Cromwell Rd. SW7. Tube: South Kensington. Open daily 10am–5:45pm (until 10pm Wed and last Fri of month). Closed Dec 24–26, Jan 1. Admission free.*
See Map 15 on p. 136, bullet 51.

Wallace Collection (p. 116, 125) MARYLEBONE Four generations of Marquesses of Hertford assembled this exquisite collection of European paintings, Sèvres porcelain, Italian majolica, and Renaissance gold, all housed in a late-18th-century mansion. Don't miss Frans Hals's *Laughing Cavalier*.... *Tel 020/7563-9500. Hertford House, Manchester Sq. W1. Tube: Bond St. Open Mon–Sat 10am–5pm, Sun noon–5pm. Closed Easter, May 1, Dec 24–26, Jan. 1. Admission free.*
See Map 14 on p. 134, bullet 11.

Westminster Abbey (p. 113, 114, 118, 122, 127) WESTMINSTER London's other ur-sight (along with the Tower), this Gothic church was founded by Edward the Confessor in 1067 on the site of a Saxon church. Inside are the Coronation Chair, on which 6 centuries of monarchs have been crowned, Poets' Corner, and many beautiful chapels, tombs, and monuments. Prepare to queue.... *Tel 020/7222-5152. Broad Sanctuary SW1. Tube: Westminster. Open Mon–Fri 9:30am–4:45pm, Sat 9:30am–2:45pm. Admission charged.*
See Map 16 on p. 138, bullet 65.

Whitechapel Bell Foundry (p. 131) WHITECHAPEL The place where Big Ben and the Liberty Bell (yes, the cracked one) were forged, this working foundry has a little exhibition and shop; phone and book to tour the foundry.... *Tel 020/7247-2599. 32–34 Whitechapel Rd. E1. Tube: Aldgate East. Open Mon–Fri 9am–4:15pm. Closed public holidays. Free admission to shop, foundry tours. Admission charged.*
See Map 17 on p. 139, bullet 81.

Whitechapel Gallery (p. 124, 131) WHITECHAPEL An excitingly curated space where group and solo shows of notable contemporary work are mounted in an Art Nouveau building.... *Tel 020/ 7522-7878. 80–82 Whitechapel High St. E1. Tube: Aldgate East. Open Tues–Sun 11am–6pm (Thurs until 9pm). Closed between exhibitions. Admission free.*

See Map 17 on p. 139, bullet 82.

White Cube (p. 124) HOXTON One of the city's newer and more cutting-edge spaces, situated in trendy Hoxton.... *Tel 020/7930-5373. Hoxton Sq. N1. Tube: Old St. Open Tues–Sat 10am–6pm. Admission free.*

See Map 17 on p. 139, bullet 80.

Windsor Castle (p. 123) WINDSOR, BERKSHIRE The queen's favorite weekend home—and the world's largest inhabited castle—makes for a classy day trip. See the State Apartments, St. George's Chapel (restored after the fire of 1992), royal carriages, and Queen Mary's Doll's House. The town of Windsor is cute, too, and Eton is right next door.... *Tel 01753/868-618. Windsor, Berkshire. BR: Windsor & Eton. Open daily 9:45am–5:15pm (Nov–Feb until 4:15pm). Closed for some state visits (call first). Admission charged.*

See Map 14 on p. 134, bullet 15.

DIVERSIONS

THE INDEX

GETTING

OUTSIDE

4

Map 19: London Orientation—Getting Outside

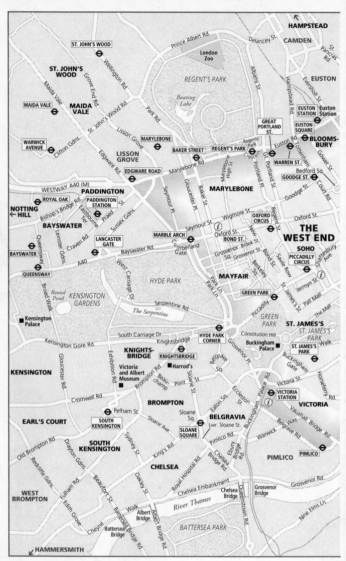

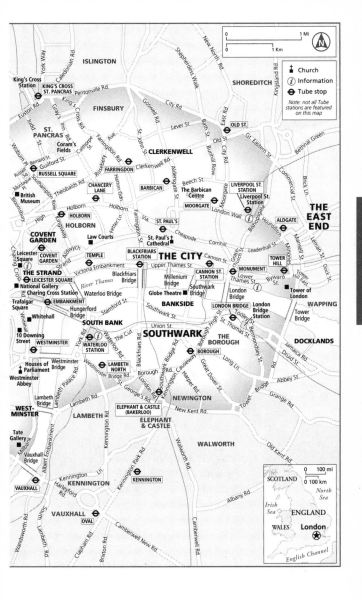

If a Londoner claims not to work out at all, believe it. The aerobic eighties did hit town, but then regular vigorous exercise immediately regained its former English image of being punitive and faintly embarrassing, not to mention incompatible with drinking and smoking. Now things have settled down somewhere between the two extremes. Games (what Americans call sports), however, are very popular, at least in theory, but although many Londoners indulge in tennis, squash, cycling, golf, and so on, they do try not to wear the right clothes. Horse pursuits, cricket, and the burgeoning American sports—especially softball—are exceptions, where the correct kit is key. You'll be surprised by the dearth of physical activity in all those acres of park. You'll see a trickle of joggers and 'bladers, miniature packs of cyclists, and a few team games (many more on summer weekends), but even in those parks most conducive to sporting fun, the players amount to a mere fraction of the volume in, say, Central Park. This does mean more space for you!

The Lowdown

Parks to get lost in… The biggest by far are outlying **Richmond Park** and **Hampstead Heath.** Wild **Richmond Park,** in the upriver town of Richmond (reachable by British Rail or riverboat; see the Diversions chapter), even has a herd of deer, but its sports appeal is limited to horseback riding and biking—outside of Regent's Park, this is true of most of London's parks. **Hampstead Heath,** in the upscale north London neighborhood of the same name (Hampstead tube stop), is all rolling hills and dells and old woods, good for long contemplative walks. On summer evenings you can pretend you're the poet Keats, who lived nearby, and sit under a tree listening for a nightingale's liquid warbling (whether you hear one is another matter). In the center of town, **Hyde Park** and its neighbor (there's no visible dividing line), **Kensington Gardens,** are vast expanses of green, and include Kensington Palace and the Serpentine Gallery, as well as sights like the Italian Gardens and the Round Pond; the famous statue of Peter Pan, and the newish Princess Diana Memorial Playground in the northwest corner of Kensington Gardens. Farther out, but still central, is **Regent's Park,** medium-size (for London, huge for elsewhere) but impossible to get lost in, because

GETTING OUTSIDE

it's encircled by a road and has a vast open space in the middle that makes it prime for sport. Check out Queen Mary's Rose Garden, and catch a Shakespeare comedy at the delightful open-air theater. The most heavenly of the heavily planted, landscaped, and manicured parks is **Kew Gardens** (officially the Royal Botanic Gardens at Kew), far upstream (reachable via British Rail or riverboat—see the Diversions chapter). Wander through its great Victorian conservatories and their micro-environments from desert to rainforest, have a brush with the tropics under the palm trees, or spend an hour waiting for a fly to land in one of the carnivorous plants.

Perfect petite parks... Locals will swear their own green patch is the best, but they're lying unless they're from **Holland Park.** These grounds of a ruined Jacobean mansion are crammed with goodies, viz: an open-air theater mounting full-scale operas and ballets; a restaurant; a youth hostel; tennis courts; an adventure playground for kids; flocks of peacocks, guinea fowl, and Canadian geese; a Japanese water garden; a cricket pitch; an art gallery; rose gardens; and rhododendrons. It's really pretty, too. If you're hitting the tourist trail in town and need respite, **St. James's Park** and, across the Mall, **Green Park,** are the obvious solutions, with the former the hands-down winner for scenery (lake, ducks, bandstand), and the latter having nothing but a weird new Canadian Air Force WWII memorial (southeast corner by Constitution Hill) and nice daffodils. The **Chelsea Physic Garden,** with its antique rock garden and medicinal herbs, is gorgeous but is only open Wednesday and Sunday afternoons, except during the Chelsea Flower Show, when it's open daily. Be sure to get afternoon tea from the lovely volunteer ladies, then go say hi to the nattily dressed Chelsea Pensioners on the Royal Hospital grounds. A great place to take a break, whether you're a bird-watcher or not, is the 42-hectare (105-acre) **WWT Wetland Centre** in Hammersmith. This environmentally friendly parcel of lakes, lagoons, and marshes is the first to be created on such a scale in any capital city anywhere. The Wildfowl & Wetland Trust shifted thousands of tons of concrete and recycled soil to turn old reservoirs into a Site of Special Scientific Interest. Paths loop out in two directions from the Discovery Centre, across little bridges and past observation hides. Turn one way for World Wetlands, where some of the world's rarest ducks, geese, and swans live in 14 mocked-up habitats, and for life in a native pond (Wildside). Turn the other for three eco-friendly designer gardens, a children's farmyard full of ducks, and wetland crafts in Waterlife. The view from the observatory is breathtaking. You can watch the wardens feed the birds at noon and 3:30pm, or take a tour at 11am or 2:30pm. Up north, between Regent's Park and the Heath, is pretty **Primrose Hill,** with panoramic skyline views, while even farther north is a bizarre slice of countryside, in the shadow of gasometers, on a street that's half light-industrial and half red-light, called **Camley Street Nature Reserve.** It's only worth visiting if you're at Camden Lock or doing a canal-side walk, but I can almost guarantee that you'll never see it described in any other London guidebook. This disreputable (and then some) neighborhood was going to be Europe's biggest building site until the plans fell through, and now it's spawning ever more interesting arts activity. It was the site of many a legendary "warehouse party" of the Ecstasy-enhanced late '80s.

Green escapes from tourism... Vest pocket–size, but useful for the West End, are the squares **Berkeley,** where the nightingale sang, and **Grosvenor,** where the U.S. Embassy stands. From Trafalgar Square, head to the Thames for **Embankment Gardens,** a pretty spot for a picnic on a nice day (takeout food and drinks available in all kinds of shops around Embankment tube station), or nip across the new Hungerford Bridge (for trains and people only) to **Jubilee Gardens** alongside the Thames for a peerless view. From Westminster Abbey, visit Rodin's *Burghers of Calais* at **Victoria Tower Gardens,** on the riverbank just south of the Houses of Parliament. For a quick fix of green during a South Ken museum marathon, penetrate the heart of the **V&A,** where there's a surprising cloister garden. If you're at the British Museum, you're near the best hidden park of all: **Lincoln's Inn Fields** (if you're at Sir John Soane's Museum, you're in it), surrounded by the beautiful 17th-century courts of law. Farther north is the 2.8-hectare (7-acre) **Coram's Fields,** next to which Charles Dickens lived (see his house at 48 Doughty St.) and drank (try the Lamb on Lamb's Conduit St.). **Covent**

Garden is dense and annoying, but find escape in the secret garden behind the "actors' church," **St. Paul's.**

Best central jogging... Any Park Lane, Piccadilly, or St. James's hotel has **St. James's** and **Green parks** on the doorstep, which together provide one of the most scenic running tracks anywhere. A **Green Park** perimeter run is 1.6km (1 mile), or you can start on Piccadilly, cross Green Park due south, and then run all around the **St. James's lake** and north back across Green Park for a 3.2km (2-mile) run. You'll pass the back door of St. James's Palace and the front gates of Buckingham Palace, and meet many species of ducks. If you're staying, say, at the Lanesborough or the Halkin, **Hyde Park** is your locale, as it is from any of the Knightsbridge hotels; starting from Hyde Park Corner, you'll find a loop right around the Serpentine, crossing its bridge and returning on the south shore, 4km (2.5 miles) long. Extend that into **Kensington Gardens** to circle around the northern section of the lake called the Long Water and you've clocked 4.8km (3 miles). To run the entire 7.25km (4.5-mile) perimeter of both parks, follow the east and west paths, both called Broad Walk, the Carriage Drives on the north side, and the riding path, Rotten Row, on the south. Increase the cardio-intensity by running on the sandy horse track, but don't do this early in the morning, when the Household Cavalry exercise their hundreds of steeds. For an unusual and scenic 1.6km (1-mile) route, head out to **Hammersmith** to run from Hammersmith Bridge along the Upper, Lower, and Chiswick malls (rhymes with "pals" and has nothing to do with shopping). If you'll never run alone, London's several running clubs welcome visitors, especially the long-established **Hash House Harriers** (www.hhh.org.uk), **"the drinking club with a running problem."**

Inline skating... The inline-skating cult starts buzzing down London's streets and through its parks as soon as there's the least sign of summer. It's a mass participation thing—kinda *Fame* meets *Sex and the City*. Every Wednesday from mid-May, hundreds of people meet up at 7pm on the north side of the Serpentine in **Hyde Park** for a 2½-hour marshaled skate. The route takes in the capital's most famous landmarks, from Big Ben to Buckingham

GETTING OUTSIDE

Palace. The hard-core don't turn round until they reach Tower Bridge, while the lightweights stop for a drink on the river. Taking part in **London Skate** (tel 0800/169-3889; www.sweatybetty.com/bettyblade) is free, as is instruction on the night if you're a little nervous about keeping up. Be warned, though—neither this event, nor the **Friday Night Skate (FNS),** which also starts at 7pm on the north side of the Serpentine, are for novices. If you need to hire skates, **Slick Willies** (tel 010/7939-3824; 41 Kensington High St. W8; Kensington High St. tube stop) charges £10 ($17) a day. You can rent skates by the hour at **Urban Chaos** (tel 020/7373-1193; 324 Old Brompton Rd.; Earl's Court tube stop), where prices are £5 ($8.25) for 1 hour, £7.50 ($12) for 2 hours, or £15 ($25) all weekend. Both shops take a big deposit.

Balls... You're not going to be able to participate in the British national sports, **cricket** and **football.** ("Football" means soccer, but nobody calls it that. What Americans call football is known here as "American football.") Both sports are played weekends in Regent's Park by teams of varying levels of seriousness; football's played in fall and winter, cricket starts in late spring. Cricket is relaxing to watch, however, even if you can't make head or tail of its rules; watch amateur games in **Regent's Park,** or more picturesquely in **Holland Park,** where there's a designated Cricket Lawn with adjacent tearoom. Professional cricket is played at **Lords** and **the Oval** (see the Entertainment chapter). In Regent's Park and also in **Hyde Park,** each spring you'll find a phenomenon of the last decade or so: **softball games.** Teams are organized, but bring your mitt and you'll probably be able to pick up a game, especially Sundays in the middle of Regent's Park. Other softball spots include **Battersea Park** and **Clapham Common.** The standard's getting pretty good, especially since most serious teams include American expat players, whose imported skills have now been thoroughly absorbed. *Time Out* lists finals in the various leagues; the men's fast-pitch team the **Zoo Crew** and the co-ed slow-pitch **London New Zealand** are worth catching. The **Seymour Leisure Centre** (tel 020/7723-8019; Seymour Place W1; Marylebone tube stop) has a hall that accommodates many sports, from badminton to five-a-side football, from circuit training to, yes, basketball; there's also a serious amateur b-ball league. The

games are played indoors, and though you're welcome to
watch, you can see better games at your local college gym.
Baseball is played in Britain, but really badly. If you're any
good, you'll probably be a welcome player, but you'd have
to be desperate, because most teams are based in the sub-
urbs. Two sports you can play here, and not at home, are
Australian Rules Football and **Camogie.** The rules in the
former are very loose—this is like gridiron crossed with
mud wrestling (look in *Time Out* for the latest team details).
Camogie is the most Irish of sports, somewhere between
hurling, lacrosse, and field hockey. **Field hockey** is called
hockey here, and hockey is called **ice hockey;** on
Hampstead Heath, there's a high-standard hockey pickup
game you're welcome to join that's been going on every
Sunday since World War II (about 300m/984 ft. past
Whitestone Ponds; to the right, near the TV antenna. Bully-
off at 3pm).

Horsing around... The English really like messing around
with large quadrupeds, and you can do it with them, either
in the center of town or, in a bigger way, by taking a tube
to the end of a line. In **Hyde Park** is **Rotten Row,** a sand-
track artery with various sand-track arterioles, which has
been handy for showing off an equestrian wardrobe and a
perfect seat (that's your form on horseback) since Charles
II had it laid. The name Rotten Row is probably a corrup-
tion of *route du roi,* a reference to that same king. Both
Ross Nye (tel 020/7262-3791; 8 Bathurst Mews W2) and
Hyde Park Stables (tel 020/7723-2813; 63 Bathurst Mews
W2; Lancaster Gate tube stop for both) can mount you
and send you off into the park, albeit not unaccompanied,
not dressed in jeans, not Western style, and not at a gallop.
It's a pretty formal affair, riding in London, and if you've
never ridden English saddle, be prepared for a shock—it's
utterly different and far more complex than Western saddle, though experienced wranglers should get the hang of
the basics pretty fast. The **London Equestrian Centre** (tel
020/8349-1345; Lullington Garth N12) is a good place,
even for beginners; all new riders get a half-hour assess-
ment lesson. **Trent Park Equestrian Centre** (tel 020/
8363-9005; Bramley Rd., Southgate, London N14;
Oakwood tube stop) has the dual advantages of being on
the end of a tube line (get the Piccadilly to Oakwood) and
having acres of "green belt" protected countryside to ride

around in, in addition to two international-sized indoor schools. You'll leave the city far behind. Hard hats and shoes with heels are a requirement to ride in the U.K.; stables can usually furnish you with a riding helmet.

Teeing off... There are many fine courses in England, and world-class ones in Scotland, but in London itself the pickings are slim. Next door to Trent Park Stables is **Trent Park Golf Club** (tel 020/8366-7432; Bramley Rd., Southgate N14; Oakwood tube stop), about the only full-scale 18-hole round of golf so accessible to downtown. A bit further out there's **Richmond Park Golf Club** (tel 020/8876-1795; Roehampton Gate, Richmond Park SW15), an 18-hole public course reputed to be quite good. To pacify your addiction, try **Regent's Park Golf School** (tel 020/7724-0643; in Regent's Park, near the zoo), where you can schedule a lesson or just putt around on the small greens—indoors or out—or drive on the ranges. The only problem is that it requires a £60 ($99) membership.

For those with slightly smaller ambitions, there is a pitch-and-putt course in **Queen's Park,** NW6 (tel 020/8969-5661). Open in summer months until 6pm, the course has nine holes and takes a half hour to an hour, depending on how busy it is...and how competent you are. The course is behind the cafe on the north side of the park.

On the water... You can watch rowing on a stretch of the Thames from Hammersmith to Putney, but you can't easily do it yourself. Real Oxford and Cambridge Boat Race–style rowing and sculling clubs are exclusively members-only. From April through September, from a hut on the Lido in Hyde Park, you can rent a rowboat and take it out on the **Serpentine.** Though it's a bargain (around £5/$8.25 an hour to rent a boat), it is really just a pale imitation of river sculling. Sailing, believe it or not, is available on the Thames in London at **Westminster Boating Base** (tel 020/7821-7389; 136 Grosvenor Rd. SW1; Pimlico tube stop) and way out in the 'burbs, on a big reservoir in the 42km-long (26 miles) **Lee Valley Park** (tel 020/8531-1129; Banbury reservoir, Harbert Rd., Chingford).

In the swim... Thanks to the climate, water is a natural element for the English, and there are consequently loads of public swimming pools in London, though surprisingly few hotels have pools. The best pools among the hotels listed in the Accommodations chapter are at **Le Meridien Grosvenor House** and **Dolphin Square.** Two unlisted (by us) hotels with spectacular pools are **Le Meridien Piccadilly** (tel 0870/400-8400; 21 Piccadilly W1), whose megabucks health club is run by the swanky spa Champneys (which charges a megabucks daily membership), and **The Berkeley** (tel 020/7235-6000; Wilton Place, Knightsbridge SW1), with a roof that peels back to expose its truly fabulous pool. If your hotel is poolless, search out a public pool. They're generally well maintained and sparkling clean, though the chlorine level is high and the changing rooms are communal. **The Oasis Sports Centre** (tel 020/7831-1804; 32 Endell St. WC2; Tottenham Court Rd. tube stop) has two pools, including a not particularly beautiful outdoor one, and it couldn't be more central, but every office worker near Covent Garden seems to be there at lunchtime. A better outdoor option is the **Serpentine Lido** pool in Hyde Park, open May through September, with a chlorinated section. Join the mad **Serpentine Swimming Club** (www.serpentineswimming club.com), which has its own changing facilities and permission to swim in the Serpentine itself at certain hours every day of the year (if you're interested in joining the club, go to the Serpentine at 8am any Sat morning and talk to one of the swimmers). These are the swimmers you see on TV when they break the ice in the year's first freeze. As far as public indoor pools go, **Swiss Cottage pool** (tel 020/ 7483-4324; Winchester Rd. NW3) is one of the biggest (37m/121 ft. long) and conveniently located next to the Swiss Cottage tube stop, but it gets crowded; the **Chelsea pool** (tel 020/7352-6985; Chelsea Manor St. SW3; Sloane Sq. tube stop) is handy for aqua-addicts staying in the southwest. **Seymour Leisure Centre** (tel 020/7723-8019; Seymour Place W1) has a good, long, four-lane lap pool just a 15-minute walk from Marble Arch. Watch out for aqua-aerobics times, though, because the Seymour Centre is well known for its fitness classes. You can also get your scuba-diving certification here.

Climbing the walls... There are no mountains in London, but rock climbing and mountaineering are popular, and Brits even win medals at it. Oldest and finest of the climbing centers is indoors at **Mile End Climbing Wall**

(tel 020/8980-0289; Cordova Rd. Bow E3; Mile End tube). It's hidden deep in the East End (call for directions) but is worth the trek for rock fans, since there are faces with many features—for bouldering (traverse climbing), competition climbing (with moveable holds), high up, medium, easy, impossible, and completely upside-down climbing. There are lessons, and it's all extremely inexpensive. The newest wall is outdoors at the **Westway Sports Centre** (tel 020/8969-0992; 1 Crowthorne Rd. W10; Latimer Road tube stop), with a 15m (49-ft.) tower, a 12m (39-ft.) pyramid, and 30m (98 ft.) of traversing wall. Both cost around £5 ($8.25) a day and offer lessons. One more wall is the 21m-high (70-footer) one at north London's **Sobell Sports Centre** (tel 020/7609-2166; Hornsey Rd. N7; Finsbury Park tube stop), an all-around sports facility that offers plenty to do.

On ice... Back in the olden days before global warming, the Thames used to freeze solid enough to accommodate a winter's fair on top of it. Even as late as the 1960s, the winters were reliably cold enough for the Round Pond in Kensington Gardens to be London's unofficial skating rink. Now, however, we must rely on a handful of artificially frozen rinks, of which the most central and glamorously romantic is in the spiffed-up courtyard of **Somerset House** (Strand W2; Charing Cross tube station). Starting in December they turn off the fountains and the courtyard is transformed into an open-air ice rink. Another choice, albeit tiny, is the October-to-April-only **Broadgate Ice Rink** (tel 020/7505-4068; 3 Broadgate EC2; Liverpool St. tube stop) in a swanky City business development and with a "skate-of-the-art" sound system.

Getting fit indoors... London's hotels are not necessarily equipped with the kind of gym you'd expect for the rates they charge; see the Accommodations chapter for the few that offer exercise facilities. If a workout is essential to your well-being, try the following multipurpose gyms offering temporary memberships or drop-in rates. The snazzy and well-equipped **London Central YMCA** (tel 020/7637-8131; 112 Great Russell St. WC1; Covent Garden tube stop), like every Y, has a pool, weight room, squash and badminton courts, cardio equipment, and a sauna. The bustling **Seymour Leisure Centre** (tel 020/7723-8019;

Seymour Place W1; Marylebone tube stop) has a gym, badminton, and morning-to-evening classes that can be a blast. **Jubilee Hall** (tel 020/7379-0008; 30 the Piazza WC2; Covent Garden tube stop) actually feels swankier and more expensive than the public facility that it is; you can do tai chi or Thai kickboxing before your step class here. The even tonier **Gym at the Sanctuary** (tel 020/7240-0695; 12 Floral St. WC2; Covent Garden tube station), attached to the women-only day spa of the same name (but operated separately), is a good place for women to sweat unobserved by Schwarzeneggers. The **Albany Fitness Centre** (tel 020/7383-7131; St. Bede's Hall, Albany St. NW1; Great Portland St. tube stop), in a former church, is fun and full of weight-training hardware for Schwarzenegger wannabes. For dance classes, **Pineapple** (tel 020/7836-4004; 7 Langley St. WC2; Covent Garden tube stop) tends toward the aerobics, hip-hop, jazz side, and also offers tai chi, while **Danceworks** (tel 020/7629-6183, 16 Balderton St. W1; Bond St. tube stop) has everything from ballet to salsa at all levels from beginner to pro, plus various aerobics innovations. Professional dancers who can't sit still might want to try **The Place** (tel 020/7388-8430; 17 Dukes Rd. WC2; Euston tube stop), attached to the London Contemporary Dance School. Tennis players should gravitate toward two new indoor tennis centers built to bring the game out of the posh exclusive clubs and to the public at large: the **Islington Tennis Centre** (tel 020/7700-1370; Market Rd. N7) is a bit remote, though 5 minutes' walk from the Caledonian Road tube stop; and the **Westway Sports Centre** (tel 020/8969-0992; 1 Crowthorne Rd. W10) is nearer to downtown and close to the Latimer Road tube station. For squash, head for **Finsbury Leisure Centre** (tel 020/7253-2346; Norman St. EC1; Old St. tube stop), **Portobello Green** (tel 020/8960-2221; 3–5 Thorpe Close W10; Ladbroke Grove tube stop), or the **Sobell Sports Centre** (tel 020/7609-2166; Hornsey Rd. N7; Finsbury Park tube stop). Isola Akay's wonderful West London boxing gym housed in a church, **All Stars Gym** (tel 020/8960-7724; 576 Harrow Rd. W10; Kensal Green tube stop; call after 5pm) welcomes all contenders to its 2-hour, no-contact KO circuit; it's the friendliest (stay for tea and biscuits after) and most challenging workout in town.

PING

5

Map 20: Central London Shopping

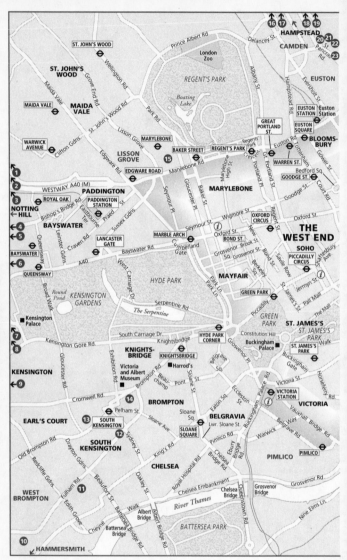

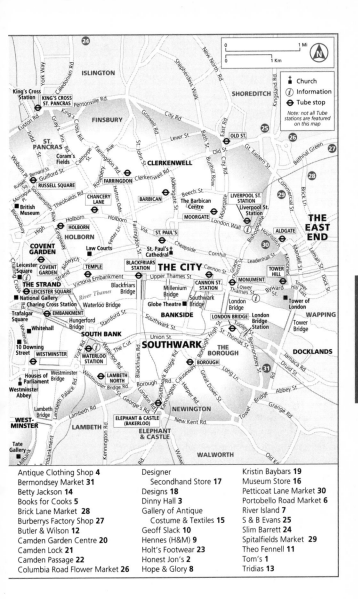

Antique Clothing Shop 4	Designer	Kristin Baybars 19
Bermondsey Market 31	Secondhand Store 17	Museum Store 16
Betty Jackson 14	Designs 18	Petticoat Lane Market 30
Books for Cooks 5	Dinny Hall 3	Portobello Road Market 6
Brick Lane Market 28	Gallery of Antique	River Island 7
Burberrys Factory Shop 27	Costume & Textiles 15	S & B Evans 25
Butler & Wilson 12	Geoff Slack 10	Slim Barrett 24
Camden Garden Centre 20	Hennes (H&M) 9	Spitalfields Market 29
Camden Lock 21	Holt's Footwear 23	Theo Fennell 11
Camden Passage 22	Honest Jon's 2	Tom's 1
Columbia Road Flower Market 26	Hope & Glory 8	Tridias 13

Basic Stuff

If you ask me—and you did—London is one of the world's great shopping cities. Sure, it's full of the international chain stores that make it difficult to discern which country you're in, but there are also plenty of interesting (well, sometimes) homegrown clothing chains. Prices aren't low, and the dollar-to-sterling exchange rate periodically makes shopping London fiendishly expensive, but you make up for that with quality and selection.

What to Buy

Anything made in the U.K. is going to be far cheaper in London than what you'd pay for it (if it were even available) in the U.S. Get **antiques,** or just lust after them. If you're not rich, trawl flea markets and so-called junk shops for treasure. Stock up on **books**—antiquarian, out-of-print, and those written by European and British writers without a U.S. publisher—then lug them home. (Books and children's clothing are the only things that don't have the 17.5% value-added tax added on.) Some of the world's best **porcelain** and **china** is indigenous to England: Royal Doulton, Spode, and Wedgwood spring to mind. Buy **clothes** here. The big European designers have at least a store each, as do the Americans, but British and other Euro designers you may not have heard of will surprise you, and they're perfectionists with the finish, especially the Brits, Dutch, and Belgians. Traditional English tailoring is famous, of course. Savile Row (it rhymes with "gravel") is the apogee, but look at the less exorbitant (but still not cheap) huntin', shootin', and fishin' outfits, elements of which work with any wardrobe. Ralph Lauren, eat your heart out. At the other extreme, look for street clothes—London's been famous for funky since the mods put Carnaby Street on the map. The word "crafts" conjures images of crude pots and Birkenstocks, but really means acres of exciting, handmade **design wares** that you can only find here. Also buy **tea**—loose leaf, not bags—and a teapot and strainer. Other food gifts and treats are **cheeses,** especially whole mini-cheddars and stiltons, and the **oatcakes** to accompany them; make sure the cheeses are vacuum-sealed or you may run into trouble getting them back into the U.S. Then there are Thornton's special toffee, and anything from Fortnum & Mason, Marks & Spencer, Waitrose, or Sainsbury's (in decreasing order of poshness) for the packaging. This is a nation of gardeners. If you share that obsession, get **gardening paraphernalia** here;

you can't bring live plants back into the U.S., but you can be inspired. Finally, London is really great for fine **toiletries**—I mean soaps, shaving gear, and bath stuff.

Target Zones

There are so many shopping districts; here's a quick whiz through. The **West End**'s artery—**Oxford Street**—is the busiest street in town, with chain stores and tacky closeout stores, plus good department stores and two swanky fashion streets on the edge (**S. Molton St.** and **St. Christopher's Place**). Around the corner is **Bond Street** (New segueing into Old), famous for top-dollar clothes, art, jewelry. **Savile Row, Jermyn Street** in **St. James's,** and the arcades of **Piccadilly** (the sine qua non of window shopping) also count as West End, as does **Regent Street** (for big stores **Liberty** and **Hamleys**), and the little streets around **Soho** and **Carnaby Street,** full of T-shirts and sneakers, plus more interesting designer-type boutiques. **Covent Garden** is sort of counted as West End but is a very fruitful shopping district in its own right. It has all the better clothing chains, plus market stalls, and many little boutiques, with the bookstores of **Charing Cross Road** and **Cecil Court** on its border. A 20-minute ride north on Bus 24 or 29, **Camden Town** has its huge teenage street market, the **Lock,** but also plenty of shops selling vintage clothes, Indian brassware, denims, funky hats and boots, kilims, and silver jewelry. Keep going north and you hit **Hampstead,** a picturesque way to shop the best clothing chains. In the west, **Knightsbridge** is the ultimate destination, with London's most famous store, **Harrods,** plus every European designer represented in shops strung along **Sloane Street** and **Brompton Road.** Keep going and you reach **Brompton Cross,** with its cluster of very fancy fashion and interiors shops. North of Knightsbridge you'll hear Kensington's main drag shortened to **Ken High Street.** It has most of the chains, plus the interesting curve of **Ken Church Street,** where antiques are expensive but of museum quality. More egalitarian antiques are found farther north, in and around famous **Portobello Road**—not just a market, but a way of life. Explore this Notting Hill neighborhood for fashion designers just starting out, stuff for interiors, and young, affordable artists. One more westerly destination is **Chelsea.** The **King's Road** is okay for trendy boutiques, midpriced antiques, and the better clothing chains. It has a **Waitrose** reputed to be a good place to shop both for groceries and a date. Its nether

SHOPPING

reaches, around **World's End,** where the designer Vivienne Westwood has her shop, are better.

Bargain Hunting

You can make London much less expensive by applying three main strategies: shopping the sales, hitting markets, and (for clothes) seeking out resale stores. The sales seasons are traditionally January and June, although these are moveable feasts that leak further into December and July every year. Lots of shops also have a permanent sale rack. I list some resale shops, but look in the *Evening Standard,* and the "Sell Out" section in *Time Out* for news of designers' "warehouse sales" or showroom clearances. Look below for how to do markets and what to get there.

Trading with the Natives

Certain rituals familiar to every American shopper are mysteries to Brits. You may find assistants less attentive than you're used to. Londoner shop staff don't wish to know how a stranger thinks some piece of clothing looks on them or whether it goes with their new jacket. You won't see WE SHIP ANYWHERE signs either. Big stores will ship, but otherwise you're usually on your own, though your hotel may help. Places that ship are usually set up for instant VAT refunds as well (see "Sales Tax," below). Delivery in London is also the exception rather than the rule, and can cost extra. As you would expect, bargaining for a lower price is *not* done in regular shops, though haggling can pay dividends in street markets.

Hours of Business

Since Sunday trading laws have been relaxed and Londoners are getting more demanding ("I want to shop and I want to shop *now*"), there's less and less uniformity to the hours London shops keep. Traditional opening hours are 9am to 5pm or 6pm, with one half-day closing (almost an extinct practice in London, but still found in the provinces) and 1 day, usually Thursday, with extended hours, till 7 or 8pm. That said, many shops these days don't open till 10am, so they're open an extra hour or so in the evening. Most shops open on Sundays, which has actually become the busiest shopping day (now that no one goes to church anymore). London shops are currently allowed to remain open for 6 hours on Sunday—it could be 10am to 4pm or 11am to 5pm or noon to 6pm.

Sales Tax

England's sales tax is called **value-added tax (VAT),** and it runs at a greedy 17.5% on so-called "nonessential goods" (which means almost everything you'll be shopping for). You can get VAT refunded by filling out a form at the time of purchase, which you then take, with the goods and receipts, to Customs at Heathrow. For this reason, always shop with your passport. For tax-refund purposes, some shops have a minimum (about £30/$50 and up), some don't want to do it at all, and some have big long lines. If you have something shipped, you can get an on-the-spot VAT refund. And remember, the total value of goods you can bring back to the U.S. is now $800, twice the former amount.

The Lowdown

The big stores... Of Oxford Street's three department stores, **Selfridges** is the best because they've poured lots of dough into a major sprucing-up program. The Food Hall and the fashion departments are now thoroughly revamped. (By the way, clothing is the core merchandise at all of these stores, unless otherwise indicated.) Still on Oxford Street, pass by **Debenhams,** the Kmart to Selfridges' Macy's, perhaps just popping in for a squint at **Jasper Conran**'s bargain "J" line, plus other designers' diffusion lines, then head to **John Lewis** (loveable for its motto, "Never Knowingly Undersold") and its excellent fabrics, notions, and haberdashery. Around the corner, in Regent Street, **Dickens & Jones** is the flagship of the nationwide House of Fraser group, which is not generally known for fashion leadership. This store, however, tries really hard with its prices in the middle range, and its great sales. Nearby is irresistible **Liberty,** which started as an Oriental bazaar and still maintains an Eastern bias in certain exotic corners of its mahogany and stained-glass interior. Down Bond Street, find slightly odd **Fenwick,** a store that often attempts to be all things to all people but isn't, except in the underwear department. The lord of department stores is **Fortnum & Mason.** It's the queen's grocer, and you shouldn't pass up the food halls with their liveried servers and towers of teas, preserves, handmade chocolates, and cans of turtle soup. But go upstairs, too, for the least frenetic cosmetics counter in town and many matronly clothes. Mega-successful nationwide chain **Marks & Spencer** is the hamburger of shops, universally known and loved. Every Londoner has Marks 'n' Sparks knickers (panties, that is), sweaters, and an addiction to some item from the food counters. In the west, **Peter Jones** (part of the John Lewis chain) is more of a sociological phenomenon than a store, the spiritual home of the Sloane Ranger and purveyor of school uniforms. The great store of the west, though, is **Harvey Nichols,** home of practically nothing but fashion—but what clothes! And what prices. It's definitely worth a visit, especially during the sales. Nearby is **Harrods.** What do you want me to say? That it's overrated? Overpriced? Over the top? Well, it is, but it's still worth a browse. This London landmark and its 230 departments do attempt to live up to the store motto *Omnia, Omnibus, Ubique* (Latin for "everything for everyone, everywhere"). Harrods recently lost its royal warrant because its owner, father of Dodi al-Fayed, killed with Princess Diana, suggested that there was something royally fishy about that car crash in Paris. In a royal huff, Prince Phillip withdrew the royal warrant.

Rattling the chains... Instead of the Gap and other places you can patronize *chez vous,* check out local stores and styles. To look like a teenage clubber in iridescent minis and Day-Glo rubber Ts, shop **Top Shop, Miss Selfridge,** and (for more formal occasions) **River Island** and **Oasis,** the best of the cheapies. Best of the best for the generation formerly known as X, though, is **Warehouse,** where stock moves so fast, it's blurred. Boys as well as girls get to shop at **Zara**. Everyone goes to **Marks & Spencer** for underwear, but it's an open secret that Marks 'n' Sparks gets fancy designers to consult on garments requiring more fabric, and there's much to discover in this formerly frumpy superchain (remember, they rioted in Paris when the Marks 'n' Sparks was going to be closed down there). A very *short* chain, but best of all for quality, and being on target aesthetically, is **Whistles.**

The big names... The shop with the mostest has to be **Browns,** from which owner Joan Burstein has led London into the appreciation and assimilation of tasty clothes for many years. Here are Galliano, Demeulemeester, Ozbek,

Rykiel, Karan, Tyler, Gigli, Sander, Muir, etc., etc. Other places where you can compare and contrast multiple makers include the tiny Knightsbridge **A la Mode,** which favors the Americans and the Belgians. Best for young Brit designers, of the edgy, envelope-pushing sort—like those famous few who stormed Paris (McQueen, Galliano, McCartney the daughter)...but I mustn't name too many names they'll probably have their own flagship stores by the time this book comes out and then I'll look stupid. Let me simply say that *all* designers you've ever heard of are in London somewhere, but highlights among those (non-British ones) with entire shops include **Prada, Dolce & Gabbana,** and **Comme des Garçons. Emporio Armani** shops are everywhere, while the memory of **Gianni Versace** is kept alive in an over-the top rococo marble folly on Bond Street. For less cash outlay than at any of the above, shop **Joseph** for enticing ranges of beautifully cut, mostly French-made, monochrome separates.

Homegrown talent... The British Isles once produced great writers, but now it's better at clothes. You may know that her ladyship **Vivienne Westwood** is one of the world's most inventive and most copied designers, but you should see her clothes close up—they're exquisitely tailored. (Wear her son's wares from **Agent Provocateur** underneath.) Easier to handle, though, are **Betty Jackson**'s slightly offbeat classics. Also check out this pair of designers who do the riding-clothes–country-tweeds–rumpled-linens look better than anyone: **Margaret Howell**'s clothes last forever; Irishman **Paul Costelloe** does the Irish version with *lots* of linen. See **Mulberry** for the most staid versions of this look, and next door to that, the secret of certain well-dressed, anti-fashion mature women, **Paddy Campbell,** who makes timeless fitted suits and separates. **Paul Smith** is the menswear king for suits with a sense of humor, plus accessories and tons of shirts, with a limited women's range, too. The other terribly famous (and deservedly so) menswear man is the clothes **Conran, Jasper,** who also dresses women. **Nicole Farhi** also swings both ways. She's London's Donna Karan. On the opposite bank, wearing work clothes in denim with something clingy, rhinestoned, and small, and a well-cut jacket, stands **Katharine Hamnett.** And, on the wilder shores, look around Neal Street in Covent Garden, in Camden at the

Lock, and along Portobello Road (best on the weekend) for street style.

For riot grrls and boys... Street wear stays out of the limelight and is found, yes, on the street: in market stalls, thrift stores (called charity shops here), and rummage sales (called jumble sales). However, to approximate a London look, try the following: the **Duffer of St. George** has the Chelsea boot-boy kitted out in vaguely threatening style; riot girls wear it, too. **The Dispensary** edits other people's lines (some from the U.S.) and makes their own to dress you not too outrageously. As for flea markets, **Camden Lock** is the biggest, but before you plunge in, pause at **Holt's Footwear,** which has been providing 20-hole Docs for punk feet for over a century. It's a cramped, not necessarily *freundlich,* cash-only shopping experience, but every Brit band, Beatles to Madness to Pulp to Cornershop, was shod here.

Labels for less... I mentioned in the intro how you should check listings in the *Standard* and *Time Out* for warehouse sales, and call the showrooms, too. Some other sources: **Labels for Less** is **Browns** outlet store, while Burberrys outlet store is called **Burberrys Factory Shop.** Of course, these days, that famed Burberry check (the beige plaid beloved of Euro tourists) is being ripped off even more than Coco's little black dress. So keep your eyes peeled because some of those fakes are smoking. **Whistles** also has an outlet, not far away. Both **Vivienne Westwood** and **Paul Smith** have permanent sale stores. Of London's consignment and used-designer-clothing shops, the best are **Designs** (for the Escada and Genny type of woman—the German well-pressed look), **Designer Secondhand Store** (a little hipper, with some Versace, Rifat Ozbek, and Paul Smith), and the Knightsbridge **Pandora** (big and well known, with racks of Alaïa, Armani, Karan, and even Chanel). For designers who are no longer designing, there's nowhere better than the incredible **Steinberg & Tolkein.** The basement here is like a funky version of the V&A Dress Collection where everything's for sale, with a ton of affordable tat alongside the Jacques Fath and historic Chanel pieces from the days of Coco herself. Nowhere except the **Antique Clothing Shop,** that is. The catch is, you have to be here Friday or Saturday for a riffle through

Sandy Stagg's bulging racks of 1930s tea dresses, flapper gowns, cricket sweaters, and frock coats.

For sir, with $$$... The famous tailors of Savile Row are moving with the times...a bit. **Richard James** is a newer face, who cuts with nontraditional cloths like denim, as well as the suitings one would expect. At 1 Savile Row is the quintessential, ultimate bespoke tailor, **Gieves & Hawkes** (that's a hard "G"), which started with Admiral Nelson and graduated to Hugh Grant's Oscar-night suit. Get your shirts made where the Prince of Wales gets his, **Turnbull & Asser.** A Savile Row suit will take maybe 6 weeks, at least three fittings, and will cost a minimum of £1,000 ($1,650), though the tab may be twice that. A minimum order of half a dozen bespoke shirts with shell buttons and collar stays of bone will set you back £600 to £900 ($990–$1,485). If you're not in that tax bracket yet, try **Favourbrook** for a brocade waistcoat (or vest), in one of their many dandy fabrics, or an entire silk-brocade dandy's suit. Nearly all these tailors will also make to measure for women.

Cutting costs... The tailoring skills of London designers have long been appreciated in the world of fashion. Surprisingly, a tailored suit (or just one that has been altered) need not cost an arm and a leg. A tailor with an impressive celeb client list is **Jackie Palmer,** with wedding outfits (for the whole team) a specialty. **Mr. Eddie** and his crew can knock up a suit in a few days if you're in a hurry, but do expect to pay a bit more for your haste. **Geoff Slack** will also work on a tight schedule, whether fashioning full-scale wedding dresses or duplicates of your favorite T-shirts. Geoff is also never happier than when working with "fetishistic" fabrics—latex wedding dress, anyone? If the outfit you love doesn't fit like a glove, you need **Couturière,** inexpensive but excellent alterations by Japanese-born Takako Sato, whose skill with a needle is legendary (it's all sewn by hand).

Your own crown jewels... The actual crown jewels are watched over by **Garrard,** where you can order your personal collection any way you like it, or try out the royal-looking work of **Theo Fennell**—his ecclesiastical goldsmithery is quite distinctive. But, let's face it, you're probably looking for something a little less *real*. The most

outrageously rhinestoned of **Butler & Wilson**'s wares fool
nobody none of the time and are irresistible to human
magpies, especially the crown brooches and earrings;
there's also great classic French gilt and a lot of jet. If you
really do require an actual crown, **Slim Barrett** is your man.
His stone-encrusted coronets and tiaras are fashion-victim
favorites. But for something to wear on a daily basis, visit
with **Dinny Hall** (who works mostly in silver), see the jewelry departments at **Liberty** and **Harvey Nichols**, or check
out the score of young designers at **Janet Fitch**.

Smelling like a rose... At **Penhaligon's** you'll have a blast
uncorking crystal flagons and sniffing precious waters.
William Penhaligon was Victoria's court barber, and the
same Blenheim Bouquet he blended is still sold. For other
superluxe, hand-milled soaps and toiletries, **Floris** on
Jermyn Street is also recommended. But for more fun and
affordable soaps, visit an outlet of all-the-rage **Lush**, where
huge cakes of handmade soaps are cut like cheeses and sold
by weight. Organic lip balm and super herbal remedies of all
kinds are sold at **Neal's Yard Remedies.** Guys who are looking for first-class shaving equipment, including badger shaving brushes, should stop in at **Taylor of Old Bond Street.**

Gifts that scream London... **Janet Fitch** is a great gift
source for your modern and design-conscious friends, and
the diamanté crown pieces from **Butler & Wilson** are cute
British gifts, or get a St. Paul's dome in umbrella form from
the **Museum Store.** There are racks and racks of that
essential English accessory at the gorgeous Victorian brolly
(umbrella to you) emporium **James Smith & Sons,** where
you can also get shooting sticks (a portable seat), silver-
topped canes, Mary Poppins parrot-top umbrellas, and riding crops. Try giving a scarf from genius **Georgina von
Etzdorf,** whose *devoré* velvets and hand-printed silk chif-
fons and opulent satins are much copied but never equaled.
For guys, what else but a tie? Check out the selection at
Liberty. For gifts in quantity, for the entire office, perhaps,
get orchid or banana tea from **The Tea House,** or
Twining's Earl Grey (the best) from **R. Twining &
Co.,** with its little tea museum on the company's original
premises; or go for smoky Lapsang Souchong and the
New York blend (made to brew with New York water—
yes, really) from **Fortnum & Mason,** which is one-stop

shopping for the entire gift list. Smellies are not boring gifts when they come from **Penhaligon's** or **Floris.** But for more fun and affordable soaps, have a few bars cut for you at **Lush,** which has opened in Canada but not yet in the U.S.; they also sell fizzing "bath bombs" that make great gifts. **Rococo** has Earl Grey tea chocolate bars, while **Thornton's** is forever coming up with gimmicky candies. If there's nothing London-themed right now, get some Special Toffee, which is the best there is. There's another Thornton's in Heathrow (this side of the gates) for emergencies.

Guy gifts... Real cigarette lighters can be picked up at **Davidoff Cigars,** which is really more for cigar smokers, with wall-to-wall Havanas in its walk-in humidor. Those who prefer an indigenous English sports souvenir will fare best at **Lillywhite's,** the amazing sports department store. Football gear, including the jerseys of all London teams, plus those of the glamorous Italian *Serie* A and other Euro footy players, is at **Soccer Scene,** while British boxers (one of the few sports for which the English supply stars) get their hands wrapped at **Lonsdale.** And if all you can think of is a tie, then head for **Liberty.** For super shaving and grooming gear visit **Floris.** They sell great-smelling shaving soaps.

> ### Cockney Rhyming Slang
> *If you wander the East End of London, you may hear a few odd word pairings that are meant to substitute for things related only inasmuch as they rhyme. For example: whistle+flute=suit, or Brahms+Liszt=pissed (=drunk, not angry), or apple+pear=stair. These are sometimes boiled down to just the first word, which then produces sentences such as, "Nice whistle, matey," meaning, "That is an elegant suit." Years of Ealing comedies and My Fair Lady have convinced much of the world that these constructions, called Rhyming Slang, are a secret language of the Cockneys. In fact, the rhyming slang used by some Londoners is really a form of wordplay common among traders in the 18th century and found as well in Australia and in the States. Its continued presence on English radio and television shows in the U.K. has given it a prominence based more on regional identity than on actual use, much like the famous Brooklyn accent in New York.*

SHOPPING

Remarkable markets... **Bermondsey Market** is for serious antiques collectors. It's where dealers buy, but very, very early (before dawn). **Camden Passage** has a picturesque setting, with its alleys and little shops, in which the prices are higher than on the stalls. Finds are also still possible among the 2,000-odd dealers at the most famous market, **Portobello Road Market.** The antiques are concentrated at the Notting Hill end; they give way to fruit-and-veg, to the flea under the Westway (great vintage clothes), then into the nether reaches of Goldborne Road, where it's all junk and rummage, character, and the important pit stop, the Lisboa Portuguese bakery. **Brick Lane Market** has antiques, too, but you'll have to sift. This East End Sunday agglomeration of *stuff*—cassettes, work tools, candies, leather jackets, wallets—has great atmo and provides you the best chance of catching old market trader's banter and maybe rhyming slang. For a "real" market smack dab in the West End, you can't beat Soho's **Berwick Street Market,** where the fruit and veg is so good that chefs shop there. For the diametric opposite, try **Camden Lock**—heaven to some (if they're under 20), hell to others. Another famous market is **Petticoat Lane Market,** which is really a lot of tat nowadays and is surpassed by its neighbors Brick Lane and the totally contrasting, covered **Spitalfields Market,** whose Sunday greenmarket is a breath of the country.

Very old things... London has rich antiques pickings in shops and at auction, as well as at the markets mentioned above. It's one area where a price tag is a mutable thing, and haggling is advisable. Annual antiques fairs—of which the three biggies are the **Grosvenor House,** the **Chelsea,** and the **British Antique Dealers' Association**—attract international buyers and carriage trade alike. Several collections of stalls under one roof are best bets for casual purchases. In the King's Road are two big ones: **Antiquarius** and **Chenil Galleries.** Between those and the West End **Grays,** you'll probably score a hit. If not, try the **London Silver Vaults** for a set of Edwardian fruit knives, **Hope & Glory** for its stock of affordable commemorative china, the wonderful **Gallery of Antique Costume & Textiles,** which also makes its own reproduction 18th-century vests and coats, or **The Button Queen** for something to jazz up your tired old jacket.

Money's no object... A tasteful way to splash some cash around is to commission a bespoke Savile Row suit, as offered by **Gieves & Hawkes** or the hipper version chez

Richard James. Speaking of which, only Hong Kong rivals London as a place to achieve perfect head-to-toe tailoring, and Hong Kong lacks the class of the bowler-hat capital. **James Lock** is your guy for that hat, even though Mr. Lock himself expired in the early 18th century after making Admiral Lord Nelson's titfers (tit-for-tat: hat). Your platinum cards will start to wiggle in anticipation when they see the beautiful, security-guard-patrolled Burlington Arcade, where the **Irish Linen Co.** has some of the world's finest pure white sheets. From there, make your way to the bathroom fittings heaven that is **Czech & Speake** before heading for Mayfair and **Marlborough Fine Art, Asprey** the jewelers, and the finest purveyor of porcelain and crystal, **Thomas Goode & Co.**

Money's too tight to mention... The **Linen Cupboard** and **Harrods' Sale** were invented for those without means who yet aspire to pristine Irish linen sheets and English bone china. But why not just forget the whole aspirational thing and go to **Neal Street East** for an enormous selection of Asian imports for the home and to **Columbia Road Flower Market** for stuff to enhance the yard. Cheap gifts that look expensive are easy. **The Tea House** supplies tea and "teaphernalia," as they call it; **Marks & Spencer** has good things to wear, and its food department packages so gorgeously, you could make a gift out of a TV dinner.

For bookworms... London's literary legacy lives on in bookstores of all sizes. In the West End resides vast and impossible to understand **Foyles** is the handsome **Hatchards,** where the staff is really helpful, and the original **Waterstone's,** which cloned itself all over the U.K. Those are the best big ones, but look for the countless little specialty stores. Around book heaven **Charing Cross Road,** browse several varieties of **Zwemmer** (the art store is especially fine) and the self-explanatory **Dance Books,** among others. There are shops stocked as exhaustively as sections of the British Library, such as **French's Theatre Bookshop,** with every English-language play; beautiful, wood-paneled **Daunt Books** for travel tomes; **Stanfords** for the maps and guides; and **Sportspages** for the obvious. Antiquarian books are a famous commodity of this town, though nowadays try **Any Amount of Books** at number 62. If you need a specific out-of-print title, go to **Skoob Books;**

for a rarity or a signed first edition, investigate the world-class dealer **Bernard Quaritch,** who quotes prices in dollars. And if you collect cookbooks, or actually like to use them, then head over to **Books for Cooks** in Notting Hill off Portobello Road; it has a fab-o little cafe where you can enjoy lunch or tea.

For aural obsessives... London's been the world's vinyl capital since the Beatles, and now that everyone's got CDs (which are ridiculously expensive here), it still is. For club music that always did and still does hit the streets in 12-inch single form, this city's number one. Try **Trax** for Euro dance (trance, house, Ballearic). For jazz, the near-legendary **Mole Jazz** is better than it ever was in its new and larger place—it's kept up with the times on the CD front, too. The Portobello **Honest Jon's** has a Blue Note collection that's sublime, plus a good secondhand section, and many new CDs. As you would guess from its name, that other Soho institution, **Reckless Records,** stocks only vinyl, and only secondhand at that, but it caters to almost all tastes except classical in two Soho stores and a third just opened in Camden Town. If you're looking for Puccini's *La Fanciulla del West* with Birgit Nilsson, trot over to **MDC Classic Music,** which specializes in opera.

For the green thumb... London is frustrating for American gardeners, since you can't take the plants home. Ideas and inspiration, however, are free. The **Chelsea Gardener** and the **Camden Garden Centre** are the city's two best outdoor emporia, with climbers and rosebushes to die for, free advice, and accessories. Ditto the pots of **S & B Evans** at the unmissable **Columbia Road Flower Market,** which is itself full of wrought iron, terra-cotta, and wooden accessories.

Small fry... Convert fractious kids into shopping experts by showing them the five floors of **Hamleys,** the "world's biggest toy store" (or is that Toys "R" Us?). Smaller and maybe better is **Humla,** a cult among grandmas, for the gorgeous European garments and wooden toys at remarkably ungreedy prices. Older girls find heaven at **Hennes,** aka H&M, a Swedish chain that does high fashion cheap and has great kids' clothes, too. If you forgot to bring something, classy, British chain **Mothercare** is fine for baby equipment and toddler stuff. Wooden and traditional toys, teddies, dolls, stationery, and games are London finds. Try well-stocked **Tridias,** or if that isn't enough, take them to nearby **Harrods,** whose phantasmagorical Toy Kingdom is the kind where the plush lions are life-size and roar. Owners of dollhouses will remember **Kristin Baybars** all their lives, so it's worth the trek.

For gastronomes and epicures... For gifts in bulk, Prince Charles has obligingly done a Paul Newman: He sells packs of his own brand; the disarmingly delicious Duchy Originals oatcakes and ginger biscuits fill every carry-on bag. The whole baby Stilton cheese for the oatcakes should be got from **Paxton & Whitfield,** the cheese shop of cheese shops since 1797 (no Monty Python references, please), or the **Neal's Yard Dairy,** in which everything is from the British Isles, or made on the premises, and you can ask for tastes. Neal's Yard products are among the epicurean riches of **Tom's.** This may stretch your credulity, but Tom is yet another Conran: brother of Jasper the clothes designer, and son of Sir Terence, whose **"Gastrodrome"** by Tower Bridge provides smoked fish and seaweed bread, French charcuterie, fruit vinegars, Tuscan olive oils, homemade English chutneys, and more, in four separate shops. There's also the **Bluebird** food emporium on the King's Road. **Fortnum & Mason,** as you know by now, also fulfills this role. Get cans of brown Windsor soup, truffled foie gras, thick-cut marmalade with Scottish whisky, the anchovy paste in decorative ceramic jars called Patum Peperium Gentleman's Relish, and English mustard, but not, as a persistent myth has it, red ants in chocolate. And, of course, the food halls at **Harrods** are legendary.

For sweet teeth... Almost as exotic as Fortnum's fictional sweetmeat are certain of master chocolatier **Gerard Ronay**'s handmade fillings, like his award-winning smoked lemon. They are available at **Selfridges.** Chocoholics dedicated to quality will enjoy **Rococo** on the King's Road, a cocoa paradise run by the founder of the Chocolate Society. Anyone preferring quantity will favor the many branches of **Thornton's** for Belgian fresh cream truffles, children's novelty shapes in creamy milk and sickly white chocolate, and the aptly named Special Toffee, which is chewy, buttery caramel, not brittle like the "English toffee" of Heath Bars.

Map 21: Shopping in the West End

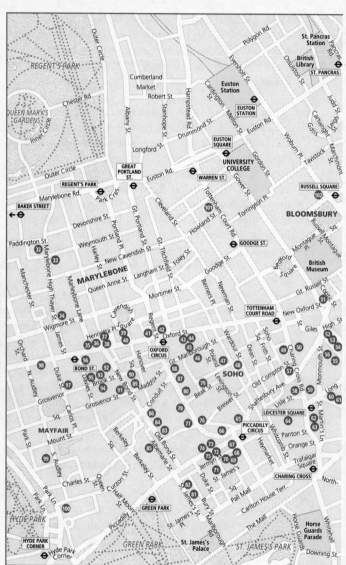

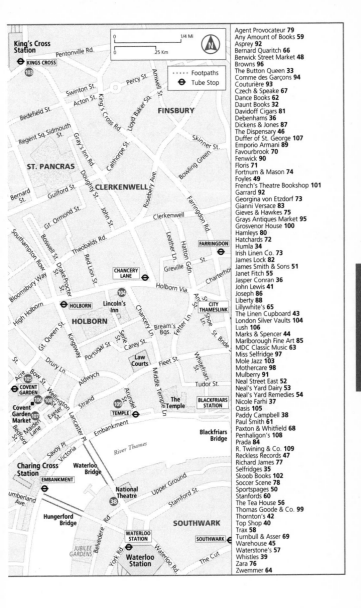

SHOPPING

Map 22: Shopping in Knightsbridge & Chelsea

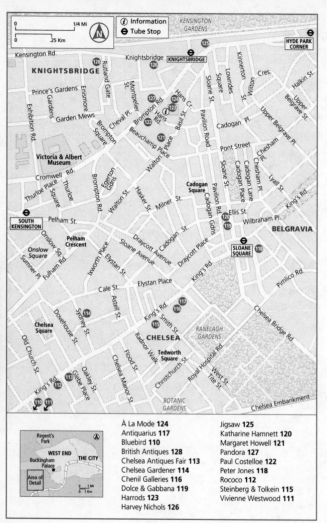

À La Mode **124**
Antiquarius **117**
Bluebird **110**
British Antiques **128**
Chelsea Antiques Fair **113**
Chelsea Gardener **114**
Chenil Galleries **116**
Dolce & Gabbana **119**
Harrods **123**
Harvey Nichols **126**

Jigsaw **125**
Katharine Hamnett **120**
Margaret Howell **121**
Pandora **127**
Paul Costelloe **122**
Peter Jones **118**
Rococo **112**
Steinberg & Tolkein **115**
Vivienne Westwood **111**

The Index

Agent Provocateur (p. 183) WEST END Joe Corré's snottily super-groovy boudoir boutique for racy undies. Get the transparent tangerine nylon with kingfisher lace–trim bra you've been look-ing for.... *Tel 020/7439-0229. www.agentprovocateur.com. 6 Broadwick St. W1. Tube: Oxford Circus. Open Mon–Sat 11am–7pm.*

See Map 21 on p. 192, bullet 79.

A la Mode (p. 183) KNIGHTSBRIDGE Opposite Harrods is this tiny *boutique* stocking the hottest designers for wardrobe invest-ments.... *Tel 020/7584-2133. 36 Hans Crescent, SW1. Tube: Knightsbridge. Open Mon–Sat 10am–6pm.*

See Map 22 on p. 194, bullet 124.

Antiquarius (p. 188) CHELSEA A long-established collection of antique dealers, with especially notable Art Deco.... *Tel 020/ 7351-5353. 131–141 King's Rd. SW3. Tube: Sloane Sq. Open Mon–Sat 10am–6pm.*

See Map 22 on p. 194, bullet 117.

Antique Clothing Shop (p. 184) NOTTING HILL This secret address is the cat's miaow for exceptional pieces circa 1880 to 1970. Kate bleedin' Moss shops here, so go figure.... *Tel 020/ 8964-4830. 282 Portobello Rd. W10. Tube: Ladbroke Grove. Open Fri–Sat 9am–6pm or by appointment.*

See Map 20 on p. 176, bullet 4.

Any Amount of Books (p. 189) WEST END Take this secondhand (as opposed to antiquarian) store on book row literally.... *Tel 020/7836-3697. www.anyamountofbooks.com. 56 Charing Cross Rd. WC2. Tube: Leicester Sq. Open daily 10:30am–9:30pm.*

See Map 21 on p. 192, bullet 59.

Asprey (p. 189) WEST END Jewelry, silver, leather goods, crystal, and bone china exquisitely served by this swanky gift emporium.... *Tel 020/7493-6767. 167 New Bond St. W1. Tube: Bond St. Open Mon–Fri 9am–5:30pm, Sat 10am–5pm.*

See Map 21 on p. 192, bullet 92.

Bermondsey Market (p. 187) SOUTH BANK Take a flashlight and join the serious antiques collectors and trade professionals here at dawn. If you go later, you miss the choicest pieces and the best atmosphere. *Bermondsey Sq. SE1. Tube: Borough. Open Fri 5am–noon.*

See Map 20 on p. 176, bullet 31.

Bernard Quaritch (p. 190) WEST END Fine rare manuscripts and antiquarian volumes, priced in dollars and pounds. Know what you want before you go.... *Tel 020/7734-2983. www.quaritch. com. 5–8 Lower John St. W1. Tube: Piccadilly Circus. Open Mon–Fri 9am–6pm or by appointment.*

See Map 21 on p. 192, bullet 66.

Berwick Street Market (p. 188) WEST END Soho's fresh fruit and veg market provides great produce and local color in every sense; bargain prices, too. *Berwick and Rupert streets W1. Tube: Leicester Sq. Open Mon–Sat 9am–6pm.*

See Map 21 on p. 192, bullet 48.

Betty Jackson (p. 183) SOUTH KENSINGTON With her kind cuts, interesting textures, and extraordinary color combos, Jackson's women's collection is always a hot seller.... *Tel 020/7589-7884. www.bettyjackson.com. 311 Brompton Rd. SW3. Tube: South Kensington. Open Mon–Fri 10:30am–6:30pm,Sat 10am–6pm, Sun noon–5pm.*

See Map 20 on p. 176, bullet 14.

Bluebird (p. 191) CHELSEA Sir Terence "omni" Conran's gastro enterprise in Chelsea, with huge *traiteur* and grocery, faux market stalls, restaurants (see the Dining chapter). Worth a miss if you don't want to feel manipulated.... *Tel 020/7559-1000. 350 King's Rd. SW3. Tube: Sloane Sq. Open Mon–Sat 9am–10pm, Sun noon–6pm.*

See Map 22 on p. 194, bullet 110.

Books for Cooks (p. 190) NOTTING HILL Thousands of tomes on food and how to prepare it, plus a lovely little cafe that serves a great inexpensive lunch or tea.... *Tel 020/7221-1992. www. booksforcooks.com. 4 Blenheim Crescent. Tube: Notting Hill Gate. Open Tues–Sat 10am–6pm. Closed Dec 24–Jan 1, last 3 weeks in Aug.*

See Map 20 on p. 176, bullet 5.

Brick Lane Market (p. 188) SHOREDITCH For our money, this is the most fun Sunday market—you'll find everything from bric-a-brac and antiques to bikes and bagels. It's best early.... *Brick Lane EC1, east to Cheshire St., north to Club Row. Tube: Shoreditch. Open Sun 6am–1pm.*

See Map 20 on p. 176, bullet 28.

British Antique Dealers' Association Fair (p. 188) KNIGHTS-
BRIDGE The newest of the big fairs happens in late March....
*Tel 020/7589-6108 for information. 20 Rutland Gate, SW7. Tube:
Knightsbridge.*
See Map 22 on p. 194, bullet 128.

Browns (p. 182, 184) WEST END One-stop shopping if you live for
fashion and have healthy plastic. All known designers live in connected shops, with Browns' own label providing missing links.
Don't forget **Labels for Less** at number 50.... *Tel 020/7491-
7833. 23–27 S. Molton St. W1. Tube: Bond St. Open Mon–Sat
10am–6:30pm.*
See Map 21 on p. 192, bullet 96.

Burberrys Factory Shop (p. 184) BETHNAL GREEN East End
outlet store for the famous plaid-lined quintessentially Brit
macs for tourists, and related clothing and paraphernalia....
*Tel 020/8985-3344. 29–53 Chatham Place E9. Tube: Bethnal
Green, then 106, Bus 253. Open Mon–Fri 11am–6pm, Sat
10am–5pm, Sun 11am–5pm.*
See Map 20 on p. 176, bullet 27.

Butler & Wilson (p. 186) WEST END Come out dripping with diamanté, multicolored rhinestones, gilt, and jet, and still managing
to look chic.... *Tel 020/7409-2955. 20 S. Molton St. W1. Tube:
Bond St. Tel 0207/352-3045. 189 Fulham Rd. SW3. Tube: South
Kensington. Open Mon–Sat 10am–6pm, Thurs 10am–7pm, Sun
noon–6pm.*
See Map 20 on p. 176, bullet 12.

The Button Queen (p. 197) WEST END An array of clothes closers,
from antique, precious, and collectible to wacky, handmade, and
just plain useful.... *Tel 020/7935-1505. www.thebuttonqueen.co.
uk. 19 Marylebone Lane W1. Tube: Bond St. Open Mon–Wed
10am–5pm, Thurs–Fri 10am–6am, Sat 10am–4pm.*

Camden Garden Centre (p. 190) CAMDEN This gardenlike
outdoor store is a living catalog for the green-thumbed....
*Tel 020/7485-8468. 2 Barker Dr., St. Pancras Way NW1. Tube:
Camden Town. Open Mon–Sat 9am–5pm, Sun 10am–4pm.*
See Map 20 on p. 176, bullet 20.

Camden Lock (p. 184, 188) CAMDEN A teeny-bopper fave, this
labyrinthine maze in warehouse and railway buildings both historic and fake 'round the Regent's Canal gets beyond busy on
sunny Sundays. *Camden Lock, Chalk Farm Rd., all down Camden
High St. NW1. Tube: Camden Town, Chalk Farm. Open Sat–Sun
10am–6pm; limited stalls daily 9:30am–5:30pm.*
See Map 20 on p. 176, bullet 21.

THE INDEX

SHOPPING

Camden Passage (p. 188) CAMDEN Twice-a-week antiques market still offers the odd bargain. Shops augment stalls.... Tel 020/ 7359-9969. Camden Passage, Upper St. N1. Tube: Angel. Open Wed 8am–1pm, Sat 10am–3pm.

See Map 20 on p. 176, bullet 22.

Chelsea Antiques Fair (p. 188) CHELSEA Twice a year (March and Sept), dealers of pre-1830 pieces congregate at Chelsea's Old Town Hall.... Tel 01444/482-514 for info. King's Rd. SW3. Tube: Sloane Sq.

See Map 22 on p. 194, bullet 113.

Chelsea Gardener (p. 190) CHELSEA The toniest of garden stores, with multitudes of ideas to steal, and yard accessories to buy.... Tel 020/7352-5656. 125 Sydney St. SW3. Tube: Sloane Sq. Open Mon–Sat 10am–6pm, Sun 11am–5pm.

See Map 22 on p. 194, bullet 114.

Chenil Galleries (p. 188) CHELSEA This sister to Antiquarius has higher price tags and more serious pieces.... Tel 020/7351-5353. 181–183 King's Rd. SW3. Tube: Sloane Sq. Open Mon–Sat 10am–6pm.

See Map 22 on p. 194, bullet 116.

Columbia Road Flower Market (p. 189, 190) SHOREDITCH Heaven for flower fans, gardeners, or people with a spare Sunday morning, this is the cut-flower, bedding-plant, and yard-accoutrement bargain center of Europe.... (add rest of ellipses) Gosset St. to the Royal Oak pub E2. Tube: Old St. Open Sun 8am–1pm.

See Map 20 on p. 176, bullet 26.

Comme des Garçons (p. 183) WEST END Rei Kawakubo's structural, collectible art clothes are augmented by her more affordable lines.... Tel 020/7493-1258. 59 Brooke St. W1. Tube: Bond St. Open Mon–Wed and Fri–Sat 10am–6, Thurs 10am–7pm.

See Map 21 on p. 192, bullet 94.

Couturière (p. 185) WEST END Inexpensive but highly skilled alterations. Let Takako Sato make the outfit you love fit you like a glove.... Tel 020/7493-1564. Second floor, 22 Brook St. W1. Tube: Bond St. By appointment.

See Map 21 on p. 192, bullet 93.

Czech & Speake (p. 189) WEST END Mecca for bathroom-hardware fanatics desirous of Italian brushed-steel faucets.... Tel 020/7439-0216. www.czechspeake.com. 39c Jermyn St. SW1. Tube: Piccadilly Circus. Open Mon–Sat 10am–6pm.

See Map 21 on p. 192, bullet 67.

Dance Books (p. 189) WEST END Also magazines and memorabilia for balletomanes.... Tel 020/7836-2314. 9 Cecil Court WC2. Tube: Leicester Sq. Open Mon–Sat 10am–6pm.

See Map 21 on p. 192, bullet 62.

Daunt Books (p. 189) MARYLEBONE This handsome galleried shop covers travel worldwide.... *Tel 020/7224-2295. 83 Marylebone High St. W1. Tube: Baker St. Open Mon–Sat 10am–6pm.*
See Map 21 on p. 192, bullet 32.

Davidoff Cigars (p. 187) WEST END Mainly Davidoff, but all the rare breeds are carried here, plus European packaged varieties in all cigar sizes, sold by appropriately snotty gents.... *Tel 020/7930-3079. 35 St. James's St. SW1. Tube: Green Park. Open Mon–Sat 10am–6pm.*
See Map 21 on p. 192, bullet 81.

Debenhams (p. 181) WEST END Not London's most exciting department store, but this part of the Burton Group empire keeps prices on the low side, and contains a few designer surprises, including Jasper Conran's "J" collection.... *Tel 020/ 7580-3000. www.debehams.co.uk. 334–338 Oxford St. W1. Tube: Bond St. Open Mon–Tues and Thurs–Fri 9:30am–8pm, Wed 10am–8pm, Sun noon–6pm.*
See Map 21 on p. 192, bullet 36.

Designer Secondhand Store (p. 184) HAMPSTEAD Does exactly what it says on the can. Expect the straighter labels— Mugler and Muir, not Ozbek and Westwood—with friendly service.... *Tel 020/7431-8618. 24 Hampstead High St. NW3. Tube: Hampstead. Open daily 11:30am–6pm.*
See Map 20 on p. 176, bullet 17.

Designs (p. 184) HAMPSTEAD This other Hampstead designer secondhand shop is the more staid of the two (Prada and Donna Karan), but everything is scrupulously as-new.... *Tel 020/7435-0100. 60 Rosslyn Hill NW3. Tube: Hampstead. Open Mon–Sat 10am–5:45pm, Thurs 10am–6:30pm, Sun by appointment.*
See Map 20 on p. 176, bullet 18.

Dickens & Jones (p. 181) WEST END With its recent face-lift, this department store went from old-fashioned to good on fashion, especially the midprice lines on the ground (first) floor.... *Tel 020/7734-7070. 224–244 Regent St. W1. Tube: Oxford Circus. Open Mon–Wed and Fri–Sat 9:30am–6pm, Thurs 9:30am–8pm.*
See Map 21 on p. 192, bullet 87.

Dinny Hall (p. 186) NOTTING HILL Jeweler Dinny favors silver, turning out wearable, beautifully crafted pieces at reasonable prices.... *Tel 020/7792-3913. 200 Westbourne Grove W11. Tube: Notting Hill Gate. Open Mon–Sat 10am–6pm, Thurs 11am–7pm.*
See Map 20 on p. 176, bullet 3.

The Dispensary (p. 184) WEST END Four branches of this hip clothes emporium serve up the longer-lasting (i.e., well-made) model of street style: Patrick Cox's Wannabes, Schott leathers, Stüssy, and its own label.... *Tel 020/7287-8145. 9 Newburgh St.*

THE INDEX

SHOPPING

(menswear at number 15) W1. Tube: Oxford Circus. Open (all branches) Mon–Sat 9:30am–6pm. Tel 020/7221-9290. 25 Pembridge Rd. W11. Tube: Notting Hill Gate. Tel 020/7727-8797. 200 Kensington Park Rd. W11. Tube: Notting Hill Gate.

See Map 21 on p. 192, bullet 46.

Dolce & Gabbana (p. 183) KNIGHTSBRIDGE Beautifully tailored, sexy, expensive clothes by Italians.... Tel 020/7235-0335. 175 Sloane St. SW1. Tube: Knightsbridge. Open Mon–Sat 10am–6pm.

See Map 22 on p. 194, bullet 119.

Duffer of St. George (p. 184) COVENT GARDEN Perennially hip club garb from this menswear street stylist, with added sports stuff and U.S. labels (Phat Farm, Antoni & Alison).... Tel 020/7379-4660. 29 Shorts Gardens WC2. Tube: Covent Garden. Open Mon–Sat 10am–6pm.

See Map 21 on p. 192, bullet 107.

Emporio Armani (p. 183) KNIGHTSBRIDGE Oh, you know what this is like. Three London branches.... Tel 0207/491-8080. 1129 New Bond St. W1. Tube: Bond St. Open (all branches) Mon–Sat 10am–6pm, Sun noon–5pm. Tel 020/7917-6882. 57–59 Long Acre WC2. Tube: Covent Garden. Tel 020/7823-8818. 191 Brompton Rd. SW3. Tube: Knightsbridge.

See Map 21 on p. 192, bullet 89.

Favourbrook (p. 185) WEST END Brocades and damasks, silks, velvets, and embroidered linens get made into exquisite vests, jackets, and frock coats at this coed tailor. Perfect wedding wear.... Tel 020/7491-2337. 55 Jermyn St. SW1. Tube: Green Park. Open Mon–Wed 9:30am–6:30pm, Thurs–Fri 9:30am–7pm, Sat 10am–6pm.

See Map 21 on p. 192, bullet 70.

Fenwick (p. 181) WEST END Four floors of fashion. Standout departments are lingerie and a designer floor with Betty Jackson, Jean Muir, Paul Costelloe, Jasper Conran, Nicole Farhi, and Georges Rech.... Tel 020/7629-9161. 63 New Bond St. W1. Tube: Bond St. Open Mon–Sat 9:30am–6pm, Sun noon–5pm.

See Map 21 on p. 192, bullet 90.

Floris (p. 186, 187) WEST END Fine soaps and scents and toiletry items (hair brushes) and grooming aids sold in a marvelous wood-paneled shop that opened in 1851.... Tel 020/7930-5336. 39 Jermyn St. SW1. Tube: Piccadilly Circus. Open Mon–Sat 10am–6pm.

See Map 21 on p. 192, bullet 71.

Fortnum & Mason (p. 178, 181, 186, 191) WEST END The ne plus ultra of grocers has the royal warrant for her very majesty, plus gifts for your entire list, and a quaint clock in front. Check out the

other lovely, pricey, old-fashioned departments, too.... *Tel 020/ 7734-8040. 181 Piccadilly W1. Tube: Piccadilly Circus/Green Park. Open Mon–Sat 10am–6:30pm, Sun noon–6pm.*
See Map 21 on p. 192, bullet 74.

Foyles (p. 189) WEST END The biggest bookstore in town is also the least organized, but this has its charm, since it's such fun to get lost in the stacks.... *Tel 020/7437-5660. www.foyles.com. 119 Charing Cross Rd. WC2. Tube: Leicester Sq. Open Mon–Sat 9:30am–8pm, Sun noon–6pm.*
See Map 21 on p. 192, bullet 49.

French's Theatre Bookshop (p. 189) BLOOMSBURY This aims to stock every play in the English language that's in print.... *Tel 020/787-9373. 52 Fitzroy St. W1. Tube: Warren St. Open Mon–Fri 9:30am–5:30pm, Sat 11am–5pm.*
See Map 21 on p. 192, bullet 101.

Gallery of Antique Costume & Textiles (p. 188) MARYLEBONE Another shop you can treat as a museum, except you'll want to walk out with a 1920s tea gown, a chenille throw, an embroidered pillow, or one of the reproduction brocade vests they fashion here.... *Tel 020/7723-9981. 2 Church St. NW8. Tube: Marylebone. Open Wed–Sat 10am–6pm, Tues by appt.*
See Map 20 on p. 176, bullet 15.

Garrard (p. 185) WEST END Paired with Asprey, this gallery shop is studded with precious gems and laden with gold. They polish the crown jewels here.... *Tel 020/7493-6767. 167 New Bond St. W1. Tube: Oxford Circus. Open Mon–Fri 9:30am–5:30pm, Sat 10am–5pm.*
See Map 21 on p. 192, bullet 92.

Geoff Slack (p. 185) SHEPHERD'S BUSH No job is too large or too small, from duplicating your fave cotton T-shirt to a customized rubber bodysuit.... *Tel 020/8743-7713. Goldhawk Rd. W12. Tube: Shepherd's Bush. Open by appointment.*
See Map 20 on p. 176, bullet 10.

Georgina von Etzdorf (p. 186) WEST END Darling of the fashion pages, Von Etzdorf produces England's most desirably opulent scarves and clothing, as well as home furnishings in precious materials.... *Tel 020/7409-7789. 1–2 Burlington Arcade W1. Tube: Piccadilly Circus. Open Mon–Sat 9:30am–6pm.*
See Map 21 on p. 192, bullet 73.

Gianni Versace (p. 183) WEST END This marble palace with the snootiest staff in the kingdom exactly matches Versace's gaudy, gilt-embossed, dominatrix-wear.... *Tel 020/7499-1862. 34–36 Old Bond St. W1. Tube: Green Park. Open Mon–Fri 10am–6pm, Sat 10am–5pm.*
See Map 21 on p. 192, bullet 83.

THE INDEX

SHOPPING

Gieves & Hawkes (p. 185, 188) WEST END One of Savile Row's best-known, yet also most approachable, bespoke tailors has fiendish rates, but for the best.... *Tel 020/7434-2001. 1 Savile Row W1. Tube: Piccadilly Circus. Mon–Fri 10am–5:30pm, Sat 10am–5pm.*
See Map 21 on p. 192, bullet 75.

Grays Antiques Market (p. 188) WEST END One of those collections of collectors, conveniently located downtown, and not over-priced.... *Tel 020/7629-7034. S. Molton Lane W1. Tube: Bond St. tube. Mon–Fri 11am–5pm.*
See Map 21 on p. 192, bullet 95.

Grosvenor House (p. 188) WEST END For a week in June, the toniest of antiquing opportunities.... *Tel 0207/399-8100. Le Meridien Grosvenor House, Park Lane W1. Tube: Marble Arch.*
See Map 21 on p. 192, bullet 100.

Hamleys (p. 179, 190) WEST END The vastest toy shop in Europe creates major problems for parents trying to reach the exit.... *Tel 020/7734-3161. 188–196 Regent St. W1. Tube: Oxford Circus. Open Mon–Wed 10am–6:30pm, Thurs 10am–8pm, Fri 10am–7pm, Sat 9:30am–7pm, Sun noon–6pm.*
See Map 21 on p. 192, bullet 80.

Harrods (p. 179, 182, 189, 191) KNIGHTSBRIDGE The one and only. Go ogle the food hall, visit the pets, covet stuff in the young-designer room, then get an olive-green-and-gold logo bag so you'll feel like you've accomplished something. The sales are essential.... *Tel 020/7730-1234. www.harrods.com. 87–155 Brompton Rd. SW1. Tube: Knightsbridge. Open Mon–Sat 10am–7pm.*
See Map 22 on p. 194, bullet 123.

Harvey Nichols (p. 182, 186) KNIGHTSBRIDGE Here are Galliano, Dolce & Gabbana, Rifat Ozbek, Claude Montana, Jil Sander, Moschino, and oh, thousands more, including new young Brits-to-watch.... *Tel 020/7235-5000. www.harveynichols.com. 109–125 Knightsbridge SW1. Tube: Knightsbridge. Open Mon–Tues, Sat 10am–7pm, Wed–Fri 10am–8pm, Sun noon–6pm.*
See Map 22 on p. 194, bullet 126.

Hatchards (p. 189) WEST END This wood-paneled store, with its royal warrant and helpful staff, is a most pleasant way to stock up on reading matter; it was Oscar Wilde's favorite.... *Tel 020/7439-9921. www.hatchards.com. 187 Piccadilly W1. Tube: Piccadilly Circus/Green Park. Open daily 10am–6pm, Sun noon–6pm.*
See Map 21 on p. 192, bullet 72.

Hennes (H&M) (p. 190) KENSINGTON The hottest fashion moments frozen in cheap materials for addicts who need high turnover, which means teenage and 20-something girls (and

boys, too). Kids' department, too.... *Tel 020/7493-8557. 481 Oxford St. W1. Tube: Oxford Circus. Tel 020/7493-4004. 261 Regent St. W1. Tube: Oxford Circus. Tel 020/7937-3329. 123 Kensington High St. W8. Tube: Kensington High St. Open Mon–Sat 10am–6pm (Thurs until 8pm), Sun noon–6pm.*
See Map 20 on p. 176, bullet 9.

Holt's Footwear (p. 194) CAMDEN Now over a century old, this wee store next to Camden tube still supplies rude boys (Madness and the Specials shopped here) with 20-hole DMs (Doc Martens), monkey boots, and house-brand Gladiator boots.... *Tel 020/7485-8505. 5 Kentish Town Rd. NW1. Tube: Camden Town. Open Mon–Sat 9:30am–5:30pm, Sun 11am–4pm.*
See Map 20 on p. 176, bullet 23.

Honest Jon's (p. 190) NOTTING HILL A vinyl destination for about 3 decades, this is black-music central, from jazz and funk to soul and reggae, vintage and rare, plus new CDs.... *Tel 020/8969-9822. 276–278 Portobello Rd. W10. Tube: Ladbroke Grove. Open Mon–Sat 10am–6pm, Sun 11am–5pm.*
See Map 20 on p. 176, bullet 2.

Hope & Glory (p. 188) KENSINGTON Commemorative china is an egalitarian antique, easily within reach of all pockets, as long as you don't mind a mere Liz's Silver Jubilee mug; more exalted anniversaries have higher prices.... *Tel 020/7727-8424. 131A Kensington Church St. W8. Tube: Notting Hill Gate. Open Mon–Sat 10am–5pm.*
See Map 20 on p. 176, bullet 8.

Humla (p. 190) WEST END Under-eights (years, that is, not size) almost welcome clothes gifts when they're colorful fun things from here and backed up by a Humla wooden toy.... *Tel 020/ 7224-1773. 23 St. Christopher's Place W1. Tube: Bond St. Open Mon–Sat 10:30am–7pm, Sun noon–6pm.*
See Map 21 on p. 192, bullet 34.

Irish Linen Co. (p. 189) WEST END Delicious, pristine bed linens and home accessories made of that crunchy, rare fabric.... *Tel 020/7493-8949. www.irish-linen.com. 35–36 Burlington Arcade W1.tube: Piccadilly Circus/Green Park. Open Mon–Sat 10am–5:30pm.*
See Map 21 on p. 192, bullet 73.

Jackie Palmer (p. 185) WEST END Allow 3 weeks (ideally) for one of Jackie's gorgeous, boned, strapless dresses. (Push-up bras? Who needs 'em?) Also specializes in maternity bridal wear (?!) and men's vests.... *Tel 020/7734-0755. W1. Tube: Piccadilly Circus. Open by appointment.*

James Lock (p. 189) WEST END Hats to the gentry since 1676. A bowler costs from about £175 ($289), but they also sell more modern headgear; for women, too.... *Tel 020/7930-5849. www.jameslock.co.uk. 6 St. James's St. SW1. Tube: Green Park. Open Mon–Sat 10am–5:30pm.*

See Map 21 on p. 192, bullet 82.

James Smith & Sons (p. 186) WEST END Every umbrella under the sun, or rain. Also riding crops, shooting sticks, walking canes, and other thwackers sold in handsome Victorian premises.... *Tel 020/7836-4731. www.jamessmith.co.uk. 53 New Oxford St. WC1. Tube: Tottenham Court Rd. Open Mon–Fri 9:30am–5:25pm, Sat 10am–5:25pm.*

See Map 21 on p. 192, bullet 51.

Janet Fitch (p. 186) COVENT GARDEN Jewelry, bags, and objets are hand-picked by Ms. Fitch, who's known to have the most perfect taste in town.... *Tel 020/7287-3789. 37a Neal St. WC2. Tube: Covent Garden. Open Mon–Sat 11am–7pm, Sun 1am–6pm.*

See Map 21 on p. 192, bullet 55.

Jasper Conran (p. 181, 183) WEST END The clothing Conran doesn't have a store of his own, but you can find his women's tailored stuff at Harrods, Selfridges, Harvey Nick's, Fenwick, and A la Mode, plus his affordable "J" collection at Debenhams....

See Map 21 on p. 192, bullet 36.

John Lewis (p. 181) WEST END "Never Knowingly Undersold" is a boast not bearing close scrutiny; still, this no-frills department store is pretty unbeatable for practical homemaking items and more.... *Tel 0207/629-7711. www.johnlewis.com. 278–306 Oxford St. W1. Tube: Oxford Circus. Open Mon–Wed and Fri–Sat 9:30am–7pm, Thurs 9:30am–8pm.*

See Map 21 on p. 192, bullet 41.

Joseph (p. 183) WEST END Joseph Ettedgui has had a major influence on how London dresses and furnishes for 2 decades. He doesn't design himself, but has an eye to buy what the English want, at midprice. Monochrome, youthful, fitted, or knitted is the tone.... *Tel 020/7629-3713. 23 Old Bond St. W1. Tube: Green Park. Open Mon–Sat 10am–6:30pm.*

See Map 21 on p. 192, bullet 86.

Katharine Hamnett (p. 183) KNIGHTSBRIDGE Half bad-girl, half environmental activist, Hamnett's clothes are similarly schizoid, with spandex and canvas, nicely cut jackets, and slut dresses, plus the good Hamnett Active jeans line.... *Tel 020/7823-1002. 20 Sloane St. SW1. Tube: Knightsbridge. Open Mon–Sat 10am–6pm.*

See Map 22 on p. 194, bullet 120.

Kristin Baybars (p. 191) HAMPSTEAD Everything for the doll's house, including the doll's house—this tiny place is unrivaled.... *Tel 020/7267-0934. 7 Mansfield Rd. NW3. BR: Gospel Oak. Open Tues–Sat 11am–6pm.*

See Map 20 on p. 176, bullet 19.

Labels for Less (p. 184) See also "Browns," above.

Liberty (p. 179, 181, 186, 187) WEST END What started as an importer of Asian goods is the most enticing department store in town, with lovely Liberty prints, good jewelry, accessories, and fashion housed in Arts and Crafts grandeur.... *Tel 020/7734-1234.www.liberty.co.uk. 214 Regent St. W1.Tube: Oxford Circus. Open Mon–Wed 10am–6:30pm, Thurs 10am–8pm, Fri–Sat 10am–7pm, Sun noon–6pm.*

See Map 21 on p. 192, bullet 88.

Lillywhite's (p. 187) WEST END Sports nirvana, with six floors of paraphernalia, kit, and garb for the usual jock competitions, British games, and cruel and unusual activities you've never heard of. The goods are high ticket, high quality.... *Tel 020/7915-4000. 24–36 Lower Regent St. SW1. Tube: Piccadilly Circus. Open Mon–Sat 10am–6pm, Sun 11am–5pm.*

See Map 21 on p. 192, bullet 65.

The Linen Cupboard (p. 189) WEST END Bargain bedclothes; good things mixed up with tat in this chaotic shop.... *Tel 020/7629-4062. 21 Great Castle St. W1. Tube: Oxford Circus. Open Mon–Sat 10am–5:30pm.*

See Map 21 on p. 192, bullet 43.

London Silver Vaults (p. 188) HOLBORN About two dozen traders have gathered under this roof since the mid–19th century. Bargains are possible.... *Tel 020/7242-3844. Chancery House, 53–64 Chancery Lane WC2. Tube: Chancery Lane. Open Mon–Fri 9am–5:30pm, Sat 9am–1pm.*

See Map 21 on p. 192, bullet 104.

Lonsdale (p. 187) WEST END The place for pugilists, and for those who just imitate them, this British answer to Everlast and Reyes does a leisurewear line.... *Tel 020/7437-1526. 47 Beak St. W1. Tube: Oxford Circus. Open Mon–Sat 10–5:30pm.*

Lush (p. 186, 187) COVENT GARDEN A chain of unique organic soap and cosmetics stores where handmade soap is cut to order and you can ladle up your own facial masks.... *Tel 020/7240-4570. www.lush.co.uk. 7–11 The Piazza, Covent Garden WC2. Tube: Covent*

THE INDEX

SHOPPING

Garden. Open (all branches) Mon–Sat 10am–6pm, Sun noon–5pm. 123 King's Rd. SW3. Tube: Sloane Sq. 96 Kensington High St. Tube: High Street Kensington. 40 Carnaby St. W1. Tube: Oxford St.
See Map 21 on p. 192, bullet 106.

Margaret Howell (p. 183) KNIGHTSBRIDGE Unpretentious, tailored English clothes that nod to the equestrian for men and women.... *Tel 020/7009-9009. www.margarethowell.co.uk. 34 Wigmore St. W1. Tube: Bond St. Tel 0207/584-2462. 29 Beauchamp Place SW3. Tube: Knightsbridge. Open Mon–Sat 10am–5:30pm.*
See Map 22 on p. 194, bullet 121.

Marks & Spencer (p. 178, 182, 189) WEST END Whatever their social strata, Londoners shop M&S for underwear and sweaters. Clothes are inexpensive, well made, and getting more exciting by the season. The food department is equally adored, and there are branches all over.... *Tel 020/7935-7954. www.marksand spencer.com. 459 Oxford St. W1. Tube: Marble Arch. Open Mon–Fri 9am–8pm, Sat 9am–7pm, Sun noon–6pm.*
See Map 21 on p. 192, bullet 44.

Marlborough Fine Art (p. 189) WEST END Where to shop for an old master—or just look like one.... *Tel 020/7629-5161. www. marlboroughfineart.com. 6 Albermarle St. W1. Tube: Green Park. Open Mon–Fri 10am–5:30pm, Sat 10am–2:30pm.*
See Map 21 on p. 192, bullet 85.

MDC Classic Music (p. 190) WEST END Everything for the opera queen, including recordings, books, postcards, and expert advice, right next to the Coliseum, where the English National Opera performs.... *Tel 020/7240-0270. www.mdcclassicmusic. co.uk. 31–32 St. Martin's Lane WC2. Tube: Leicester Sq. Open Mon 10am–6pm, Tues–Sat 10am–7:30pm.*
See Map 21 on p. 192, bullet 63.

Miss Selfridge (p. 182) WEST END Hip high-school girls find con-stantly metamorphosing clothing here to gratify short attention spans and modest allowances.... *Tel 020/7318-3833. 40 Duke St. W1. Tube: Bond St. Open Mon–Wed 10am–7pm, Thurs–Fri 10am–8pm, Sat 10am–7pm, Sun noon–6pm.*
See Map 21 on p. 192, bullet 97.

Mr. Eddie (p. 185) WEST END Over 35 years in the biz; this is another store with a big celeb clientele. Large stock of fabric (including Austin Powers' shagadelic velvet) means fast turn-around for a simple suit.... *Tel 020/7437-3727. 52 Berwick St. W1. Tube: Piccadilly Circus. Open Mon–Fri 8:30am–5:30pm, Sat 8:30am–1pm.*

Mole Jazz (p. 190) ST. PANCRAS Probably the best of all London's excellent jazz stores, with a load of rare stuff and comprehensive stacks of new CDs, too. Also runs a thrice yearly mail auction—

check out the website.... *Tel 020/7278-8623. www.molejazz.co. uk. 311 Gray's Inn Rd. WC1. King's Cross. Open Mon–Sat 10am– 6pm.*

See Map 21 on p. 192, bullet 103.

Mothercare (p. 190) WEST END One-stop shopping for baby and toddler needs; low prices, high quality.... *Tel 020/7629-6621. 461 Oxford St. W1.Tube: Marble Arch. Open Mon–Sat 9:30am– 6pm, Sun noon–6pm.*

See Map 21 on p. 192, bullet 98.

Mulberry (p. 183) KNIGHTSBRIDGE Tweed hacking jackets, cord jodhpurs (but not for riding in), leather purses, belts, and wal- lets, tailored separates and staid dresses—not bargain, but top quality.... *Tel 020/7493-2546. 11 Gees Court W1. Tube: Bond St. Tel 020/7225-0313. 185 Brompton Rd. SW3. Tube: Knightsbridge. Open Mon–Sat 10am–5pm.*

See Map 21 on p. 192, bullet 91.

Museum Store (p. 186) HAMPSTEAD Collected goodies from museums around the world—from reproduction ancient artifacts to arty scarves; last-minute gifts that make you look like you shopped your heart out.... *Tel 020/7431-7156. 4 Perrins Court NW3. Tube: Hampstead. Open Mon–Sat 10am–6pm, Sun 11am– 5pm.*

See Map 20 on p. 176, bullet 16.

Neal Street East (p. 189) COVENT GARDEN Gorgeous gifts on a budget, many penny toys, kitchenware, and knickknacks from Asia make this long-running store fun.... *Tel 020/7240-0135. 5 Neal St. WC2. Tube: Covent Garden. Open Mon–Wed 11am–7pm, Thurs–Sat 10am–7pm, Sun noon–6pm.*

See Map 21 on p. 192, bullet 52.

Neal's Yard Dairy (p. 191) COVENT GARDEN Cheeses from the British Isles, many rare, unpasteurized farmhouse specials.... *Tel 020/7379-7646. 17 Shorts Gardens WC2. Tube: Covent Garden. Open Mon–Sat 9am–7pm, Sun 11am–5pm.*

See Map 21 on p. 192, bullet 53.

Neal's Yard Remedies (p. 186) COVENT GARDEN London's best holistic-healing, herbalist, massage therapist, natural-foods cen- ter; wonderful natural remedies in cobalt-blue bottles.... *Tel 020/7379-7222. 15 Neal's Yard (off Shorts Gardens) WC2. Tube: Covent Garden. Open Mon–Sat 10am–6pm, Sun 11am– 5pm.*

See Map 21 on p. 192, bullet 54.

Nicole Farhi (p. 183) WEST END Wearable, well-made suits and separates in muted colors and natural fibers, and at medium fashionability and cost for both male and female grown-ups.... *Tel 020/7499-8368. 158 New Bond St. W1. Tube: Bond St. Open* *(all branches) Mon–Sat 10am–6pm. Tel 020/7497-8713. 11 Floral St. WC2. Tube: Covent Garden. Tel 020/7486-3416. 26 St. Christopher's Place W1. Tube: Bond St. Tel 020/7235-0877. 193 Sloane St. SW1. Tube: Knightsbridge.*

See Map 21 on p. 192, bullet 37.

Oasis (p. 182) COVENT GARDEN Inexpensive, reasonably trendy clothes for young career girls. Color is a strong suit.... *Tel 020/ 7240-7445. 13 James St. WC2. Tube: Covent Garden. Open Mon–Sat 10am–7pm (8pm Thurs), Sun noon–7pm.*

See Map 21 on p. 192, bullet 105.

Paddy Campbell (p. 183) WEST END Campbell's suits and frocks in natural fabrics and non-hysterical cuts come off as if tailored just for you, and swift alterations are offered at her boutique.... *Tel 020/7493-5646. 8 Gees Court, St. Christopher's Place W1. Tube: Bond St. Open Mon–Fri 10am–6pm, Thurs 10am–7pm, Sat 10:30am–6pm.*

See Map 21 on p. 192, bullet 38.

Pandora (p. 184) KNIGHTSBRIDGE There is so much top-quality used designer garb here that there are entire Armani and Chanel sections. Plenty of other names and labels, too.... *Tel 020/ 7589-5289. 16–22 Cheval Place SW7. Tube: Knightsbridge. Open Mon–Sat 9am–6pm.*

See Map 22 on p. 194, bullet 127.

Paul Costelloe (p. 183) KNIGHTSBRIDGE Best known for midprice Dressage collection of Irish linens and tweed suits. Costelloe also offers a high-fashion line.... *Tel 020/7589-9480. 156 Brompton Rd. SW3. Tube: Knightsbridge. Open Mon–Sat 10am– 6pm.*

See Map 22 on p. 194, bullet 122.

Paul Smith (p. 183, 184) WEST END The king of quirk has a flagship store in the heart of hip Notting Hill, and another just for the ladies with their little sprogs.... *Original flagship store: Tel 020/ 7379-7133. 40–44 Floral St. WC2. Tube: Covent Garden. Sale shop: Tel 020/7493-1287. 23 Avery Row W1. Tube: Bond St. Tel 020/7727-3553. 122 Kensington Park Rd. W11. Tube: Notting Hill. Tel 020/7589-9139. 84–86 Sloane Ave. SW3. Tube: Sloane Sq. Open Mon–Sat 10am–6pm.*

See Map 21 on p. 192, bullet 61.

Paxton & Whitfield (p. 191) WEST END The cheese shop of your dairy dreams is the oldest in the land, in beautiful period premises.... *Tel 020/7930-0259. 93 Jermyn St. SW1. Tube: Piccadilly Circus. Open Mon–Sat 9:30am–6pm.*

See Map 21 on p. 192, bullet 68.

Penhaligon's (p. 186, 187) COVENT GARDEN Gorgeous glass flagons with classic smells for your delectation. Founded by Victoria's court barber.... *Tel 020/7836-2150. www.penhaligons. com. 41 Wellington St. WC2. Tube: Covent Garden. Open Mon–Sat*

10am–6pm, Sun noon–6pm. Tel 020/7629-1416. 16 Burlington Arcade W1. Tube: Piccadilly Circus. Open Mon–Sat 9:30am–5:30pm. Tel 020/7493-0002. 20a Brook St. W1. Tube: Bond St. Open Mon–Sat 10am–6pm.

See Map 21 on p. 192, bullet 108.

Peter Jones (p. 182) KNIGHTSBRIDGE Where the Sloane Ranger mummy gets the cricket sweater and prep school uniform, plus her own twin set and pearls. Part of the John Lewis chain, PJ is also good for home wares and furnishings.... *Tel 020/7730-3434. www.peterjones.co.uk. Sloane Sq. SW1. Tube: Sloane Sq. Open Mon–Sat 9:30am–7pm.*

See Map 22 on p. 194, bullet 118.

Petticoat Lane Market (p. 188) THE CITY Famous street stalls of cheap leather jackets, underwear, CDs, and old gold; past its heyday, but still very cheap. *Middlesex/Goulston/Old Castle/Cutler Streets, Bell Lane. Tube: Liverpool St. Open Sun 9am–2pm.*

See Map 20 on p. 176, bullet 30.

Portobello Road Market (p. 188) NOTTING HILL Several markets in one, from the 2,000 antiques dealers of the Notting Hill end, past the fruit-and-veg traders, to the trendy stalls of vintage stuff under the Westway, and on into the junk of Goldborne Road. London's best, or at least most famous.... *Portobello Rd. W11–W10. Tube: Ladbroke Grove/Notting Hill Gate. Open: antiques Sat 7–5:30pm; general Mon–Sat 9am–5pm; closes 1pm Thurs.*

See Map 20 on p. 176, bullet 6.

Prada (p. 183) WEST END Every fashion victim and fashion editor's favorite fashion fetish.... *Tel 020/7235-0008. 43–5 Sloane St. SW3. Tube: Sloane Sq. Tel 020/7647-5000. 15–18 Old Bond St. Tube: Green Park. Open Mon–Sat 10am–6pm.*

See Map 21 on p. 192, bullet 84.

Reckless Records (p. 190) WEST END Here's another venerable vinyl destination, not a genre specialist, but well stocked with secondhand rock, pop, soul, jazz.... *Tel 020/7437-4271. 30 Berwick St. W1. Tube: Oxford Circus. Open daily 10am–7pm.*

See Map 21 on p. 192, bullet 47.

Richard James (p. 185, 189) WEST END The groovy face of Savile Row. You can preview his bespoke style by eyeing up the waiters at the Atlantic and the Ivy.... *Tel 020/7434-0605. 29 Savile Row W1. Tube: Piccadilly Circus. Open Mon–Fri 10am–6pm, Sat 11am–6pm.*

See Map 21 on p. 192, bullet 77.

River Island (p. 182) KENSINGTON Trendy, inexpensive fashion from this High Street chain, with the Charlotte Halton line going upmarket in suits and dresses for dressing up.... *Tel 020/7937-0224. 124 Kensington High St. W8. Tube: High Street*

Kensington. Open Mon–Sat 9am–6pm (Thurs 10am–7:30), Sun 11am–5pm.

See Map 20 on p. 176, bullet 7.

Rococo (p. 187, 191) KNIGHTSBRIDGE Chocoholic heaven, way beyond Hershey's, and even Valrhona—get sophisticated, organic, high-cocoa-content confections, and funny-shape novelties.... *Tel 020/7352-5857. 321 King's Rd. SW3. Tube: Sloane Sq. Open Mon–Sat 9am–7pm, Sun 10am–2pm.*

See Map 22 on p. 194, bullet 112.

R. Twining & Co. (p. 186) WEST END Where Twining's tea was brought into the world is still a shop, with a tea museum-ette attached.... *Tel 020/7353-3511. 216 Strand WC2. Tube: Temple. Open Mon–Sat 9:30am–6pm.*

See Map 21 on p. 192, bullet 109.

S & B Evans (p. 190) SHOREDITCH Pots for yards, in the Columbia Road Market for gardeners.... *Tel 020/7729-6635. 7a Ezra St. E2. Tube: Old St. Open Sun 8am–1pm.*

See Map 20 on p. 176, bullet 25.

Selfridges (p. 181, 191) WEST END A venerable department store, founded by an American. Food, fashion, and cosmetics are strong.... *Tel 020/7629-1234. 400 Oxford St. W1. Tube: Bond St. Open Mon–Wed 10am–7pm, Thurs–Fri 10am–8pm, Sat 9:30am–7pm, Sun noon–6pm.*

See Map 21 on p. 192, bullet 35.

Skoob Books (p. 189) BLOOMSBURY Well-stocked secondhand-book mecca, for when you know what you're after.... *Tel 020/7278-8760. www.skoob.com. 10 Brunswich Centre, Russell Sq. WC1. Tube: Russell Sq. Open Mon–Sat 11am–7pm, Sun noon–5pm.*

See Map 21 on p. 192, bullet 102.

Slim Barrett (p. 186) ISLINGTON This hip jeweler makes crowns for our times, and also home accessories.... *Tel 020/7354-9393. Studio 6, Shepperton House, 83–93 Shepperton Rd. N1. Tube: Angel. Open by appointment.*

See Map 20 on p. 176, bullet 24.

Soccer Scene (p. 187) WEST END Impress your teammates back home with an Arsenal uniform or a pair of British spikes.... *Tel 020/7439-0778, 56–57 Carnaby St. W1. Tel 020/7437-1966 (the year the English won the World Cup). 17 Foubert's Place W1. Tube (for both): Oxford Circus. Open Mon–Sat 10am–6pm, Sun 11am–5pm.*

See Map 21 on p. 192, bullet 78.

Spitalfields Market (p. 188) SPITALFIELDS An indoor collection of permanent stalls with a changing center; Sunday is greenmarket and crafts day.... *Tel 020/7247-6590. Commercial/Brushfield St. E1. Tube: Liverpool St. Open Mon–Fri, Sun 11am–3pm.*

See Map 20 on p. 176, bullet 29.

Sportspages (p. 189) WEST END The place for that unusual cricket tome you've been hunting for, or any other Brit-sport book.... *Tel 020/7240-9604. Caxton Walk, 94–96 Charing Cross Rd. WC2. Tube: Tottenham Court Rd. Open Mon–Sat 9:30am–7pm, Sun 11:30am–5pm.*

See Map 21 on p. 192, bullet 50.

Stanfords (p. 189) WEST END Maps, travel guides, and even globes in great abundance; international in scope.... *Tel 020/ 7836-1321. www.stanfords.co.uk. 12–14 Long Acre WC2. Tube: Leicester Sq. Open Mon and Wed–Sat 9am–7:30pm, Tues 9:30am–7:30pm, Sun noon–6pm.*

See Map 21 on p. 192, bullet 60.

Steinberg & Tolkein (p. 184) CHELSEA Museum-quality pre-1960 clothing in classy thrift-shop ambience downstairs; mountains of vintage costume jewelry upstairs.... *Tel 020/7376-3660. 193 King's Rd. SW3. Sloane Sq. Open Mon–Sat 10:30am–7pm.*

See Map 22 on p. 194, bullet 115.

The Tea House (p. 186, 189) COVENT GARDEN More varieties of tea than you can count, plus strainers, trivets, pots, and cozies.... *Tel 020/7240-7539. 15 Neal St. WC2. Tube: Covent Garden. Open Mon–Sat 10am–7pm, Sun noon–6pm.*

See Map 21 on p. 192, bullet 56.

Theo Fennell (p. 185) SOUTH KENSINGTON Gold ecclesiastical/ Renaissance-inspired shapes with cabochon gems, and exquisitely detailed silver miniatures are what Fennell does best. Top dollar.... *Tel 020/7591-5000. 169 Fulham Rd. SW3. Tube: South Kensington. Open Mon–Sat 10am–6pm, Sun noon–5pm.*

See Map 20 on p. 176, bullet 11.

Thomas Goode & Co. (p. 189) MAYFAIR The ultimate store for bone china and porcelain, crystal glassware, and related costly goods.... *Tel 020/7499-2823. 19 S. Audley St. W1. Tube: Green Park. Open Mon–Sat 10am–6pm.*

See Map 21 on p. 192, bullet 99.

Thornton's (p. 178, 187, 191) WEST END The confectioner that took over the U.K. started with Special Toffee (and it is), and progressed to Belgian-style cream truffles, kids' novelties, ice cream, and other goodies.... *Tel 020/7434-2483. 254 Regent St. W1. Tube: Oxford Circus. Open Mon–Sat 9:30am–7pm (Thurs until 7:30pm), Sun 11:30am–5:30pm.*

See Map 21 on p. 192, bullet 42.

Tom's (p. 191) NOTTING HILL Another son-of-Terence-Conran shop, this one from the food end, and a cornucopian deli it is.... *Tel 020/7221-8818. 226 Westbourne Grove W11. Tube: Notting Hill Gate. Open Mon–Sat 10am–6pm, Sun noon–4pm.*

See Map 20 on p. 176, bullet 1.

Top Shop (p. 182) WEST END Loud clothes in a loud shop; cheap, colorful, and tight, mostly for teenagers, who find them stylish.... *Tel 020/7636-7700. 214 Oxford St. W1. Tube: Oxford Circus. Open Mon–Sat 9:30am–7pm, Sun noon–6pm.*

See Map 21 on p. 192, bullet 40.

Trax (p. 190) WEST END The best Soho place for Soho club–type groove music of every ilk.... *Tel 020/7734-0795. www. traxrecords.co.uk. 55 Greek St. W1. Tube: Tottenham Court Rd. Open Mon–Sat 11am–7pm.*

See Map 21 on p. 192, bullet 58.

Tridias (p. 212) SOUTH KENSINGTON Toys tending toward traditional, with science sets, coloring pens, and games galore; near the big museums.... *Tel 020/7584-2330. 25 Bute St. SW7. Tube: South Kensington. Open Mon–Sat 10am–6pm, Sun noon–5pm.*

See Map 20 on p. 176, bullet 13.

Turnbull & Asser (p. 185) WEST END The minimum first order for customized shirts is a half dozen, from £100 ($165) apiece, but these are the world's best shirts. Ready-made also available.... *Tel 020/7930-0502. 71 Jermyn St. SW1. Tube: Piccadilly Circus. Open Mon–Sat 10am–5:30pm.*

See Map 21 on p. 192, bullet 69.

Vivienne Westwood (p. 180, 183, 184) CHELSEA The ultimate style queen, who constantly invents fashion movements and is copied by the world about 3 years later.... *Tel 020/7352-6551. World's End, 430 King's Rd. SW10. Tube: Sloane Sq., then Bus 11 or 22. Open Mon–Sat 10am–6pm.* **Sale Shop:** *Tel 020/7439-1109. 44 Conduit St. W1. Tube: Oxford Circus. Open Mon–Sat 10am–6pm, Sun noon–5pm.*

See Map 22 on p. 194, bullet 111.

Warehouse (p. 182) WEST END High turnover for high fashion; not top quality in the finish, but far from top prices, Warehouse keeps getting better.... *Tel 020/7734-5096. 19 Argyll St. W1. Tube: Oxford Circus. Open Mon–Sat 10am–6pm.*

See Map 21 on p. 192, bullet 45.

Waterstone's (p. 189) WEST END A terribly successful and likeable chain of bookstores, many of which run readings and signings.... *Tel 020/7434-4291. 121–125 Charing Cross Rd. W1. Tube: Leicester Sq. Open Mon–Sat 9:30am–8pm, Sun noon–6pm. Branches all over.*

See Map 21 on p. 192, bullet 157.

Whistles (p. 182, 184) WEST END The tiniest and trendiest of chains racks clothes by shade, has its own label, and sells European designer-wear in bright and spacious shops.... *Tel 020/7487-4484. 12 St. Christopher's Place W1. Tube: Bond St. Open Mon–Sat 10am–6pm, Sun noon–5pm.*

See Map 21 on p. 192, bullet 39.

Zara (p. 182) WEST END The Spanish chain that is taking the world by storm owes its success to producing rip-offs from the runway hours after a show takes place in practical, hard-wearing fabric and at prices that are hard to beat.... *Tel 020/7534-9500. 118 Regent St. W1. Tube: Piccadilly Circus. Branches. Open Mon–Sat 10am–7pm, Thurs 10am–8pm, Sun noon–6pm.*

See Map 21 on p. 192, bullet 76.

Zwemmer (p. 189) WEST END Well-stocked bookstores in two arty varieties: fine arts and photography/cinema.... *Tel 020/ 7240-4158. 24 Litchfield St. WC2. Tel 020/7240-4157. 80 Charing Cross Rd. WC2. Tube (for both): Leicester Sq. Open Mon–Sat 10am–6pm, Sun noon–5pm.*

See Map 21 on p. 192, bullet 64.

THE INDEX

SHOPPING

NIGH

TLIFE

6

Map 23: London Pubs, Clubs & Bars

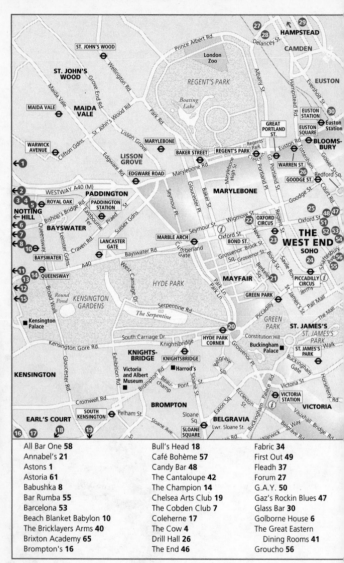

NIGHTLIFE

All Bar One **58**
Annabel's **21**
Astons **1**
Astoria **61**
Babushka **8**
Bar Rumba **55**
Barcelona **53**
Beach Blanket Babylon **10**
The Bricklayers Arms **40**
Brixton Academy **65**
Brompton's **16**

Bull's Head **18**
Café Bohème **57**
Candy Bar **48**
The Cantaloupe **42**
The Champion **14**
Chelsea Arts Club **19**
The Cobden Club **7**
Coleherne **17**
The Cow **4**
Drill Hall **26**
The End **46**

Fabric **34**
First Out **49**
Fleadh **37**
Forum **27**
G.A.Y. **50**
Gaz's Rockin Blues **47**
Glass Bar **30**
Golborne House **6**
The Great Eastern
    Dining Rooms **41**
Groucho **56**

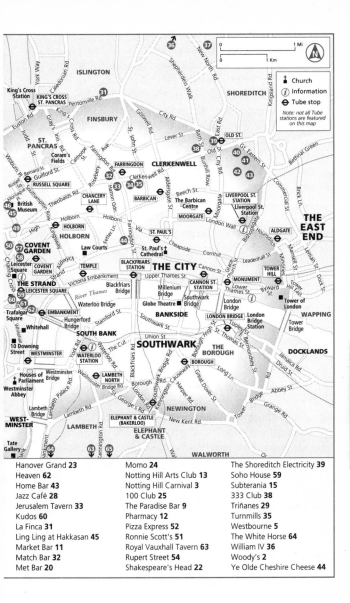

Hanover Grand **23**	Momo **24**	The Shoreditch Electricity **39**
Heaven **62**	Notting Hill Arts Club **13**	Soho House **59**
Home Bar **43**	Notting Hill Carnival **3**	Subterania **15**
Jazz Café **28**	100 Club **25**	333 Club **38**
Jerusalem Tavern **33**	The Paradise Bar **9**	Triñanes **29**
Kudos **60**	Pharmacy **12**	Turnmills **35**
La Finca **31**	Pizza Express **52**	Westbourne **5**
Ling Ling at Hakkasan **45**	Ronnie Scott's **51**	The White Horse **64**
Market Bar **11**	Royal Vauxhall Tavern **63**	William IV **36**
Match Bar **32**	Rupert Street **54**	Woody's **2**
Met Bar **20**	Shakespeare's Head **22**	Ye Olde Cheshire Cheese **44**

Basic Stuff

The age-old debate about licensing laws rears its head wherever *Britain* and *nightlife* are mentioned in the same sentence. Well, the good news is that things are beginning to loosen up...a little. PM Tony Blair, known as El Presidente among the masses, seems to advocate a change in the legal boozing hours, even though his teenaged son was picked up pickled in Leicester Square a couple of years back. The draconian "licensed" hours of yesteryear date back to World War I, when the government wanted to make sure its munitions workers got home at a decent hour and would be able to carry on their duties the next day. The laws were never really challenged until recently, and now the direction the U.K. is going in is definitely more in line with its Euro neighbors (where drink is sold 24/7). As things stand now, 11am is opening time and 11pm is still standard closing time. However, most neighborhoods have at least one venue with a later license than that on weekend nights. The best thing to do is to ask wherever you are drinking, as these things can and do change constantly.

Of course, whether your pub closes at 11pm or 2am, there will always be a closing time. At 20 minutes before the appointed hour, most venues ring a bell or flash lights or some such to signify "last orders." This is the signal for Pavlov's Lush to down as much beer as possible before the pub closes up shop. Alcohol is not the only fuel for a good time, of course, but Londoners—well, the British in general—prefer a wet bar to a juice bar, however modish those ginseng-guarana-spirulina cocktails might be. Londoners like to drink. Proof is provided by the ubiquity of the age-old British pub. The full title, *public house,* describes exactly what a good pub offers: a warm environment where many people feel at home. Music is also important to the London soul, whether pop, jazz, indie bands, world music, or the indigenous folk traditions of the British Isles. As for clubbing and youth culture, fashion worldwide always has an eye to what young London is wearing and saying and how it's dancing in its constantly changing array of "one-nighters," warehouse parties, and restaurants *du moment.*

The Soho gay scene has helped make London friendlier than it's ever been. The hippest gay clubs here are often the hippest clubs, period. Those legendary "Summer of Love II" warehouse parties, full of technobeat and Vicks Vaporub–enhanced trance-dancing, really did exist. That phenomenon has yet to be equaled for pure nighttime mayhem and depravity, although there are a lot of people trying to equal it every

Saturday night. These revelers have spawned such cross-cultural music-led scenes as an Asian underground and ever more subdivisions of techno, drum 'n' bass, and rave. Pick up flyers anywhere hip, or be handed them as you exit somewhere sweaty, and follow the paper trail.

Sources

For an all-around picture of music, clubs, and the student scene, pick up the weekly *Time Out* (out Wed, Tues in the city center). The tone is irritatingly smug, but it does a grand job of listing nearly everything there is to do. *Time Out*'s club listings aren't bad, but there are several magazines dedicated to the scene that go deeper. *MixMag* is a good one, and so are the weekly (out Thurs) music papers, especially the *NME (New Musical Express)*. The gay scene, for both genders, is conveyed through the monthly *Gay Times* and the weeklies *Boyz* and *QX;* these free papers are available in gay establishments all over town.

The Lowdown

Personality pubs... There used to be a pub for every taste; then the big breweries (landlords of most pubs) suddenly converted every dear old grungy, down-home barroom into a small Edwardian theme park, with antiquarian books by-the-mile, a fake log fire, brass rails, and stuffed owls, then stripped them down to bare floorboards, wooden tables and plain color-washed walls, with salady, Tuscan food chalked on a blackboard. Go into any **All Bar One** to see this in action or **Shakespeare's Head** a kitschy Soho pub always packed with tourists. It's annoying when what one really wants in a pub is authenticity. The real thing still exists, although **Ye Olde Cheshire Cheese,** for instance, which is about 330 years old, is terribly touristy. On the other hand, its sawdust floors, low, wood-beamed ceilings, and 14th-century crypt are just the same as when Dickens drank there. Don't get too excited by that last part: Either Dickens drank nearly everywhere in London, or publicans are congenital liars.

Beards and real ale... Oh, how the British like their beer. They like it warm, they like it dark, they like it flat, they like it strong—they like it any way but cold and gassy and in a bottle. Well, most of them. In truth, millions of Londoners have acquired an American taste in beer, and

Rolling Rock, Bud, et al., are omnipresent, as is Corona with a slice of lime wedged in the neck. But "real ale" is true British beer, similar to U.S. microbrewery output, yet older. Its traditional image is mixed up with men who wear sandals with socks and grow unruly beards, but it has become trendy. Try the **Jerusalem Tavern** for proof (and good ale) or go to any of the pubs with "**...& Firkin**" (a kind of barrel used in beer making) in their names, like the **Pheasant & Firkin,** and have a pint of "rail ale" with medical students in their cups, to see how popular this game really is. For good Irish stout, **The Cow** is more salubrious than echt Irish pubs along the Kilburn High Road, and it's usually good for the *craic,* too.

Cruising, schmoozing, meeting (straight)... A designated singles scene really doesn't exist in London, because the unwritten rules of dating are not the same here. Exactly how, I couldn't say (these are unwritten rules), but see if you notice a difference at **Beach Blanket Babylon,** where the decor is suitably gothic for the throbbing mass of smooth-skinned (i.e., young) humanity convening weekend nights, especially in summer. If you can force someone to get you into the **Groucho,** you'll certainly see "chatting-up" in progress, though you'll need a strong stomach to deal with the rampant elitism. Despite being named after the man who wouldn't join a club that would take him as a member, the most famous media-movie-journo hangout is liable to look down its nose at you unless it knows you. Precisely the opposite is true of London's two best high-summer fests: the West Indian **Notting Hill Carnival,** and the **Fleadh,** the Celtic party in Finsbury Park. Whatever you did tonight, whomever you met, wherever (within reason) you are, you'll probably end up having an espresso at **Bar Italia,** scoping or dishing other clubbers. The **Hanover Grand** is where you might have been, if you're young. Or, for the best sound system in London, perhaps **The End,** in which case you're probably deaf now.

Cruising, schmoozing, meeting (gay)... The gay earth revolves around "the Compton," Soho's always lively Old Compton Street that underwent a metamorphosis and is now almost New Yorky in its hours and up-frontness. As we've said, places mostly welcome a mix (permutations of gay-straight-men-women), but men are the target customers of the biggest and busiest, **The Yard,** while little **First Out** peacefully purveys caffeine and alcohol. Gay cafe/bars hit the Soho scene a few years back and are popular at lunch time, after work, and into the evening. Best of the lot: **Kudos** and **Rupert Street.** The dyke scene doesn't really center on Soho, nor on any one place, although the bi-level **Candy Bar** is Soho-centric. Bloomsburyish **Glass Bar** on Euston Road, with a "smart casual" dress code, is the city's largest all-gal watering hole. **Drill Hall,** the West End arts center, runs loads of women-only events plus it has a girls' bar–night on Mondays. It's a fair bet that that long-running 1-night-a-week club will endure. Let's all hope the **Royal Vauxhall Tavern** never closes either. It's just a "local," but a faggy, sometimes dykey, one with a great vibe and an amateur drag cabaret dating from way back. **Heaven** is heaven for dancing, and **G.A.Y.** is a must scene, too. Before Soho became the gay universe, the queer action was in Earl's Court, and there are still a couple of places to check out there: **Brompton's,** for it's post-pub dancing and cruising, and the denimy **Coleherne.** If you want a good gay pub close to Notting Hill, check out the chatty **Champion** on Bayswater Road.

East meets West... but only rarely. The media-hyped rivalry between East (Shoreditch, Hoxton, Dalston) and West (Notting Hill, Kensal, Queen's Park) is becoming something of a London joke. The truth is, both areas are fashionable and both have a range of fashionable watering holes to suit all tastes, many of which also serve excellent food. Hooray. The East, or at least this area of it, has long been a purely commercial district; this means that opening hours are less rigid for bars. Recently, however, it was reinhabited by artists craving the space of warehouse conversions, which has made the area unrelentingly fashionable. The end result is a succession of trendy, late-opening bars. Since the big-spending city slickers are absent on the weekends, there is some closure in the area, notably on Sunday nights, so phone ahead for opening times. On Charlotte Road are the popular **Bricklayers Arms** (dress down) and the more suity **Cantaloupe** bar. Just opposite are **The Great Eastern Dining Rooms,** often filled with a buzzing crowd, especially on Fridays, and the **Home Bar.** In nearby Hoxton Square are **The Shoreditch Electricity Showrooms** (which is actually a bar and not a toaster shop) and the **Lux Cinema** (see the Diversions chapter). When you've sampled all these, you can go to the **333 Club** for a bit of a dance. Nearer the center of town is Farringdon, home to two of London's most popular nightclubs, the long-established **Turnmills** and the *enfant terrible* **Fabric.** Conveniently close to both of these dens is the **Match Bar,** the ideal spot to meet before a night of debauchery; indeed, it is quite capable of playing host to small-scale debauchery all on its own. Although Notting Hill has in recent years become overrun by rich, glamorous yuppies, the area has managed to retain a unique character, with its colorful collection of bars and restaurants, the Portobello Road Market, and Notting Hill Carnival. Portobello is really the center of the action; and you could do worse than check out the **Market Bar.** If you head eastward a bit you will come to the ultraglam **Westbourne,** opposite the more understated **Cow.** From here, an arc to the north and west will yield **Babushka,** with its chocolate vodkas, DJs, and upstairs parties (often private, but easily gate-crashed); the new **Golborne House,** for the last word in ice-chilled cool; **The Paradise Bar,** just as chilled but not quite as cool; **Astons,** the new kid on the block, very chilled with excellent food and fantastic sitar around a log fire (the garden rocks in summer, too); and lastly, the **William IV,** a saggy-armchaired heaven for Sunday lunch. Despite its reputation as a hedonistic funfest, Notting Hill and its environs are not a good place for late drinking. If you're lucky enough to know a member, the obvious choice is **The Cobden Club** or **Woody's,** West London's answers to Soho House. If you're not so well connected but still want to stay out late, however, you could go to the **Pharmacy,** artist Damien Hirst's conceptual bar, which is overpriced and decorated as, you guessed it, a pharmacy. My tip, however, is the less pristine **Notting Hill Arts Club,** a venue that, although basically a bar, is committed to supporting other artistic endeavors—films, exhibitions, performances, and the like.

Late license... The **Atlantic Bar and Grill** began to transform London's nights when it won a 3am alcohol license back in 1993. Others followed, but the revolution—despite a few auspicious signs—has yet to hit. The divey **Barcelona** and its neighbor **Café Bohème** are both very central, with late licenses, but neither has much else to recommend it beyond permission to drink. Candidate for most sordid and steamy dive in town is the compulsory stop-in-if-you're-in-the-neighborhood **Triñanes,** a Spanish restaurant (don't eat here) kittty-corner from the **Forum,** that Kentish Town hall of rock. Triñanes's earlier-evening flamenco nights can actually be pretty authentic and fabulous. The most genuine, diviest late-night bar is one you can't really visit without an invitation. It's at Bayswater's **Commodore** hotel, where the hippest not-too-famous bands stay, and drink all night if that's the sort of thing they do.

Two-step, waltz, salsa, and boogie... If you want to make like Fred and Ginger, there aren't that many places to go. All the regular dances are in hotels, and the best are, unsurprisingly, found in the best hotels including **Claridge**'s and the Terrace at the **Dorchester.** All have dinner dances with prix-fixe menus, inclusive of cover, and all but the Savoy hold the events on Friday and Saturday nights only (till 1am); the Savoy does it every night but Sunday. Tunes tend to be more Sinatra than Strauss at all of the hotel hops. Meanwhile, Latin dance has become mucho popular. Several places follow the same pattern of an early-evening class for the gringos to prepare for the night of nonstop salsa. Check the listings for these, though the Islington tapas bar, **La Finca,** and the West End **Bar Rumba** have all been running them for some time. Teddy boys and girls, ska and rock-steady fans, jivers, and rockers have two places to go: **Gaz's Rockin Blues,** which is probably Soho's longest-running "one-nighter" club, or the **100 Club,** which has been holding its chief R&B night Mondays. Medium-to-large venues to rock out in include the north London **Forum** and the central **Astoria.** Even hipper than those are the **Brixton Academy** in the wilds of South London, and **Subterania,** in the wilds of the West.

Where to be invited by members... Grouchy **Groucho** thinks it's the center of the publishing/TV/publicity/literary world, and, unfortunately, it's right. After a decade, the irreverent club that's secretly establishment still has what it takes, to the extent that if you yourself move in these worlds, you'll find it more challenging to avoid Groucho than to be invited. A place with a rep you'll have more trouble entering is near-legendary **Annabel's,** which is a surreal mix of early-Jackie-Collins–novel discotheque and black-tie supper club. Yes, rollicking royals really do drop in on occasion, and a glass of champagne costs 20 quid. Less predictable, and even older, is the wonderfully housed **Chelsea Arts Club,** with its gardens, bedchambers, dimly lit dining, and snooker tables in the bar. It's disreputable by design, but really is often full of drunk sculptors taking their clothes off, having fist fights, or simply falling over. Among newer clubs, the **Soho House** has found its niche after its first few years. It's for the end of the Groucho crowd with shorter skirt, higher alcohol tolerance, bigger drug habit, louder mouth, and more likely to be in movies 'n' videos than books 'n' newspapers. In the West those with the connections head to **Woody's,** while Clapham to the south offers **The White Horse.** All three of these are open to the public but with large separate bars for members and their guests. If you're gorgeous and make a living from it, head to the **Met Bar.** Another loucher, warmer choice for you beauties is the cash bar at the casbahm **Momo.**

Cocktail, anyone?... So you've had that splendid dinner and you fancy a fancy drink before bedtime. The center of town offers up **Ling Ling at Hakkasan,** a New York–style ultra-chichi little Asian lounge bar with a late license (3am Thurs–Sat) and gorgeous cocktails. A fave is the Minnie Mushka, a rhubarb and lemongrass flavored vodka-thon. In the south, cocktails are the preserve of **The White Horse,** with mojitos and martinis topping the list. Westward, check out **Woody's** for a cipirinha and a little boogie in the very little basement "Southall bar." Southall is a massive Indian community in West London, so expect kitsch decor and Ganesha the elephant god at **The Great Eastern Dining Rooms,** where a mango and bisongrass vodka bevy called Mango Street wins the prize.

Jazz standards... This week's big name in town will be found at **Ronnie Scott's,** where the cover charge seems less exorbitant since everywhere else has caught up. **Pizza Express** is in a similar mainstream-but-musically-hip vein to Ronnie's, but serves far better pizza. For the absolute coolness of the cutting edge, you'll need to leave downtown and go north to the **Jazz Café,** in sunny Camden Town, or northeast to the **Vortex** in way-out-yonder Stoke Newington. Higher quality than most, though way out in Barnes, is the riverside **Bull's Head.**

The Index

All Bar One (p. 219) WEST END Why am I listing this chain? Because all couple dozen are clean, well-lighted places. This is the Leicester Square one.... *Tel 020/7747-9921. Leicester Sq. WC2. Tube: Leicester Sq. No cover.*

Annabel's (p. 223) WEST END Whatever the opposite of a dive is, this members-only boutique is it. Nobs, snobs, and hoorays (braying, chinless Hooray Henry is the Sloane Ranger's brother) are those members. Surprisingly, it can be a blast.... *Tel 020/7629-1096. 44 Berkeley Sq. W1. Tube: Green Park. Members only.*

Astons (p. 222) KENSAL GREEN West London gastropub with excellent fish restaurant on the side. Cozy and friendly.... *Tel 020/8969-2184. 2 Regent St. NW10. Tube: Kensal Green. No cover.*

Astoria (p. 223) WEST END Very central, at the top of Oxford Street, this big hall has a pleasantly louche vibe and is open late, for wrecks in their twenties to see bands on the up.... *Tel 020/7434-9592. 157 Charing Cross Rd. WC2. Tube: Tottenham Court Rd./Leicester Sq. Cover.*

Atlantic Bar and Grill See the Dining chapter.

Babushka (p. 222) WESTBOURNE PARK A dark, atmospheric bar just north of Portobello Road. Check out the chocolate-flavored vodkas. Live DJs and a function room upstairs.... *Tel 020/7727-9250. 41 Tavistock Crescent W11. Tube: Westbourne Park. No cover.*

Barcelona (p. 222) WEST END A divey Spanish-ish bar with tapas; useful for being Soho central and managing to stay open late.... *Tel 020/7287-9932. 17 Old Compton St. W1. Tube: Leicester Sq. No cover.*

THE INDEX

NIGHTLIFE

Bar Italia See the Dining chapter.

Bar Rumba (p. 223) WEST END A conveniently located West End place that offers a free salsa class before the bargain Tuesday night "Salsa Pa'Ti."... *Tel 020/7287-2715. 36 Shaftsbury Ave. W1. Tube: Piccadilly Circus. Cover.*
See Map 23 on p. 216, bullet 55.

Beach Blanket Babylon (p. 220) NOTTING HILL As a bar, restaurant, and a place to meet fellow twenty/thirties, this gothique Portobello joint rocks on weekends.... *Tel 020/7229-2907. 45 Ledbury Rd. W11. Tube: Notting Hill Gate. No cover.*
See Map 23 on p. 216, bullet 10.

The Bricklayers Arms (p. 221) SHOREDITCH Much frequented by artists and excellent for weekend breakfasts. Do not dress up! The look is deconstructed to the point of apocalyptic. If you're lucky, you might be sneered at by a prize-winning artist.... *Tel 020/7739-5245. 63 Charlotte Rd. EC2. Tube: Old St. Cover*
See Map 23 on p. 216, bullet 40.

Brixton Academy (p. 223) BRIXTON A huge hall in South London's reggae-culture neighborhood tends to be very hip and pretty young, and has bands playing most nights, as well as club events; open late.... *Tel 020/7924-9999. 211 Stockwell Rd. SW9. Tube: Brixton. Cover.*
See Map 23 on p. 216, bullet 65.

Brompton's (p. 221) EARL'S COURT A huge and popular gay men's cruise/dance bar open until 2am Monday through Saturday and midnight on Sunday, but completely dead before 11pm.... *Tel 020/7370-1344. 294 Old Brompton Rd. SW5. Tube: Earl's Court (Warwick Rd. exit). Cover.*
See Map 23 on p. 216, bullet 16.

Bull's Head (p. 224) BARNES By the Thames in Barnes, this pretty pub has attracted serious jazz buffs (those with beards, who whoop during bass solos) for years and years.... *Tel 020/8876-5241. 373 Lonsdale Rd. SW13. BR: Barnes Bridge or Buses 209 or 419. Cover.*
See Map 23 on p. 216, bullet 18.

Café Bohème (p. 222) WEST END This well-bred, Parisian-styled corner bistro-cafe-bar in Soho mutates into a standing-room-only free-for-all after the pubs decant at 11pm.... *Tel 020/7734-0623. 13 Old Compton St. W1. Tube: Leicester Sq. No cover.*
See Map 23 on p. 216, bullet 57.

Candy Bar (p. 221) WEST END The country's newest (and only) double-decker lesbian bar-club is *the* hot scene for women; men welcome as guests.... *Tel 020/7494-4041. 4 Carlisle St. W1. Tube: Tottenham Court Rd. No cover.*
See Map 23 on p. 216, bullet 48.

The Cantaloupe (p. 221) THE CITY Popular after-work haunt for the funkier suits in the city. Reasonable food, if not cheap, and excellent Bloody Marys.... *Tel 020/7613-4411. 35–42 Charlotte Rd. EC2. Tube: Old St. or Liverpool St. No cover.*

See Map 23 on p. 216, bullet 42.

The Champion (p. 221) BAYSWATER Large Victoria-era gay pub draws a low-key but cruisey crowd.... *Tel 020/7229-5056. 1 Wellington Terrace, Bayswater Rd. W2. Tube: Notting Hill Gate. No cover.*

See Map 23 on p. 216, bullet 14.

Chelsea Arts Club (p. 224) CHELSEA Progenitor of the infamous Chelsea Arts Club Ball, wherein artists and artistes pose in teeny costumes and disgrace themselves; neither Club nor Ball are as naughty as they once were, though an invitation to penetrate the private white walls is still cause for joy.... *Tel 020/7376-3311. 143 Old Church St. SW3. Tube: Sloane Sq. Members only.*

See Map 23 on p. 216, bullet 19.

Claridge's See the Accommodations chapter.

The Cobden Club (p. 222) KENSAL Media darlings galore; the Soho House of West London, where more than a few familiar faces crop up.... *Tel 020/8960-4222. 170–2 Kensal Rd. W10. Tube: Westbourne Park. Members only.*

See Map 23 on p. 216, bullet 7.

Coleherne (p. 221) EARL'S COURT One of London's landmark gay pubs for denim and leather guys has had a recent face-lift and is busier than ever.... *Tel 020/7224-5951. 261 Old Brompton Rd. SW5. Tube: Earl's Court. No cover.*

See Map 23 on p. 216, bullet 17.

Commodore See the Accommodations chapter.

The Cow (p. 220, 222) KENSAL Tom, the deli Conran, created this cozy oyster and Guinness Irish-ish pub with a good restaurant upstairs; it's a fulcrum of the Notting Hill scene and gets crammed.... *Tel 020/7221-0021. 89 Westbourne Park Rd. W2. Tube: Royal Oak. No cover.*

See Map 23 on p. 216, bullet 4.

The Dorchester See the Accommodations chapter.

Drill Hall (p. 221) WEST END This deep West End, woman-centric arts center runs many a girlish event, and does a women-only bar on Mondays.... *Tel 020/7631-1353. 16 Chenies St. W1. Tube: Goodge St. Cover by event.*

See Map 23 on p. 216, bullet 26.

THE INDEX

NIGHTLIFE

The End (p. 220) WEST END Banging tunes from the best sound system in London. Not for the old, wrinkled, or faint of heart.... *Tel 020/7419-9199. 18 W. Central St. WC1. Tube: Tottenham Court Rd. Cover.*
See Map 23 on p. 216, bullet 46.

Fabric (p. 222) HOLBORN Three floors, 2,000 capacity, big-name DJs, residents and guests, and DTPM, the famous gay Sunday night out—oh my lord, the mind boggles. A must.... *Tel 020/ 7490-0444. 77A Charterhouse St. EC1. Tube: Farringdon. Cover.*
See Map 23 on p. 216, bullet 34.

...& Firkin (p. 220) EVERYWHERE They are everywhere, these firkin Firkins, and all featuring puns like that one, brewed-on-premises pints of Dogbolter, stripped-pine floorboards, and student types. The first microbrewery pubs in London, long since bought out by the big boys.... *Everywhere. No cover.*

First Out (p. 221) WEST END The name is exact: If you're walking into Soho from Oxford Street, and are gay, the relaxed, friendly coffee cafe/bar is the first landmark.... *Tel 020/7240-8042. 52 St. Giles High St. WC2. Tube: Tottenham Court Rd. No cover.*
See Map 23 on p. 216, bullet 49.

Fleadh (p. 220) FINSBURY PARK Finsbury Park's annual Celtic music fest in mid-June is pronounced "flah," and is practically guaranteed to feature Van Morrison, Sinead O'Connor, and whichever Pogues still have functioning livers.... *Tel 020/8963-0940. Tube: Finsbury Park. Cover.*
See Map 23 on p. 216, bullet 37.

Forum (p. 223) HAMPSTEAD A well-loved and well-frequented former ballroom in the north hosts medium-famous, medium-hip bands, usually for the twenties set, though older performers do attract older kids.... *Tel 020/7284-2200. 9–17 Highgate Rd. NW5. Tube: Kentish Town. Cover.*
See Map 23 on p. 216, bullet 27.

G.A.Y. (p. 221) WEST END The biggest gay dance venue in Europe opens its doors every Saturday from 10:30pm to 5am. A smaller version is held Monday, Thursday, and Friday in Astoria basement, same hours.... *Tel 020/7734-6963. Astoria, 157 Charing Cross Rd. WC2. Tube: Tottenham Court Rd. Cover.*
See Map 23 on p. 216, bullet 50.

Gaz's Rockin Blues (p. 223) WEST END One of this town's oldest 1-night-per-week clubs, Gaz (son of blues man John) Mayall's friendly R&B, ska, and rock 'n' roll Thursdays are still going strong.... *Tel 020/7437-0525. St. Moritz, 159 Wardour St. W1. Tube: Tottenham Court Rd. Cover.*
See Map 23 on p. 216, bullet 47.

Glass Bar (p. 221) BLOOMSBURY Lipstick lesbians like the comfy couches and candlelit atmosphere at this popular diva dive; smart-casual dress code.... *Tel 020/7837-6184. West Lodge, Euston Sq. Gardens, 190 Euston Rd. NW1 2EF. Tube: Euston. No cover.*
See Map 23 on p. 216, bullet 30.

Golborne House (p. 222) NORTH KENSINGTON The new jewel in the West London drinking crown is relaxed, informal, and very cool. The food's not bad either.... *Tel 020/8960-6260. 36 Golborne Rd. W10. Tube: Westbourne Park. No cover.*
See Map 23 on p. 216, bullet 6.

The Great Eastern Dining Rooms (p. 221, 224) SHOREDITCH Often-crowded after-work pub/bar/restaurant. No dress code, but frequented by lots of suits. Located in the heart of the Eastern drinking zone.... *Tel 020/7613-4545. 54 Great Eastern St. EC2. Tube: Old St. No cover.*
See Map 23 on p. 216, bullet 41.

Groucho (p. 220, 223) WEST END You can't get in unless you know a member, but this is so integral to the life of the London intelligentsia (drinking division) that it can't be left out.... *Tel 020/7439-4685. 45 Dean St. W1. Tube: Leicester Sq. Members only.*
See Map 23 on p. 216, bullet 56.

Hanover Grand (p. 220) WEST END At press time, very hip, but by now who knows? A West End, two-tier wonderland of swanky decor and heaving dance floor; open late.... *Tel 020/7499-7977. 6 Hanover St. W1. Tube: Oxford Circus. Cover.*
See Map 23 on p. 216, bullet 23.

Heaven (p. 221) WEST END A venerable (23 years old) and vast (mostly) gay dance club under the arches behind Charing Cross has the boomingest bass, and laser lights that give you the bends; open late.... *Tel 020/7930-2020. Off Villiers St. WC2. Tube: Charing Cross. Cover.*
See Map 23 on p. 216, bullet 62.

Home Bar (p. 221) SHOREDITCH This, the most fashionable of the East London watering holes, has now extended its dining facilities and doubled in size. Great for the 20-somethings.... *Tel 020/7684-8618. 100 Leonard St. EC2. Tube: Old St. No cover.*
See Map 23 on p. 216, bullet 43.

Jazz Café (p. 224) CAMDEN A converted bank in downtown Camden hosts the hottest combos from all over, and consistently swings. It's worth getting tickets in advance, and booking a table if you're having dinner.... *Tel 020/7916-6060. 7 Parkway NW1. Tube: Camden Town. Cover.*
See Map 23 on p. 216, bullet 28.

THE INDEX

NIGHTLIFE

Jerusalem Tavern (p. 220) THE CITY In the most happening media folks' nabe is this remade Georgian. It was from here the Knights of St. John set out on the Crusades. Kind of.... *Tel 020/ 7490-4281. 55 Britton St. EC1. Tube: Farringdon. No cover.*
See Map 23 on p. 216, bullet 33.

Kudos (p. 221) WEST END Popular gay cafe/bar serving snacks and offering flyers for reduced-price entry to G.A.Y. and Heaven.... *Tel 020/7379-4573. 10 Adelaide St. WC2. Tube: Charing Cross. No cover.*
See Map 23 on p. 216, bullet 60.

La Finca (p. 223) ST. PANCRAS This tapas bar/restaurant has salsa classes and dance nights in its upstairs club.... *Tel 020/ 7837-5387. 96 Pentonville Rd. N1. Tube: Angel. Cover (waived for diners).*
See Map 23 on p. 216, bullet 31.

Ling Ling at Hakkasan (p. 224) WEST END This moody temple of Asian chic is hidden down a back alley with a junkie past. Very *Indiana Jones....* *Tel 020/7927-7000. 8 Hathaway Place W1. Tube: Tottenham Court Rd. No cover.*
See Map 23 on p. 216, bullet 45.

Market Bar (p. 222) NOTTING HILL A Portobello institution, all Gothic candles and flowing locks (dreadlocks, that is). Good Thai food upstairs as well.... *Tel 020/8460-8320. 240 Portobello Rd. W11. Tube: Ladbroke Grove. No cover.*
See Map 23 on p. 216, bullet 11.

Match Bar (p. 222) CLERKENWELL Ultra-styled cocktail bar that serves food as well. Ideally located for preclub drinks (Turnmills and Fabric are 'round the corner).... *Tel 020/7250-4002. 45–7 Clerkenwell Rd. EC1. Tube: Farringdon. No cover.*
See Map 23 on p. 216, bullet 32.

Met Bar (p. 224) WEST END Members-and-hotel-guests–only scene. The place is titchy, overpriced, and overrated, but if a crowd wedged firmly up its own ass is your cup of tea, this is the place for you.... *Tel 020/7447-1000. Metropolitan Hotel, Old Park Lane W1. Tube: Hyde Park Corner. Members/hotel guests only.*
See Map 23 on p. 216, bullet 20.

Momo (p. 224) WEST END Unless you're a member, you'll have to dine in the restaurant upstairs to gain entrance to this mosque-lamped, mud-walled slice of old Morocco, and even then you can only drink before you eat.... *Tel 020/7434-4040. 25 Heddon St. W1. Tube: Piccadilly Circus. Members/diners only.*
See Map 23 on p. 216, bullet 24.

Notting Hill Arts Club (p. 222) NOTTING HILL This dance club on Notting Hill Gate is open late. Friendly staff and a varied menu of cool sounds. Phone for details, but check out Thursday's

Brazilian Love Affair and Sunday's Lazy Dog.... *Tel 020/7460-4459. 19 Notting Hill Gate W11. Tube: Notting Hill. Cover.*
See Map 23 on p. 216, bullet 13.

Notting Hill Carnival (p. 220, 222) NOTTING HILL A 2-day street party of genuine Island vibes, heaving merengueing crowds, sound stages, parades, curried goat, Red Stripe, and ganja; it all takes place during the August bank holiday.... *No phone. Centered around the Westway, Portobello Rd. Tube: Ladbroke Grove.*
See Map 23 on p. 216, bullet 3.

100 Club (p. 223) WEST END A venerable dive. Rock and jazz, blues and R&B, with live bands and dance nights.... *Tel 020/7636-0933. 100 Oxford St. W1. Tube: Oxford Circus. Cover.*
See Map 23 on p. 216, bullet 25.

The Paradise Bar (p. 222) KENSAL GREEN Chilled hangout bar with restaurant out back and dancing till midnight (sometimes) upstairs.... *Tel 020/8969-0098. 19 Kilburn Lane W10. Tube: Ladbroke Grove, then Bus 52 north. No cover.*
See Map 23 on p. 216, bullet 9.

Pharmacy (p. 222) NOTTING HILL Rich, self-promoting, conceptual artist Damien Hirst (he of the bisected cow) opened this ultra-cool but ultimately bland and boring bar a few years back; great idea if you're into drugstores.... *Tel 020/7221-2442. 150 Notting Hill Gate W11. Tube: Notting Hill. No cover.*
See Map 23 on p. 216, bullet 12.

Pizza Express (p. 224) WEST END A big jazz venue, as well as London's best pizzas. This tends to host mainstream performers.... *Tel 020/7437-9595. 10 Dean St. W1. Tube: Tottenham Court Rd. Cover.*
See Map 23 on p. 216, bullet 52.

Ronnie Scott's (p. 224) WEST END London's best-known and most-loved jazz venue is missing the late, great saxophonist Ronnie, but is still hosting hot line-ups at high-end prices.... *Tel 020/7439-0747. 47 Frith St. W1. Tube: Leicester Sq. Cover.*
See Map 23 on p. 216, bullet 51.

Royal Vauxhall Tavern (p. 221) SOUTH BANK Just an old South London pub that hosts a drag show.... *Tel 020/7582-0833. 372 Kennington Lane SW8. Tube: Oval. No cover.*
See Map 23 on p. 216, bullet 63.

Rupert Street (p. 221) WEST END Most culinarily ambitious of the gay Soho cafe-bars, always filled with a hip, lively, youngish crowd.... *Tel 020/7292-7141. 50 Rupert St. W1. Tube: Piccadilly Circus. No cover.*
See Map 23 on p. 216, bullet 54.

THE INDEX

NIGHTLIFE

Shakespeare's Head (p. 219) SOHO At primetime it's almost impossible to find a place to sit or slump or even to be waited on in this kitschy Soho pub, but that doesn't stop droves of drinkers (many of them tourists wandering down Carnaby St.) from stopping in. The Bard's visage looks down from an upstairs window and fake Bardophrenalia decorates the interior.... *Tel 020/7734-2911. 29 Great Marlborough St. W1. Tube: Oxford St. No cover.*
See Map 23 on p. 216, bullet 22.

The Shoreditch Electricity Showrooms (p. 221) SHOREDITCH Open-plan bar with good atmosphere.... *Tel 020/7739-6934. 39a Hoxton Sq. N1. Tube: Old St. No cover.*
See Map 23 on p. 216, bullet 39.

Soho House (p. 222, 224) WEST END Another members-only Soho haunt of media types, more the TV, movie sort than its rival's, Groucho's, hacks.... *Tel 020/7734-5188. 40 Greek St. W1. Tube: Leicester Sq. Members and guests only.*
See Map 23 on p. 216, bullet 59.

Subterania (p. 223) NOTTING HILL A groovy duplex dive beneath the Westway, in Notting Hill. Happening bands and late-late clubbing.... *Tel 020/8960-4590. 36 Acklam Rd. W10. Tube: Ladbroke Grove. Cover.*
See Map 23 on p. 216, bullet 15.

333 Club (p. 222) SHOREDITCH Three floors of varied music and a hip, grungy crowd. Dance, sweat, and meet.... *Tel 020/7739-1800. 333 Old St. EC1. Tube: Old St. Cover.*
See Map 23 on p. 216, bullet 38.

Triñanes (p. 223) KENTISH TOWN An open-late spot where everyone goes when booted out of the Forum, across the street. The tapas are not why, but the flamenco performers are a weekend plus.... *Tel 020/7482-3616. 298 Kentish Town Rd. NW5. Tube: Kentish Town. No cover.*
See Map 23 on p. 216, bullet 29.

Turnmills (p. 222) CLERKENWELL Famous venue for Trade (9-year-old gay after-hours club) is also worthwhile on other nights. If you like your music hard, Trade is a must, straight or gay.... *Tel 020/7250-3409. 636 Clerkenwell Rd. EC1. Tube: Farringdon. Cover.*
See Map 23 on p. 216, bullet 35.

Vortex (p. 224) STOKE NEWINGTON Serious jazz buffs should make the trek out to Stokey, a residential neighborhood, with Asian/vegetarian restaurants and some good pubs, for the cutting edge of the London scene.... *Tel 020/7254-6516. 139–141 Stoke Newington Church St. N16. BR: Stoke Newington. Cover.*

Westbourne (p. 222) WESTBOURNE GREEN Wrap your shades 'round your head and pose like your life depended on it. The large terrace is a must in summer, but the bar will be a scrum.... *Tel 020/7221-1332. 101 Westbourne Park Villas W2. Tube: Royal Oak. No cover.*
See Map 23 on p. 216, bullet 5.

The White Horse (p. 224) CLAPHAM Funky late venue for 20-something South Londoners. Try to get an invite to the first-floor members' lounge or the second-floor private dining rooms. Food is excellent, too.... *Tel 020/7498-3388. 65 Clapham Park SW4. Tube: Clapham Common. Cover.*
See Map 23 on p. 216, bullet 64.

William IV (p. 222) KENSAL GREEN Gorgeous on Sundays: the sun streams through the windows, the food is delicious, and the place is filled with children playing.... *Tel 020/8969-5944. 786 Harrow Rd. NW10. Tube: Kensal Green. No cover.*
See Map 23 on p. 216, bullet 36.

Woody's (p. 222, 224) WESTBOURNE GROVE Although the service here doesn't always match up to the price, it really is *the* place for late drinks in the Portobello neighborhood.... *Tel 020/7266-3030. 41–43 Woodfield Rd. W9. Tube: Westbourne Park. No cover.*
See Map 23 on p. 216, bullet 2.

The Yard (p. 221) WEST END This gay-oriented Soho cafe-bar does, indeed, have a little courtyard for coffee or beer, as well as two floors of bars that buzz by night.... *Tel 020/7437-2652. 57 Rupert St. W1. Tube: Piccadilly Circus. No cover.*

Ye Olde Cheshire Cheese (p. 219) THE CITY Ye original hokey tourist hostelry, with sawdust-strewn floors and great blackened beams, but it's been open for over 3 centuries, so go anyway.... *Tel 020/7353-6170. 145 Fleet St. EC4. Tube: Blackfriars. No cover.*
See Map 23 on p. 216, bullet 44.

THE INDEX

NIGHTLIFE

INMENT

Basic Stuff

As you are probably only too aware, what London is most famous for is theater. Well, is its snob reputation deserved? The scope and bravery of the best theater companies here is certainly wide and sometimes innovative, too—although the very newest in physical theater tends to come from elsewhere in Europe. Those European companies visit London, though, so you end up with the best of all worlds: indigenous highbrow, Shakespeare, West End (London's Broadway), homegrown experimental, and imported avant-garde. Look out for the June London International Festival of Theatre (LIFT) for concentrated doses of Catalan mimes and French nouvelle clowning. Crossover genres like physical theater (Théâtre de Complicité is a master of this), new circus (look for Ra Ra Zoo and Archaos), narrative dance (Yolanda Snaith), and comedic performance (Rose English, for instance) are worth seeking out here if you're a true fan of living theater, and not just worshiping at the shrine of the traditional proscenium arch and three acts. Not that there's anything wrong with the **National Theatre** and the **Royal Shakespeare Company,** or the big name stars (at least they're big names in London) who regularly trod the boards in big West End productions. Because that's one thing you will find in spades: good to great acting....

If theater sends you to sleep, London's got plenty of music, from opera to classical to jazz and all points in between: dance, ballet to aforementioned experiments; and comedy (this is the home of *Monty Python* and *Absolutely Fabulous*) to keep you amused. There are even sports.

Sources

At the risk of sounding like an infomercial, I have to give the estimable *Time Out* another plug here. If you buy only one "what's on" guide, this should be it. It's the nearest thing to having a clued-in Londoner on your team (which, naturally, is an even better way into the mysteries of this town). This weekly publication has the most complete entertainment listings, with information on music, dance, and London's diverse theater scene. Visit Time Out's web page at www.timeout.co.uk. You'll find the magazine at many international newsstands in the United States and Canada. In London, it can be picked up almost anywhere. The reviews can be bitchy and unfair, as in any other periodical, but they are thorough in their coverage of all of London's different entertainment scenes. The second-best source of entertainment information is the *Evening Standard;* especially its weekly "Hot Tickets" magazine (free with the paper on Thurs). Both these publications give plenty of background to their listings, so you'll get a feel for what's hot at this moment.

Getting Tickets

Prices for shows vary from £18 to £70 ($28–$109), depending on the theater and the seat. Matinees, performed Tuesday through Saturday are cheaper than evening performances. Evening performances begin between 7:30 and 8:30pm, midweek matinees at 2:30 or 3pm, and Saturday matinees at 5:45pm. West End theaters are closed Sundays. Many theaters accept telephone bookings at regular prices with a credit card. They'll hold your tickets for you at the box office, where you pick them up at show time with a credit card.

The best way to get theater tickets is to go to the box office of the theater itself, or to call it and charge your tickets. There's nothing wrong with ticket agents, like **First Call** (0207/420-0000) or **Ticketmaster** (0207/413-3321), unless you hate to pay the booking fee, and they do come up trumps for major rock gigs or for when you're having a theater orgy and want to book several shows. If that's you, **Keith Prowse** can be called before you leave home, at the New York office (212/398-1430 or 800/669-8687). If you're cheap, broke, or smart, wait till you're in London and line up at the indispensable **Tkts Half Price Ticket Booth** (no phone) on the southwest corner of Leicester Square, which has same-day-only tickets for about 25 theaters (Mon–Sat 1–6:30pm for evening shows; Tues–Sun from noon for matinees. MasterCard and Visa accepted; £2/$3.30 service charge). Traditionally, theaters have been dark on Sundays, but there has been a recent smattering of Sunday performances, so check the listings. Hotels—including those with a dedicated theater desk—charge a bigger fee than the phone bookers and are only worth using if you're lazy, loaded, or longing to see the latest hot musical, in which case the best of them (**The Savoy,** the **Athenaeum, The Dorchester**) may come up with the impossible, pricey, ticket. Those big hit shows, predictably, are the most likely to harbor a crop of **scalpers** (known as **ticket touts** here) outside the theater. Just say no. Never buy from a guy furtively brandishing a fistful of tickets: Common sense will tell you when there's someone with a legitimate extra one. If you feel that you must deal with a scalper, you should know that by law the tout must tell you the face value of the ticket at the time of sale so you can see how much he's marking it up, and be warned that it will be more than generous. Know the top prices of the show you want to see and remember that very few are regularly sold out. Every single theater keeps at least one row of **house seats** back till the last possible moment (for emergency oversales and unexpected situations) plus a dozen or two **returns.** Policies on how these are dispensed vary, but be prepared to stand in line, possibly in the morning, probably an hour before curtain, with no guarantee of success. On the other hand, day-of-show queuing at some venues may land you an £85+ ($140+) seat at the Royal Opera House for about £22 ($36). Failing that, if it's a big new show, you don't want to spend your vacation in line, and money's no object, check out the **classified ads** in the *Evening Standard* for sort-of-legitimate scalpers who bought blocks of tickets and are unloading them at a premium. This is your only hope for major sporting events, like the FA (Football Association) Cup Final, or the late rounds of the men's singles, center court, Wimbledon. Apart from those, the toughest London ticket to acquire is the season's hottest fringe production (often called **Off–West End** in imitation of New York's off-Broadway appellation).

The Lowdown

The West End and the Nationals... "West End" refers to the 50-odd mainstream houses, most of which are in that neighborhood, with a few exceptions. The weird thing about West End is its ever-closer resemblance to New York's Broadway, with productions transferring back and forth across the Atlantic like so much stock from the Gap. To be fair, though, downright West End disappointment usually arises from a combo of overinflated expectations, a large dent in the pocketbook, and a bad pick. If you hate musicals, the London *Les Miserables* (nicknamed "The Glums" by some) or any of the vapid Lloyd Webber monstrosities will please you about as much as a high-school production of *Fiddler on the Roof.* Look for the houses that pitch their brow higher—like the **Haymarket Theatre Royal,** the **Aldwych,** the **Arts Theatre,** the **Cambridge,** the **Comedy Theatre,** the **Garrick,** the **Old Vic,** and more. The easiest, safest way to go is to select from the current season at the **National Theatre** or Royal Shakespeare Company (RSC). For decades the RSC made its London home exclusively at the **Barbican Arts Centre,** but the Barbican is now only one of the RSC venues and they have upped their West End profile by mounting productions (with big stars) at the **Gielgud** and the Haymarket Theatre Royal. Many screen stars—from Ralph Fiennes to Patrick Stewart—earned their stripes with the RSC. The other guaranteed ticket is to the South Bank Centre's National Theatre, home of three stages: the huge **Olivier,** the medium-size **Lyttelton,** and the small **Cottesloe,** where embarrassing juvenilia alternates with exciting edge-of-the-seat new talent.

On the fringe... The fringe denotes all the other theaters—about the same number again. It's where the new and more exciting stuff is, where the much-vaunted British reverence for the stage is still at large. The best of the fringe venues known nowadays as Off–West End do theater as it might have been in its premovie heyday, with passion, conviction, infectious adoration of the medium. Those with the best track record for supplying chills of awe are the **Almeida,** the **Bush,** the little **Gate, The Riverside Studio,** the **Donmar Warehouse** (actually West End, but nobody remembers), the **Greenwich Theatre,** and the increasingly exciting **Young Vic.** The Almeida demands a trek north, but this place hardly ever misses. Others often worth traveling for include the **Theatre Royal Stratford East,** the **Battersea Arts Centre,** that beauteous old music hall the **Hackney Empire,** and the Kilburn **Tricycle.** Don't overlook the **Royal Court** (£5/$8.25 seats on Mon) or the **Lyric Studio,** which mount works experimental, debut, or in the round.

Way out on the fringe... With little fringe places, usually secreted above pubs, behind cafes, or way out in the sticks, you're on your own. Quality, degree of professionalism, amount of scenery, size of audience—everything is so utterly variable that generalization would be foolish and misleading. If they're good enough for long enough, they get sucked into the Off–West End list, like the Gate, the Bush, and the Almeida's neighbor, the original pub theater, the **King's Head.** However, there are a few pub joints that enjoy a good reputation: The Battersea **Latchmere Theatre** (formerly the Grace), **Jacksons Lane** up north, the Chelsea **Man in the Moon,** and the Islington **Old Red Lion,** for instance, are long-standing. You might also find something good playing at the **Canal Café Theatre** in lovely Little Venice.

Verdi to Schnittke... Opera is big in London. A first night at the newly renovated **Royal Opera House** is once more a hot ticket. Every bit as good as the Royal Opera, and far more adventurous, is the **English National Opera,** which lives at the humongous **Coliseum,** off Trafalgar Square. As far as repertoire is concerned, the main differences between the two houses are that the ENO costs less to see, commissions new works, and their performers sing in English. The Royal Opera gets more of the international stars, and projects "surtitles" over the stage. The ENO is far more likely to mount Philip Glass or Schnittke or Janacek, while the Royal Opera will be first with your Wagner. Another theater with an opera program is the Islington **Sadler's Wells,** which is where to find the D'Oyly Carte, founded by the Englishissimo Gilbert and Sullivan, and still performing *The Yeomen of the Guard, The Pirates of Penzance,* et al., plus other people's operettas. If the music is not your top priority—although the standard is rising each year— then don't pass up the **Holland Park Open-Air Theatre,** wherein little opera companies stage full-scale productions of *La Traviata* and *Tosca*—and *The Yeomen of the Guard*— accompanied by the screeches of roosting peacocks and, if you're lucky, a Technicolor sunset

Mozart to Martinu... Indigenous world-famous orchestras and ensembles include the Royal Philharmonic Orchestra, which plays in the **Royal Festival Hall,** and the **London Symphony Orchestra,** which performs at the **Barbican Arts Centre** with the English Chamber Orchestra. You'll find a lot of Henry Purcell and Thomas Tallis around—not just because they're English, but because Baroque is in vogue. As for venues...a lot goes on in a few places. Between them, the **South Bank Centre** and the **Barbican** have most of the major recitals and concerts sewn up. The South Bank Centre has three halls of diminishing size: the big **Royal**

Festival Hall for symphony concerts, the smaller **Queen Elizabeth Hall,** and the **Purcell Room,** used for recitals and chamber music. Other than these there's the glorious and acoustically blessed **Wigmore Hall,** behind Oxford Street, and the aforementioned (in Diversions) **Royal Albert Hall,** which is most remarkable for the wonderful summer series of Henry Wood Promenade Concerts, or **Proms.** Good for a gentle evening is a recital at one of these two historic houses: Holland Park's **Leighton House** and Hampstead's **Burgh House.** Summer outdoor concerts are performed at lovely **Kenwood House** in Hampstead.

Pew music... Some of the major classical-music venues, and certainly the most numerous, are churches. A few, like the leader of the pack, **St. John's Smith Square,** are deconsecrated; others, including the other big cheese, **St. Martin-in-the-Fields,** retain their pasture, and operate a double life as house of entertainment/house of God. (The latter is the home of the famous Baroque ensemble, the Academy of St. Martin-in-the-Fields, by the way.) Others of the genre include several churches in the City, like **St. Giles** in the Barbican and Wren's **St. James's Garlickhythe,** plus the **St. James's Piccadilly,** a Wren with a plastic (okay, fiberglass) spire. **Southwark Cathedral** is a major venue, and look out for the program at Nicholas Hawksmoor's **Christ Church Spitalfields** because the building's as glorious as the music. There's a very good festival there in June and September. Concerts in churches are big bargains, and often they're entirely free, especially at lunchtime.

The dance... This city's up there with the best, in both the classical and young choreographers departments. The ballet is biggest and glossiest when given by the Royal Ballet at the **Royal Opera House.** Stars they own include Irek Mikhamedov and Darcey Bussell, but visiting feet dance here, too, as they do at the other big ballet place, **Sadler's Wells,** where there's also flamenco and tango and whichever specialty dancers are dropping by. The English National Ballet performs at the **Coliseum.** If you prefer newer stuff, look out for dance festivals, like the summer Dance Umbrella, the springtime Spring Loaded, and the Islington Dance Festival; get the program from **The Place,** which is the center of new dance.

Music under the stars... You have three very good choices, but they occur only in summer, as you might expect. Firstly, you can hear opera, mostly the familiar warhorses, and ballet at **Holland Park Theatre,** a lovely stage in a ruined Jacobean mansion smack dab in the middle of Holland Park. A tent is set up so rain won't stop the show. Then there's the **Regent's Park Open-Air Theatre,** which has been staging dramas and Shakespearean comedies since way back in 1932. Lastly, there's the lovely lakeside setting of **Kenwood House,** perfect for picnics, where you can hear classical faves that usually end with a fireworks display.

Ha ha ha ha... Comedy is huge and growing and places to see it are legion. The one that kicked off the thing called "alternative comedy," which became the mainstream in the '80s (and still is), is the **Comedy Store.** Since way before *Monty Python,* Britain has had a special affinity for comedy, but any attempted explanation of the scene, or of the British sense of humor, is bound to fail. You'll have to figure it all out yourself, using the exhaustive comedy listings in *Time Out.* **Jongleurs** has three spots, and counting, and hosts incredibly popular, and therefore pretty reliable, line-ups. Killing them on TV are Vic Reeves, Bob Mortimer, Paul Whitehouse, and Charlie Higson of *The Fast Show,* which you can see live at **Labatt's Apollo,** if you hit the right season. Totally recommended.

Jolly good sports... On the whole, Londoners like watching other people do sports more than they like exerting themselves. One of the best sports to watch is football (soccer). London has three clubs in the elite Premier League. Catch Spurs (Tottenham Hotspurs) at **White Hart Lane,** or **Arsenal** or **Chelsea** at their respective grounds. Rumors about football hooliganism have been greatly exaggerated, although it is true that Chelsea fans like to chant "You're going home in a London ambulance" to the opposing side's fans. By comparison, cricket is as genteel as the afternoon tea that stops play at 4pm. See the quintessential English game at **Lords** or **The Oval.** On the violence scale, rugby falls somewhere in between. The game's like gridiron without padding; the players are known for singing ditties with filthy lyrics ("rugby songs") in the showers and for their large quadriceps. It's an upper-class sport played at public (read: exclusive, private) school, and also the passion of the entire Welsh nation. The 13-a-side professional game's Rugby League Final is played at **Wembley Stadium;** the purists'-preferred 15-a-side amateur Rugby Union, aka rugger, is played at **Twickenham.** What everybody wants during the last week of June and first week of July is Wimbledon tickets. Well, sorry, but those are allocated on a lottery system in January. However, during the first week, it's a cinch to see grand-slam, big-shot players up close on the outer courts.

Map 24: Entertainment

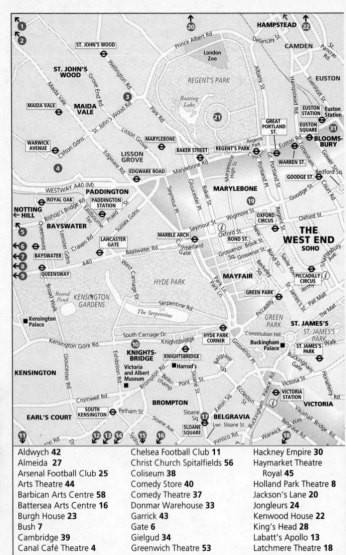

Aldwych **42**	Chelsea Football Club **11**	Hackney Empire **30**
Almeida **27**	Christ Church Spitalfields **56**	Haymarket Theatre
Arsenal Football Club **25**	Coliseum **38**	Royal **45**
Arts Theatre **44**	Comedy Store **40**	Holland Park Theatre **8**
Barbican Arts Centre **58**	Comedy Theatre **37**	Jackson's Lane **20**
Battersea Arts Centre **16**	Donmar Warehouse **33**	Jongleurs **24**
Burgh House **23**	Garrick **43**	Kenwood House **22**
Bush **7**	Gate **6**	King's Head **28**
Cambridge **39**	Gielgud **34**	Labatt's Apollo **13**
Canal Café Theatre **4**	Greenwich Theatre **53**	Latchmere Theatre **18**

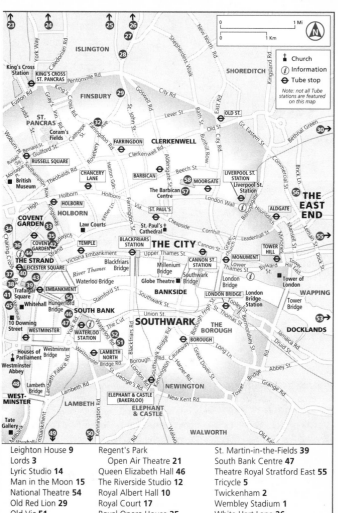

Leighton House **9**	Regent's Park	St. Martin-in-the-Fields **39**
Lords **3**	Open Air Theatre **21**	South Bank Centre **47**
Lyric Studio **14**	Queen Elizabeth Hall **46**	Theatre Royal Stratford East **55**
Man in the Moon **15**	The Riverside Studio **12**	Tricycle **5**
National Theatre **54**	Royal Albert Hall **10**	Twickenham **2**
Old Red Lion **29**	Royal Court **17**	Wembley Stadium **1**
Old Vic **51**	Royal Opera House **35**	White Hart Lane **26**
The Oval **50**	Sadler's Wells **32**	Wigmore Hall **19**
The Place **31**	St. Giles in the Barbican **57**	Wimbledon **49**
Proms **10**	St. John's Smith Square **48**	Young Vic **52**

ENTERTAINMENT

The Index

Aldwych (p. 238) WEST END A West End theater.... *Tel 020/ 7416-6003. The Aldwych WC2. Tube: Covent Garden.*
See Map 24 on page 244, bullet 42.

Almeida (p. 239) ISLINGTON Possibly London's best Off–West End theater and better than ever after its refurbishment; it's always exciting, once you've tracked it down.... *Tel 020/7359-4404. www.almeida.co.uk. Almeida St. N1. Tube: Angel.*
See Map 24 on page 244, bullet 27.

Arsenal Football Club (p. 242) HIGHBURY Emotions run high for all the soccer teams, but Arsenal fans may be the most fanatical of all.... *Tel 020/7704-4000. www.arsenal.co.uk. Avenell Rd. Highbury N5. Tube: Arsenal. Season runs Aug–May.*
See Map 24 on page 244, bullet 25.

Arts Theatre (p. 238) WEST END A West End theater.... *Tel 020/ 7836-2132. 6 Great Newport St. WC2. Tube: Leicester Sq.*
See Map 24 on page 244, bullet 44.

Barbican Arts Centre (p. 239, 240) THE CITY This major arts center's two theaters are venues for the Royal Shakespeare Company (tel 020/7628-8891, www.rsc.org.uk), and its auditorium are where the London Symphony Orchestra (www.lso.co.uk) and English Chamber Orchestra (www.englishchamberorchestra.co. uk) perform. All unsold seats for London Symphony concerts go on sale an hour before for an amazingly low £8 ($13).... *Tel 020/7638-8891 box office; 24-hour info: 020/7382-7297. Silk St. EC2. Tube: Barbican/Moorgate.*
See Map 24 on page 244, bullet 58.

Battersea Arts Centre (p. 239) BATTERSEA Aka the BAC—a long way out, but often worth it.... *Tel 020/7223-2223. www.bac.org. uk. Lavender Hill SW11. BR: Clapham Junction.*
See Map 24 on page 244, bullet 16.

Burgh House (p. 241) HAMPSTEAD An elegant Hampstead chamber-music venue.... *Tel 020/7431-0144. New End Square NW3. Tube: Hampstead.*
See Map 24 on page 244, bullet 23.

Bush (p. 239) SHEPHERD'S BUSH Off–West End venue with some-times controversial tastes.... *Tel 020/7610-4224. Shepherds Bush Green W12. Tube: Goldhawk Rd.*

See Map 24 on page 244, bullet 7.

Cambridge (p. 238) WEST END A West End theater.... *Tel 020/7494-5080. Earlham St. WC2. Tube: Covent Garden.*

See Map 24 on page 244, bullet 39.

Canal Café Theatre (p. 240) LITTLE VENICE Its Little Venice water-side location is a bonus; there's often a late cabaret after the play.... *Tel 020/7289-6054. Bridge House Pub, Delamere Terrace W2. Tube: Warwick Ave.*

See Map 24 on page 244, bullet 4.

Chelsea Football Club (p. 242) FULHAM Wear dark blue to see a match at the most geographically accessible London soccer ground.... *Tel 020/7385-5545. www.chelseafc.co.uk. Stamford Bridge, Fulham Rd. SW6. Tube: Fulham Broadway.*

See Map 24 on page 244, bullet 11.

Christ Church Spitalfields (p. 241) SPITALFIELDS Nicholas Hawksmoor's church is a concert venue in June and December.... *Tel 020/7377-0287. Commercial St. E1. Tube: Liverpool St.*

See Map 24 on page 244, bullet 56.

Coliseum (p. 240, 241) WEST END Mammoth theater is home of the English National Opera and English National Ballet; unsold seats go on sale at reduced prices three hours before.... *Tel 020/7632-8300. www.eno.org. St. Martin's Lane WC2. Tube: Charing Cross.*

See Map 24 on page 244, bullet 38.

Comedy Store (p. 242) WEST END The first and if not the best, at least one of the most reliable, of the funny clubs.... *Tel 020/7344-0234. Oxendon St. SW1. Tube: Piccadilly Circus.*

See Map 24 on page 244, bullet 40.

Comedy Theatre (p. 238) WEST END A West End theater, not a comedy club.... *Tel 020/7369-1731. Panton St. SW1. Tube: Piccadilly Circus.*

See Map 24 on page 244, bullet 37.

Cottesloe See "National Theatre," below.

Donmar Warehouse (p. 239) WEST END Is it West End? Is it Off? Is it fringe? Cabaret? Who cares—this centrally located theater nearly always has something worth seeing.... *Tel 0207/369-1732. www.donmarwarehouse.com. 41 Earlham St. WC2. Tube: Covent Garden.*

See Map 24 on page 244, bullet 33.

Garrick (p. 238) WEST END A West End theater.... *Tel 020/ 7494-5085. Charing Cross Rd. WC2. Tube: Leicester Sq.*
See Map 24 on page 244, bullet 43.

Gate (p. 239) NOTTING HILL This tiny, ambitious, and well-known theater has been around forever.... *Tel 020/7229-0706. 11 Pembridge Rd. W11. Tube: Notting Hill Gate.*
See Map 24 on page 244, bullet 6.

Gielgud (p. 239) WEST END West End theater that's now one of the venues used by the Royal Shakespeare Company... *Tel 020/7494-5085. Shaftesbury Ave. W1. Tube: Piccadilly Circus.*
See Map 24 on page 244, bullet 34.

Greenwich Theatre (p. 239) GREENWICH A West End theater far from the West End.... *Tel 020/8858-7755. www.greenwichtheatre. org.uk. Crooms Hill SE10. Tube: Greenwich.*
See Map 24 on page 244, bullet 53.

Hackney Empire (p. 239) HACKNEY A loverly old theater in the East End, where a lot of comedy happens; also plays and music. It's just had a £15 million ($24,750,000) refurb.... *Tel 020/ 8985-2424. www.hackneyempire.co.uk. 291 Mare St. E8. BR: Hackney Central.*
See Map 24 on page 244, bullet 30.

Haymarket Theatre Royal (p. 238, 239) WEST END A West End theater that's one of the venues used by the Royal Shakespeare Company.... *Tel 0870/901-3356. Haymarket SW1. Tube: Piccadilly Circus.*
See Map 24 on page 244, bullet 45.

Holland Park Theatre (p. 240, 242) HOLLAND PARK The cutest stage in town is in the ruins of a Jacobean mansion; alfresco opera and dance performed April through August.... *Tel 020/ 7602-7856. www.operahollandpark.com. Holland Park W8. Tube: Holland Park.*
See Map 24 on page 244, bullet 8.

Jacksons Lane (p. 240) HIGHGATE A place in the north, mainly for dance, usually nonindigenous, with some comedy and experimental theater. A veggie cafe offers a community feel.... *Tel 020/8341-4421. www.jacksonslane.org.uk. 269 Archway Rd. N6. Tube: Highgate.*
See Map 24 on page 244, bullet 20.

Jongleurs (p. 242) CAMDEN Eight venues nationwide, with two in London, that consistently round up funny comedians, at least judging by the popularity. This one has a picturesque canal-side setting.... *Tel 0870/787-0707. www.jongleurs.co.uk. Dingwalls Building, Middle Yard, Camden Lock NW1. Tube: Chalk Farm.*
See Map 24 on page 244, bullet 24.

Kenwood House (p. 241, 242) HAMPSTEAD July and August lakeside concerts on the grounds of a lovely Palladian mansion; popular classics and fireworks finales.... *Tel 020/7413-1443. www.picnicconcerts.com. Hampstead Lane NW3. Tube: East Finchley.*
See Map 24 on page 244, bullet 22.

King's Head (p. 240) ISLINGTON A very long-standing pub theater; at this one you can drink during the play.... *Tel 020/7226-1916. 115 Upper St. N1. Tube: Angel.*
See Map 24 on page 244, bullet 28.

Labatt's Apollo (p. 242) HAMMERSMITH Pop and popular concert venue.... *Tel 020/7416-6022. Queen Caroline St. W6. Tube: Hammersmith.*
See Map 24 on page 244, bullet 13.

Latchmere Theatre (p. 240) BATTERSEA Above the Latchmere pub in Battersea is this very good, newly energized fringe theater first known as the Gate, then the Grace.... *Tel 020/7978-7040. www.latchmeretheatre.com. 503 Battersea Park Rd. SW11. BR: Clapham Junction.*
See Map 24 on page 244, bullet 18.

Leighton House (p. 241) KENSINGTON Hear chamber music in Victorian splendor.... *Tel 020/7602-2316. 12 Holland Park Rd. W14. Tube: Kensington High St.*
See Map 24 on page 244, bullet 9.

Lords (p. 242) ST. JOHN'S WOOD The hallowed turf of British cricket since 1811.... *Tel 020/7432-1066. www.lords.org/mcc/welcome.asp. St. John's Wood Rd. NW8. Tube: St. John's Wood.*
See Map 24 on page 244, bullet 3.

Lyric Studio (p. 239) HAMMERSMITH Experimental works, plus classics and music theater.... *Tel 020/8741-2311. www.lyric.co.uk. King St. W6. Tube: Hammersmith.*
See Map 24 on page 244, bullet 14.

Lyttelton See "National Theatre," below.

Man in the Moon (p. 240) CHELSEA Another pub fringe theater, this one in Chelsea.... *Tel 020/7352-5075. 392 Kings Rd. SW3. Tube: Sloane Sq., then Bus 11 or 22.*
See Map 24 on page 244, bullet 15.

National Theatre (p. 236, 239) SOUTH BANK The South Bank Centre's trio of theaters—Olivier, Lyttelton, Cottesloe—are the playgrounds for the occasionally star-flecked, ever-changing, often brilliant Royal National Theatre Company.... *Tel 020/7452-3000. www.nt-online.org. South Bank SE1. Tube: Waterloo.*
See Map 24 on page 244, bullet 54.

THE INDEX

ENTERTAINMENT

Old Red Lion (p. 240) SHOREDITCH Here's yet another pub theater, this one conveniently close to the tube stop.... *Tel 020/ 7837-7816. 418 St. John's St. N1. Tube: Angel.*
See Map 24 on page 244, bullet 29.

Old Vic (p. 238) SOUTH BANK West End, but off the path, this theater stages consistent crowd-pleasers.... *Tel 0207/928-7616. www.oldvictheatre.com. Waterloo Rd. SE1. Tube: Waterloo.*
See Map 24 on page 244, bullet 51.

Olivier See "National Theatre," above.

The Oval (p. 242) KENNINGTON The not-quite-as-hallowed-as-Lords turf of British cricket.... *Tel 020/7582-6660. Kennington Oval SE11. Tube: Oval.*
See Map 24 on page 244, bullet 50.

The Place (p. 241) MARYLEBONE Practically the center of the world for contemporary dance.... *Tel 020/7387-0161. www.theplace. org.uk. 17 Duke's Rd. WC1. Tube: Euston.*
See Map 24 on page 244, bullet 31.

Proms (p. 241) SOUTH KENSINGTON Famous and wildly popular Henry Wood Promenade Concerts take place at Royal Albert Hall from mid-July through mid-September; queue on day of for ultra-cheap standing-room seats...*Tel 020/7589-8212. Royal Albert Hall, Kensington Gore SW7. Tube: High St. Kensington.*
See Map 24 on page 244, bullet 10.

Purcell Room See "South Bank Centre," below.

Regent's Park Open-Air Theatre (p. 242) REGENT'S PARK A summer (June to early September) tradition since 1932, staging summer drama and usually a Shakespeare comedy.... *Tel 020/ 7486-2431. www.openairtheatre.org. Inner Circle, Regent's Park NW1. Tube: Baker St. or Regent's Park.*
See Map 24 on page 244, bullet 21.

Queen Elizabeth Hall See "South Bank Centre," below.

The Riverside Studio (p. 239) HAMMERSMITH This happening arts complex is hidden by the Thames near Hammersmith Bridge.... *Tel 02/08237-1111. www.riversidestudios.co.uk. Crisp Rd. W6. Tube: Hammersmith.*
See Map 24 on page 244, bullet 12.

Royal Albert Hall See "Proms," above.

Royal Court (p. 239) KNIGHTSBRIDGE This West End theater made its name with groundbreaking plays back in the 1960s and still invites as much controversy as possible; seats sell for £5 ($8.25) on Monday nights; nice cafe, too.... *Tel 020/7565-5000. www.royalcourttheatre.com. Sloane Sq. SW1. Tube: Sloane Sq.*
See Map 24 on page 244, bullet 17.

Royal Festival Hall See "South Bank Centre," below.

Royal Opera House (p. 238, 240, 241) COVENT GARDEN The historic 19th-century opera house reopened after massive refurbishments and houses the Royal Opera and the Royal Ballet. Tickets cost a fortune unless you queue starting at 10am on day of performance.... *Tel 020/7304-4000. www.royalopera.org. Bow St. WC2. Tube: Covent Garden.*

See Map 24 on page 244, bullet 35.

Sadler's Wells (p. 240, 241) ISLINGTON This Islington theater is best known for dance, but also transfers European theater and music productions.... *Tel 020/7863-6000. www.sadlers-wells. com. Rosebery Ave. EC1. Tube: Angel.*

See Map 24 on page 244, bullet 32.

St. Giles in the Barbican (p. 241) THE CITY A City church with a classical concert program.... *No phone. Fore St. EC2. Tube: Barbican.*

See Map 24 on page 244, bullet 57.

St. James's Garlickhythe See the Diversions chapter.

St. James's Piccadilly See the Diversions chapter.

St. John's Smith Square (p. 241) WESTMINSTER BBC Radio often broadcasts concerts from this deconsecrated church, the major minor concert hall.... *Tel 020/7222-1061. Smith Sq. SW1. Tube: Westminster.*

See Map 24 on page 244, bullet 48.

St. Martin-in-the-Fields (p. 241) WEST END Beautiful church, beautiful music. See if you can catch the Academy of St. Martin-in-the-Fields on its home turf, or a concert performed by candlelight.... *Tel 020/7839-8362. Trafalgar Sq. WC2. Tube: Charing Cross.*

See Map 24 on page 244, bullet 39.

South Bank Centre (p. 239, 240) SOUTH BANK The center of usually-very-good mainstream theater (see "National Theatre," above) and classical music at the three concert halls (Royal Festival Hall, Queen Elizabeth Hall, Purcell Room).... *Tel 020/7960-4242. www.sbc.org.uk. South Bank SE1. Tube: Waterloo.*

See Map 24 on page 244, bullet 47.

Southwark Cathedral See the Diversions chapter.

Theatre Royal Stratford East (p. 239) STRATFORD EAST This Off–West End theater is hit or miss, since it stages a lot of brand-new work and young playwrights' stuff. When it hits, it's great.... *Tel 020/8534-0310. www.stratfordeast.com. Gerry Raffles Sq. E15. Tube: Stratford.*

See Map 24 on page 244, bullet 55.

Tricycle (p. 239) KILBURN This well-loved Off–West End theater almost closed due to lack of funds but now thrives again.... *Tel 020/7328-1000. www.tricycle.co.uk. 269 Kilburn High Rd. NW6. Tube: Kilburn.*

See Map 24 on page 244, bullet 5.

Twickenham (p. 243) TWICKENHAM The Rugby Union Valhalla where the Pilkington Cup is fought in early May.... *Tel 020/8892-8161. Whitton Rd., Twickenham Middlesex. Tube: Twickenham BR.*

See Map 24 on page 244, bullet 2.

Wembley Stadium (p. 243) WEMBLEY The FA (Football Association) Cup Final is fought here, as is the Rugby League (as opposed to the Union) Silk Cut Trophy. Since you'll never get tickets to either, go see another match at this 70,000-seater.... *Tel 020/8902-0902. www.wembleynationalstadium.co.uk. Empire Way, Wembley Middlesex HA9. Tube: Wembley Park.*

See Map 24 on page 244, bullet 1.

White Hart Lane (p. 242) TOTTENHAM Home of the Spurs, the Tottenham Hotspurs footy team.... *Tel 020/8365-5050. 748 High Rd. N17. Tube: Turnpike Lane.*

See Map 24 on page 244, bullet 26.

Wigmore Hall (p. 241) MARYLEBONE This lovely, recently restored concert hall behind Oxford Street has a really accessible program.... *Tel 020/7935-2141. www.wigmore-hall.org.uk. 36 Wigmore St. W1. Tube: Bond St.*

See Map 24 on page 244, bullet 19.

Wimbledon (p. 238, 243) WIMBLEDON For a chance at tickets to the tennis tournament, write with a SASE and International Reply coupon between August and December. *For information, call 020/8971-2473 (not during the tournament). All England Lawn Tennis & Croquet Club, P.O. Box 98, Wimbledon SW19 5AE. Tube: Southfields.*

See Map 24 on page 244, bullet 49.

Young Vic (p. 239) SOUTH BANK An excellent Off–West End theater with two auditoria and a great cafe.... *Tel 020/7928-6363. www.youngvic.org. 66 The Cut SE1. Tube: Waterloo.*

See Map 24 on page 244, bullet 52.

HOTLINES & OTHER BASICS

Airports... The one you'll almost definitely land at is **Heathrow.** The best way into town from there is undoubtedly the **Heathrow Express** train, leaving for Paddington every 15 minutes from 5am until midnight, with a journey time of 15 minutes; tickets are just under £12 ($20). Otherwise, it is a 40- to 60-minute journey by tube. Take the Piccadilly Line for £3.70 ($6.10) to Central London. By changing lines, you can get virtually anywhere without rising above ground, but if you have heavy bags, the sometimes endless walks between tube lines could be a major drag. The other cheap way into town is the **Airbus.** Both routes, A1 (to Victoria) and A2 (to Russell Sq.) depart all four terminals every 15 to 30 minutes, take about an hour, and cost £8 ($13) one-way. The buses run 5am to 8am; the tube, 5:30am to midnight (Sun 7am–11:30pm); after that you'll have to take a taxi, for around £45 ($74), plus tip. One more lesser-known option: Tell the information desk you want a **minicab** into London. They keep a secret list of local firms, with whom a trip into central London is more like £30 to £35 ($50–$58).

There's a chance your flight will land at the other main London airport, **Gatwick,** in which case you can most easily get into Central London by taking the **Gatwick Express;** it leaves for Victoria Station every 15 minutes (every 30 minutes between 1am and 5am), for £11 ($18) one-way, and takes 30 to 40 minutes. London has three additional airports (Luton, Stansted, and London City), but they only service charter flights or flights to the Continent. There are easily accessible public transportation options to and from all three.

Babysitters... Both the **Nanny Service** (tel 020/7935-3515; 6 Nottingham St. W1; www.nannyservice.co.uk) and **Universal Aunts** (tel 020/7386-5900; P.O. Box 304 SW4ONN) are tried and trusted.

Buses... Those red double-deckers that are synonymous with London are the cheapest tourist attraction in town. During rush hour (8–9:30am and 4:30–6pm) it's best not to hop on a bus if you're in a hurry; otherwise it's a scenic, if round-about, way to travel. By no means are all buses double-deckers, but all are hailed the same way—by waiting at the concrete post with a flaglike sign on its top. If the sign is red, it's a "request stop," and you stick out your arm; other-wise the bus stops automatically (unless there isn't room on it). An oblong sign lower down the post illustrates the routes of the buses that stop there, but also check the des-tination sign in front of the bus, since many fail to run the whole route. Fares are £1 ($1.65) if your journey is within Zone 1 (Central London) and 70p ($1.15) for everything outside of that. Night buses charge £1.50 ($2.50). Show your card or pay your coins to the conductor (who often doubles as the driver) and get free bus maps from **Travel Information Centres** at main tube stations. **Travelcards** are valid for both bus and tube.

Car Rental... I strongly advise you not to drive in London. You have to do it on the left, use a stick shift, and park (no spaces and exorbitant fees). If you must rent a car, though, your own driver's license is all you'll need. You'll find **Alamo** (tel 800/327-9633 in the U.S., 0800/272-200 in the U.K.), **Avis** (tel 800/331-1212 U.S., 0990/900-500 U.K.),

Budget (tel 800/527-0700 U.S., 0541/565656 U.K.), and **Hertz** (tel 800/654-3131 U.S., 0990/6699 U.K.) at the airports and at other locations in London, charging somewhat higher rates than you may be used to, with unlimited mileage at around £60 to £80 ($99–$132) per day for a midsize, plus tax, insurance, and extras like collision damage waiver. You don't have to reserve in advance but it will probably be cheaper if you do.

Climate... The climate is just as unpredictable as you've heard. Summer 1999 (like 1975) saw a 90°F+ (32°C+) heat wave, for instance, while 1997 saw the hottest August since records began, and the wettest June since 1860. Snow may fall one year but then be absent for the next three. Unless you hit those extremes, you can pretty much count on **rain**—often a soaking drizzle that can go on for days—and mild temperatures, on the cool side (40°F–50°F) from November through March, and hovering around 70°F (21°C) from June to September.

Consulates and embassies... The **U.S. Embassy** is at 24 Grosvenor Square W1A 1AE (tel 020/7499-9000); the **Canadian High Commission** is nearby, at 1 Grosvenor Square, W1 (tel 020/7258-6600). The **Australian High Commission** is in Australia House, Strand WC2 (tel 020/7379-4334). The **New Zealand High Commission** is at 17 Grosvenor House, 80 Haymarket at Pall Mall SW1 (tel 020/7930-8422).

Currency... Pounds sterling and pence are still the money here, with notes in denominations of £5, £10, £20, and £50; coins in 1p, 2p, 5p, 10p, 20p, 50p, £1, and £2 sizes. The exchange rate hovers around the £1 = $1.65 mark.

Dentists... The best bet for emergency dental work is **Guys Hospital** (tel 020/7955-5000; St. Thomas St. SE1), which is central and has the longest hours: Monday to Friday 8:45am to 3:30pm, Saturday and Sunday 9:30am to 5pm. If your abscess blows up at dinner, trek to **King's College Hospital** (tel 020/7346-3591; Denmark Hill SE5), open 6 to 10pm Monday to Friday, 9am to 4pm weekends.

Doctors... For doctors on call 24 hours, call 07000/372-255. Central London hospitals with 24-hour emergency rooms are: **Charing Cross** (tel 020/8846-1234; Fulham Palace Rd., Hammersmith W6), **Guys** (tel 020/7955-5000; St. Thomas St. SE1), and **St. Thomas's** (tel 020/7928-9292; Lambeth Palace Rd. SE1).

Electricity... It's 240-volt, 50-cycle AC (alternating current), instead of the 110-volt, 60-cycle AC in the U.S., and the wall outlets accept three-prong plugs. Adapters or transformers are necessary for any electrical gadgets, gizmos, or laptops brought from the U.S.

Emergencies... Dial 999 (it's a free call) from any phone for police, fire department, or ambulance.

Festivals & Special Events...

JANUARY: The **New Year's Day Parade** has cheerleaders, floats, marching bands, and the lord mayor of Westminster. From 12:30 to 3pm at Westminster Bridge–Berkeley Square.

FEBRUARY: Lion dancers and lots of food and crafts stalls on the streets of Chinatown. Midmonth, date changes yearly. Gerrard and Lisle streets.

APRIL: **Oxford & Cambridge Boat Race on the Thames** from Putney to Mortlake, and the **Flora London Marathon** (tel 020/7620-4117; www.london-marathon.co.uk).

MAY: **Chelsea Flower Show** (tel 0870/906-3781; Chelsea Royal Hospital, Swan Walk, 66 Royal Hospital Rd. SW3; www.rhs.org.uk): **Football Association FA Cup Final** (tel 020/8902-0902; Wembley Stadium).

JUNE: **Trooping the Colour**—the queen's birthday parade (tel 020/7414-2279; Horse Guards, Whitehall) on June 4. For tickets, send a SASE between January 1 and February 28 to: Ticket Office, Headquarters, Household Division, Chelsea Barracks, London SW1H 8RF.

JUNE–JULY: **Royal Academy Summer Exhibition** (tel 020/7439-7438; Burlington House, Piccadilly W1; www.royalacademy.org.uk)—world's largest juried art exhibition and usually mobbed. **City of London Festival** (tel 020/7377-0540; www.colf.org) is a 3-week musical extravaganza that takes place in City locales not usually open to visitors. **Wimbledon Lawn Tennis Championships** (tel 020/8944-1066; Church Rd., Wimbledon SW19 5AE; www.wimbledon.com).

JULY: **Pride in the Park** (tel 020/7494-2225; www.london
mardigras.com), celebrating gay pride, is a huge gay and
lesbian costumed march and parade from Hyde Park to
Parliament Square followed by live music and dancing; last
Saturday of July. **Hampton Court Palace Flower Show**
(tel 0870/752-7777; East Molesey, Surrey).

AUGUST: **Notting Hill Carnival** (Portobello Rd., Ladbroke
Grove, All Saints Rd.). Bank Holiday weekend—the big
Caribbean extravaganza.

JULY–SEPTEMBER: **Henry Wood Promenade Concerts** (the
Proms) (tel 020/7589-8212; Royal Albert Hall, Kensington
Gore SW7).

SEPTEMBER: **London Open House Weekend** (tel 0900/
6000061; www.londonopenhouse.org). The third weekend
of the month, hundreds of historic London buildings not
usually open to the public...are.

OCTOBER: **Pearlies Harvest Festival** (tel 020/7766-1100; St.
Martin-in-the-Fields Church, Trafalgar Sq. SW1).
London's famous Pearly Kings and Queens with their
button-encrusted outfits celebrate Harvest Festival the first
Sunday of the month.

NOVEMBER: **State Opening of Parliament** (tel 020/020/7291-
4272; Whitehall and Parliament Sq; www.parliament.uk).
All hail the queen as she rides in her golden coach to
deliver the government's upcoming program to the people.
November 5: **Guy Fawkes Day.** Day when the lack of success of a 1605 attempt to blow up the Houses of Parliament
is commemorated with fireworks and bonfires on which
effigies of Mr. Fawkes are incinerated. **Lord Mayor's Show.**
Band, floats, razzmatazz as lord mayor is hauled from
Guildhall to the Royal Courts of Justice in his gilded
coach; a fair in Paternoster Square, fireworks in each borough (tel 020/7971-0026).

DECEMBER: Christmas tree in Trafalgar Square, many carol-
singing sessions; lighting ceremony.

Gay and lesbian hotlines... London Lesbian & Gay
Switchboard (tel 020/7837-7324; www.llgs.org.uk),
24-hour info and advice.

Holidays... New Year's Day (Jan 1), Easter (Good Friday,
Easter Monday), May Day Bank Holiday (first Mon in
May), Spring Bank Holiday (last Mon in May), August

Bank Holiday (last Mon in Aug), Christmas Day and Boxing Day (Dec 25–26).

Hotel hotline... The London Tourist Board's credit card accommodation booking service (tel 020/7932-2020).

The Internet... You'll find Internet cafes all over London. Most hotels and many entertainment venues now take bookings via the Internet. Some useful sites: www.visit britain.com (official travel information site); www.visit london.com (info from the London Tourist Board); www. officiallondontheatre.co.uk (The Society of London Theatre offers a comprehensive listing of plays, dance, opera, and so on).

Newspapers... London drowns in newsprint. The daily broadsheets, or "Qualities," are: the *Times,* the *Guardian, The Independent,* the *Daily Telegraph,* and the *Financial Times,* while the awful but entertaining tabloids are the *Express,* the *Mirror,* the *Mail,* the egregious *Sun,* and even worse *Star.* There is also the valuable evening paper, the *Evening Standard,* out weekdays before lunchtime.

Opening and closing times... Banks, Monday through Friday 9:30am to 4:30 or 5:30pm in some branches, plus Saturday morning in some cases. **Shops,** typically Monday through Saturday 9am to 6pm, with many now open Sunday. **Pubs,** Monday to Saturday 11am to 11pm (some shut 3–5:30pm), Sunday noon to 10:30pm (some shut 3–7pm). **Museums,** average opening hours are Monday to Saturday 10am to 6pm, Sunday noon to 5pm, but always check, especially during holiday periods. **Post offices,** Monday to Friday 9am to 5:30pm, Saturday 9am to 1pm.

Parking... You've already been warned not to drive, but if you insist, know that parking is hell, thanks to the usual meters and restrictions, and also the dread "Denver Boot," or wheel clamp, an immobilizing device administered by independent operators, which costs about £120 ($198) to get removed. **NCP (National Car Parks)** lots are open throughout London, but they fill up quickly and they're expensive: £10 ($17) for 3 hours in most places, and up to

£15 ($25) in others. Parking **on the street** is no less expensive, nor easy. Meters take varying amounts, anywhere from 5p to £1 (80¢–$1.65), and it must be in coin; 20p (30¢) will usually buy between 6 and 20 minutes of time, depending on location.

Passports and visas... Citizens from the U.S., Canada, Australia, and New Zealand need a valid passport to enter the U.K. for stays of up to 3 months.

Pharmacy... They're called *chemist shops* in the U.K. **Boots** is ubiquitous and much-used for prescription drugs and all kinds of other stuff. Get late-night drugs from **Bliss** (tel 020/7723-6116; 5 Marble Arch W1).

Postal Service... Mailboxes are rather attractive scarlet cylinders or wall mounts with the times of collection posted on the front. Get stamps from post offices, many newsagents, and shops. Rates at press time are: 47p (80¢) for airmail letters up to 10g and 42p (70¢) for postcards to the U.S. The post office at **Trafalgar Square** (tel 020/7495-4915; 24–28 William IV St. WC2) keeps long hours: Monday to Saturday 8am to 8pm.

Radio Stations... There are five national radio stations: **1FM,** 98.8FM (mainstream pop music, with some more interesting stuff, including John Peel's great indie and alternative show Tues–Thurs at 10:10am); **Radio 2,** 89.1FM (easy listening); **Radio 3,** 91.3FM (classical, some talk); **Radio 4,** 93.5FM, 198/720AM (talk, news, game shows, drama. A beloved national institution, especially *The Archers*—a 30-year-old radio soap about country folk); **Radio 5,** 693 AM (sports, talk); plus the **World Service,** 648 AM. The principal London stations are: **Capital FM,** 95.8 (pop); **Kiss FM,** 100FM (dance/club music; probably the hippest station in town); **JFM,** 102.2FM (jazz); **Classic FM,** 101.6 (heavily commercial classical); **GLR,** 94.9FM (talk, music); **Virgin,** 105.8FM (pop and rock music); **London News,** 97.3FM; **Magic,** 105.4FM (easy listening and golden oldies, ironically, rather hip); and **Talk,** 1053AM (like an only slightly more civilized aural Jerry Springer).

Standards of measure... England is supposed to be metric, like the rest of Europe, but you'll see as many feet and inches, pounds and ounces, as meters and centimeters, kilos, and grams. Human weight is given in stones and pounds; 1 stone = 14 pounds. Clothing sizes: For women, increase one size for English wear across the board; men's suit and shirt sizes are the same. Clothing sizes tend to vary wildly anywhere, however. Shoes are often sold in European sizes. For men: European 41 = U.K. 7 = U.S. 8. For women: European 41 = U.K. 7 = U.S. 10.

Subways... See "Tubes," below.

Taxes... Value-added tax (VAT) adds 17.5% to all purchases except books, groceries, and children's clothing, and is often refundable (except, of course, for hotel and restaurant charges). U.K. airport departure tax is £10 ($17) per person.

Taxis... Hail one when the orange FOR HIRE light on the roof is lit. An empty one may stop even if its light is off, since drivers sometimes use this method to screen passengers at night. London cabbies are among the best in the world; they all have an encyclopedic grasp of London's geography, having passed an exhaustive exam called "The Knowledge." Of this they are justly proud; don't insult your driver by offering directions. Metered fares are £1.40 ($2.30) for the first 378.6m (1,242 ft.) or 81.6 secs; thereafter 20p (30¢) for 189.3m (621 ft.) or 40.8 secs until the fare reaches £110 ($18); then it's 20p (30¢) for 126.2m (414 ft.) or 27.2 secs. Surcharges apply to and from airports and stations; for carrying pets, excess luggage, or extra passengers; and for traveling after 8pm.

Unlicensed taxis, called minicabs, must be booked by phone or in person at the office. Most hotels and restaurants keep numbers of local services, and will call one for you. You can also call 0800/654-321 (free) for instant connection to your nearest minicab office. Fares are about 25% lower than for black cabs.

Telephones... Public phones are either those familiar scarlet boxes or else nondescript booths; both accept coins, prepaid BT (British Telecommunications) cards, and/or credit cards. **Coin phone boxes** accept 20p (30¢) as the minimum payment. **Cardphones** take BT Cards, which you can buy in units from 10 (£1/$1.65) to 100 (£10/$17) and more from newsagents and general stores. Slot in the card, and a display shows how much time is left; the card is returned when you replace the receiver. **Credit cards** are used by swiping the magnetic stripe. Many pay phones now offer e-mail and cellular phone text messaging, too. The British ring is a double chirrup; repeated short beeps mean the line is busy, and a continuous beep means the number is "unobtainable"—either it's cut off or you dialed the wrong prefix. The system for phone numbers is as follows: the 01 and 02 prefixes denote normal rates; 03, 08, and 09 prefixes denote special rates (for example: 0800 = free; 0345 = local rate; 0839 = 50p/80¢ per minute); the 07 prefix denotes a cellular phone number. London numbers all begin with 020. When in London, drop the 020 and call an eight-digit number beginning in 7 or 8. Standard rate: Monday to Friday 8am to 6pm; cheap rate: 6pm to 8am and weekends. The international access code is 00; for the international operator, credit card, or collect calls, dial 155. For international directory inquiries, dial 153; domestic is 192. For the operator, dial 100. Hotels often whack on a big surcharge, so consider using a U.S. calling card. Some access numbers are: **AT&T USA Direct** (tel 0500/890-011), **MCI Call USA** (tel 0800/890-222), and **Sprint Express** (tel 0800/890-877).

Tipping... Hotels and restaurants often add a 10% to 15% service charge automatically, so look before you pay twice. Don't tip theater ushers or bartenders. Do tip: washroom attendants (about 20p/30¢ in the saucer), taxi and minicab drivers (10%), porters and bellhops (£1/$1.65 per bag carried), doormen (£1/$1.65 or £2/$3.30 for hailing cabs, etc.), concierges (at your discretion, for exceptional services like procuring difficult theater tickets or dinner reservations), hairdressers, beauty parlor technicians, and so on (15%).

Tours... Sightsee on an open-topped double-decker bus with **Original London Sightseeing Tours** (tel 020/8877-1722; April–Oct daily 9am–7pm; Nov–March 10–5. Board at Trafalgar Square or Green Park tube outside the Ritz Hotel), which follow four different routes over 90 stops, including all the greatest hits; you can hop on or off anywhere along the route. Tickets last 24 hours and cost £15 ($25) for adults, £7.50 ($12) for kids. The absolute coolest tour is the 80-minute road-and-river trip run by the fabulously loopy **London Frog Tours** (tel 020/7928-3132) on adapted World War II amphibious troop carriers. You're picked up on Chicheley Street, behind the London Eye, then rumble through Westminster and up to Piccadilly, passing many of London's major tourist sites. Then the vehicle splashes into the Thames at Vauxhall for a 30-minute cruise up as far as the Houses of Parliament. It costs £17 ($27) for adults, £11 ($18) for kids. The best walking tours are led by **The Original London Walks** (tel 020/7624-3978; www.londonwalks.com). **Stepping Out** (tel 020/8881-2933; www.walklon.ndirect.co.uk) is also reliable. Customized tours are given by cabbies with "The Knowledge," in **Black Taxi Tours of London** (tel 020/ 7289-4371), or, if you want to leave London, by **British Tours** (tel 020/7734-8734).

Travelers with disabilities... Hotlines include the **Artsline** (tel 020/7388-2227) for advice on accessibility of arts events, and the **Holiday Care Service** (tel 0845/ 1249971; www.holidaycare.org.uk) for help with accommodations questions. **London Transport** (www.london transport.co.uk) has a **Unit for Disabled Passengers** (tel 020/7222-5600), which includes the **Stationlink** service, a wheelchair-accessible "midibus" between nine BritRail stations and Victoria Coach Station. **RADAR (the Royal Association for Disability and Rehabilitation;** tel 020/7250-3222; 12 City Forum, 250 City Rd., London EC1 8AF) publishes travel information for the disabled in Britain.

Tubes... The London subway is the fastest way to get around...usually. There are 12 lines, plus the Docklands Light Railway (DLR). They all run Monday to Saturday from 5:30pm to midnight, Sunday 7am to 11:30pm (approximately), and the average waiting time is 5 to 10 minutes. **Tube fares** are assessed in zones, with the price rising according to how many of the six you pass through. The most expensive way to travel is by single ticket (£1.60/$2.65–£3.70/$6.10). Better: Get a **Travelcard** (from

£4.10/\$6.75 per day, £2/\$3.30 for children), valid all day from 9:30am for tube and bus, or an **LT Card** (from £8/\$13, children £3.50/\$5.80), without time restrictions. For Weekly and Monthly Travelcards purchased in London, you don't you need a photo for a **Visitor's Travelcard,** which you get in the U.S. from Rail Europe (tel 877/257-2887 in the U.S., 800/362-RAIL in Canada; www.raileurope.com); 3, 4, or 7 days cost \$31, \$42, or \$62; \$14, \$17, or \$26 for children, which includes discount vouchers to London sights. You can be fined on the spot for traveling without a valid ticket.

Visitor information... Contact **Visit Britain** (formerly the British Tourist Authority): In the U.S. and Canada, call 800/462-2748 or surf www.visitbritain.com; the main office is at 551 Fifth Avenue, Seventh Floor, New York, NY 10176.

The London Tourist Board operates the main **Tourist Information Centre** at Victoria Station Forecourt, Monday to Saturday 8am to 8pm (until 9pm in summer), Sunday 8am to 6pm; others are at Heathrow Airport (Terminals 1, 2, and 3), Liverpool Street tube station, and Waterloo International station, all open to personal callers only. For phone information, you will pay premium rates (60p/\$1) per minute at all times, plus any hotel/payphone surcharge.

GENERAL INDEX

Accommodations